Burnt Cork

Burnt Cork

TRADITIONS AND LEGACIES OF BLACKFACE MINSTRELSY

Edited by
STEPHEN JOHNSON

UNIVERSITY OF MASSACHUSETTS PRESS Amherst & Boston

Printed in the United States of America
LC 2012007995
ISBN 978-1-55849-934-8 (paper); 933-1 (library cloth)

Designed by Jack Harrison
Set in Adobe Minion Pro
Printed and bound by Thomson-Shore, Inc.

Library of Congress Cataloging-in-Publication Data

Burnt cork : traditions and legacies of blackface minstrelsy /
edited by Stephen Johnson.
p. cm.
Includes bibliographical references and index.
ISBN 978-1-55849-934-8 (pbk. : alk. paper) —
ISBN 978-1-55849-933-1 (library cloth : alk. paper)
1. Minstrel shows—United States—History. 2. Blackface entertainers—United States.
3. Minstrel shows—Social aspects—United States. 4. United States—Race relations—History.
5. Racism in popular culture—United States. 6. Whites—Race identity—United States.
I. Johnson, Stephen, 1954–
PN1969.M5B87 2012
791'.120973—dc23

2012007995

British Library Cataloguing in Publication data are available.

Contents

Illustrations

Acknowledgments

My thanks to the Centre for Drama, Theatre and Performance Studies, the Cinema Studies Institute, Faculty of Music, Centre for Diaspora and Transnational Studies, Centre for the Study of the United States, Jackman Humanities Institute, and Connaught Foundation, all at the University of Toronto, as well as that institution's School of Graduate Studies and Faculty of Arts and Science, for their support during this project's life, in a formative 2008 colloquium, and in its subsequent development. The university has assisted financially at a time when this is not easily done, and I am grateful for it. The Social Sciences and Humanities Research Council of Canada has also provided significant assistance. Thanking academic "institutions" is all well and good, but the fact is that individuals decide what happens to resources. This project's early stages received encouragement, financial and otherwise, from Charlie Keil, Gage Averill, Ato Quayson, and Elspeth Brown. I particularly thank Charlie Keil for his ongoing commitment to this project and for his willingness to listen. Thanks to my colleagues and co-contributors Nic Sammond and Alice Maurice for their support, and their very practical, reasonable advice. Indeed, all of the contributors provided me with sound advice and continued encouragement, graciously given and gratefully received. Finally, my thanks to everyone at University of Massachusetts Press, and in particular Clark Dougan, who has provided me with the very best counsel at every turn.

In the research, database development, and website creation for my own larger project, including work on this volume—particularly its Web presence—I was helped by a number of excellent research assistants from the Graduate Drama Centre. I cannot name all of them here—you know who you are (your names are listed in the credits at www.utm.utoronto.ca/~3minstr). In particular, I am indebted to Beth Marquis, Alexis Butler, Justin Blum, and Mark David Turner for bringing a personal commitment and passion to a project they made their own. My thanks also to Seika Boye, who assisted with the illustrations for this final product, and to Michael Reinhart, who gathered research for the website that provides materials supplementary to this volume. Finally, I thank Beth Marquis (again) for her excellent scholarly and technical work on that website, and Emma W. Johnson for creating the index.

Although this takes me back some years, I believe it is appropriate to thank Sally R. Sommer and Brooks McNamara, who introduced me to the complex history of blackface performance, both of them in ways that stressed its significant legacy in contemporary popular culture. That idea has stayed with me, in teaching and in research. Thanks, finally, to all my family and friends for their support and honest reflection, and most especially to WW.

Burnt Cork

Introduction

The Persistence of Blackface and the Minstrel Tradition

STEPHEN JOHNSON

If it hadn't a' been for Cotton-Eye Joe
I'd'a been married a long time ago.
Oh, where did you come from, where did you go?
Where did you come from, Cotton-Eye Joe?
—From a 1994 recording of an early minstrel song by the Swedish band Rednex

Not long ago I was approached by the Canadian Broadcasting Corporation in Toronto, where I teach, to be interviewed on a radio talk show regarding the question "Why has there been a resurgence in the use of blackface in contemporary society?" The interview did not take place—more newsworthy events took precedence—but the question remains. Although I cannot anticipate the experience of the reader of this volume, in my own experience, in just the past few years (as of this writing), I have been repeatedly confronted by blackface in almost every "walk" of my life as a spectator.[1] In film, *Tropic Thunder* featured Robert Downey Jr. in permanent blackface in a parody of the overzealous "method" actor. On cable television, Sarah Silverman sported blackface for an episode of her comedy series, and a character in *Mad Men,* set in the 1960s, blacked up to serenade his fiancée at a public gathering. In the British sketch series *Little Britain,* performers in traditional "golliwog" blackface appeared in a series of sketches as a "typical" minstrel family. In the reality series *America's Next Top Model,* a fashion "shoot" involved the contestants mixing and matching cultural groups, including both "traditional" costuming and face painting.[2] Off-off-Broadway, the Wooster Group has used blackface to denote and then deconstruct the performance of race.[3] Off-Broadway, Branden Jacobs-Jenkins's play *Neighbors* cast actors in blackface for roles named Zip, Jim, and Topsy. On Broadway, the musical *The Scottsboro Boys* used a traditional minstrel show (whatever that may be; see the discussion later in this introduction) as an organizing format, and included a "blacking up" scene. Closer to my own local culture, a student paper's annual satirical issue mocked "experimental" theater productions by advertising a (fictitious) radical reinterpretation of *You're a Good Man, Charlie Brown,* in blackface; and a group of undergraduates won a Halloween costume contest dressed in blackface as the characters from the Jamaican bobsled comedy *Cool Running.*[4] I could add to this list at some length.

Having established that there is, indeed, a resurgence of blackface in contemporary society, I would ask just one follow-up question: Did "blackface" ever go away? It seemed largely to disappear from television, film, and other popular mass media from at least the 1960s. But in fact, I don't believe it did, or could, disappear entirely. By way of illustration, when I first began teaching in the late 1980s, I invited the students of a senior seminar at McMaster University in Hamilton, Ontario, to bring in some evidence of the theater in their local community. One young man brought in a videotape that, when played for the class, showed a recording of his local community service club's annual charity fundraiser: a fully produced blackface minstrel show, with makeup and woolly wigs, white gloves, and dialect jokes. The students were shocked and outraged, raised as they were in a post–civil rights North America (and in southern Ontario, a terminus of the Underground Railroad). They had never seen anything like this; and yet there it was, on video, no more than a year or two old, sufficiently popular in its community to raise funds for charity. In our class discussion, we wondered aloud what would have happened if we had gone to the men who had produced this event and confronted them with their clearly racist portrayals; my own suspicion was and is that they would have looked at us dumbfounded, and then angrily denounced us as the "real" racists, reading derogatory portrayals into what was to them a de-racialized (or never racialized), abstract, clownlike performance of comedy and song. Their argument would not have been disingenuous; they would have believed what they were saying, however much we might have disagreed.

The fact is that the blackface minstrel tradition has never left us, not since the early nineteenth century, when white men (and black men, and sometimes women) applied a coal-black makeup made from burnt cork, and behaved in front of an audience as if they were African Americans. There are narratives of origin rehearsed later in this introduction and elsewhere in this volume: folk traditions of misrule and charivari; a culture of exhibition that included in this case the southern plantation slave. There are questions of intent: whether blackface performance was integrationist, working class, and populist, parodying and complaining about those in power and disseminating a uniquely (African) American music and dance; or whether it was segregationist and derogatory, reinforcing a white status quo of superiority and dehumanizing a clearly delineated population. Or both. This volume addresses the complex intentions and receptions of blackface, and in particular, it explores the "themes and variations" that have persisted from the day when T. D. Rice first "jumped Jim Crow" up to the present. If there is a single articulated contribution that this volume can make, it is to emphasize that phrase "or both." Every essay emphasizes the complexity of intention and reception in blackface performance, in each case arguing that the complexity builds up in layers over time, adding radical meaning to the accepted imagery without entirely erasing the old, haphazardly accumulating ways of reading blackface that reshape, refocus, and redirect its intentions—like barnacles on the hull of a very old ship that, despite its age, won't stop, won't sink.

Traditions of blackface performance, most often allied with the American minstrel show, have long been a significant part of Anglo North American culture. It is true that for a while—a brief time only, perhaps from the 1950s—it was not an active part of the mass media of film and television, and was (briefly) less visible in popular culture. Hence the question asked by the CBC. The answer to the question of its resurgence is, I believe, quite simple on the face of it. One has only to go to YouTube or to Google and type "blackface" into the search engine to see that over the last few years everything has become available to everyone, and no institutional—or personal—opinion can prevail against the Web. As a visitor to the Web, I have been able to accumulate almost the entire history of blackface performance in the twentieth century, since the advent of filmed performance. There was Edwin S. Porter's 1903 version of *Uncle Tom's Cabin*, preserving the long-standing tradition of melodramatic and minstrel blackface as part of the single most popular play in American history. There were clips from D. W. Griffith's *Birth of a Nation*, portraying the full range of minstrel and melodramatic stereotypes in blackface; and also, by way of contrast, there was Bert Williams's *Natural Born Gambler*, with this superb black performer in his signature (and imposed) blackface makeup. From the 1920s and 1930s, Al Jolson, the most successful entertainer of his day, can still be found on YouTube, singing in blackface in settings as diverse as a painted plantation backdrop, and onstage as part of a re-creation of a minstrel show. From the same time period you will also find clips of "Stepin Fetchit" (Lincoln Perry), for a time the highest-paid black performer in Hollywood, portraying a particularly demeaning minstrel character in virtual blackface. And so it goes.[5]

If they are still available on YouTube when you read this introduction, I would direct you to two particular examples of the change that did—and did not—take place in the mass media during the 1960s and 1970s. In the first instance, from the early 1970s, the deadpan comedian Pat Paulsen appears on Merv Griffin's TV talk show, walking on in blackface and traditional minstrel costume.[6] The audience and the hosts are all in an uproar, embarrassed and (I would suggest) physically titillated. Paulsen proceeds to complain to the audience about how terrible racism is on the stage, and demonstrates it by telling several racist jokes (Polish and Chinese, not African American). The audience laughs—at the jokes, and also because of its discomfort at laughing at the jokes. The co-hosts, visible in the background, slink off, embarrassed. Paulsen dances, poorly, then leaves. The episode was censored by the television network and never aired. (It is unclear to me how it managed to find its way onto YouTube.) This is a good example of the transition taking place in American media at the time; Paulsen still thought he could get away with blackface in the context of satire, but he couldn't. The audience immediately recognized the style of performance and reacted with familiarity to the humor, at the same time acknowledging by their reaction that this was "wrong" (now) and that they should no longer be willing to witness such things.

By way of contrast, also on YouTube are a number of clips from the British *Black and White Minstrels*, including at least one from 1978.[7] This long-running television series watched by so many in the United Kingdom featured choruses of singing and dancing men in full minstrel blackface and white lips, wearing in general oversized floral-patterned shirts, woolly wigs, and the other accoutrements of minstrelsy. Audiences for this show seem not to have experienced the same ethical dilemma as the audience for Paulsen, though it is true that Paulsen was purposely challenging his audience to be (or not to be) racist, despite the makeup. The audiences for the *Black and White Minstrels* somehow justified what was by this point no longer possible in the mass media in North America, perhaps through nostalgia and an attribution of archaism—the argument that this is "old-fashioned" entertainment that has lost its relevance, and thus its capacity to offend.

I am convinced that the conflicting and conflicted audience reactions to these two performances are not unusual. As the contributors to this volume will attest—every one of them—the intentions of blackface performance have always been flexible and its reception widely divergent. This is as true today as it was at minstrelsy's inception, and throughout its history. Consider the contemporary instances of blackface I have just noted. The use of blackface appears to be an accepted feature of theatrical culture on and off Broadway (though it must be said, *The Scottsboro Boys* drew some protest). Downey in blackface received mostly praise. There were no doubt some complaints about the episode of *America's Next Top Model,* but not so much as to invoke censorship. At the local level, by contrast, the story has been quite different. The newspaper parody noted earlier received widespread protest from student groups, and the Halloween masqueraders were the subject of a vigorous blog discussion, a letter-writing campaign, and a town hall meeting attracting at least 250 students. It would appear that at the level of the mass media, there is either acceptance or resignation in confronting blackface; but at the local level, where people believe that change is possible, there is interrogation and protest. The depiction of blackface might otherwise be quite similar, but the means (and authority) of dissemination differ.

The question I receive most commonly while working in this area of research, I find, is "Why?" Why are *you* studying *that?* In the case of blackface minstrelsy, the question can take a particularly skeptical tone. My answer is as unhesitant as it is, to most people, surprising. When I was first exposed to minstrelsy's historical tradition many years ago, I instantly recognized it. I recognized the costuming, the tunes, the lyrics, the dance, the gesture, the bad-punning humor, the dialect—particularly the dialect—and the image of the artificially darkened shiny burnt-cork face, with red or white lips and woolly wig. It was not *recognition* as some distant cultural memory, or an image or two from early television—it was more immediate, more visceral than that. I recognized it as present in the fabric of my own personal, familial, and local culture, inextricably intertwined into my life. I recognized it in that sense, and yet I was (am) a white male born in the 1950s and raised about sixty miles west of Toronto in a fairly secluded area of rural Ontario. That being the case, I am left wondering: How did *that* (performance tradition) get *there* (into my own, local culture)?

That question is central to my own research, even as I stray to other centuries and other countries. And I am not alone. Not a month goes by that I am not contacted by someone reporting a personal or family memory of blackface-related performance, or some reference to blackface in a published source. This leads me to think that my *recognition* of blackface is far from unique.[8] It is in some measure addressed by all the essays in this volume.

Where Did You Come From? Where Did You Go?

Where did it come from, this strange, and yet persistent performance idiom? This will always be shrouded in mystery, lost in the undocumented haze of popular culture;[9] but research published since the early 1990s has made it clear that its sources and contexts ranged widely. Some have stressed evocative folk and ritual sources: the existence of a folk character among southern black Americans called Jim Crow, a trickster figure with roots in Africa; western European traditions of charivari and carnival, which included blacked-up devil figures, some also cross-dressed; and even proposed connections with the tradition of the Harlequin of commedia dell'arte—another trickster with a black mask, a patchwork costume, and a strong dialect. Others have proposed important sources in a vibrant, uniquely diverse street culture. According to this scenario, there existed in the port and waterway cities of America (and the Atlantic more generally) a chaotic, hybridized culture consisting of the languages, songs, dances, and humor of a full range of northern European and Mediterranean immigrant cultures, commingling in the out-of-doors working world of barges and ships and the seaport world of dancehalls, saloons, brothels, and tenements. Into this mix, during the first half of the nineteenth century, came a large influx of freed and runaway slaves from the southern United States, whose uniquely combined African and American cultures tended to co-opt and be co-opted by these European cultures. Thus percussive clog, jig, and flamenco dance from Ireland, Lancashire, and Spain commingled with a very different aesthetic from western Africa, and British folksong with syncopation. Someone witnessing a performing body with a blacked-up face, then, coming to it with an experience of such folk traditions and "street culture," would read into that body a good deal more than we can understand or recognize today.[10]

And where did it go, then? The first, short answer is "into show business," at first the working-class circuses, variety houses, and theaters of the first half of the nineteenth century. There performers in blackface prospered, surely honing much of their song and dance style, informal patter, and stage presence in such venues, tapping into both the performance traditions of their audiences and the cultural negotiations they indulged in just outside the door, in the city streets of the northern United States. They were favorites in such working-class venues, producing celebrities both local and international—represented most prominently by George Washington Dixon and T. D. Rice, among others (see the first three essays in this volume).

But the longer answer to the question "Where did it go?" is "into the minstrel show," and thus into the business of "showing" race. Earlier blackface performers presented themselves as imitating a type of African American, to be sure; but beginning in the 1840s, blackface entertainments became popular as a stand-alone evening's entertainment, at which point, while retaining some of its folk and popular roots and its wild, carnivalesque tone, the form increasingly became associated with an alleged "authentic" depiction of southern plantation slave culture—hence the common epithet "Ethiopian delineators." Eric Lott, in his influential work *Love and Theft*, assesses the resulting complex of relationships between performer and audience—particularly working-class white male audiences—that remained significant for the minstrel show thereafter.[11]

His picture of minstrelsy is ambivalent in the extreme. On the one hand, he depicts it as racially motivated and demeaning toward freedmen and runaways, mocking their incompetence at anything ostensibly civilized: fashion, dance, song, language, and understanding. It was in this sense meant to bind the audience in a position of superiority, the black body standing in for any immigrant group, for women, for any "other." On the other hand, in these early days of the use of the term "wage slave," the laboring classes could identify both with any depiction of a powerless culture and with the backhanded mockery toward the middle class generated from having an "inferior" character imitate it "badly." The white performer used the role of the black trickster to mock everyone's "betters," and this was by all accounts extraordinarily popular with those first male audiences. Anarchy, apparently, was encouraged. The blackface clown resonated—out of control, angrily inept, and unable to fit into a "white" society, all in lyric, choreography, and narrative.

The fact that a group of men in blackface could carry a full evening's entertainment on their own, without benefit of alternative plot or variety, was a surprise; in effect, these entertainers set themselves up in opposition to, and as a parody of, an existing touring business of concert and variety performers. Later minstrel writing—these performers were very keen to record their own history—expressed a good deal of pride in this ability to compete, and emphasized the hermetic qualities of minstrelsy's society and skill set. Minstrel performers specialized in that one form for their entire career, founded fraternities, promulgated "myths" of origin, and moved to increase the respectability, audience, and commercial power of their "industry"; they rated a separate category in lists of touring professionals in the trade papers, coequal with the "legitimate" touring industry and vaudeville. It is important to understand that, however marginalized it seems now, minstrelsy was at the center of the entertainment industry for a very long time.

Indeed, as it persisted, prospered, and perhaps ossified over the next century, blackface minstrelsy became arguably the most widely disseminated and commercially successful entertainment form of the nineteenth century. After the Civil War it took on a standard set of characteristics familiar to popular memory, including clownlike "endmen" and a stentorian "interlocutor" trading jokes, a prevalence of multipart male harmonies, costumes formulaically alternating between formal evening wear and "plantation" rustic. In its early, antebellum years, however, such rules did not necessarily apply, and anything might have happened on the stage, in any (dis)order.

At the very core of the form—whatever other characteristics it possessed, and however the "business" of minstrelsy changed over time—the one thing all such events had in common was the consistent alteration of the performer's body.

This body had an applied black face created from burnt cork mixed with grease; it was black without shading, and usually darkened to an artificial extreme. This basic makeup was typically interrupted by red (also white) greasepaint around the mouth, creating the appearance of artificially large lips. On top of the head was a wig of short, curly black hair. Costuming varied widely but can generally be characterized as rustic and distressed, with rips and patches, or as garish and urban, ill-fitting, and with bold mismatched colors. There was a strong tendency toward accessorizing associated with the clown, in particular oversized shoes and collars (into which, in some extreme instances, the head could disappear on cue), and striped pants or stockings at odds with the rest of the costume. To all of this might be added specialty costuming, especially for the near-universal "wench" dance, in which a cross-dressed male performer was serenaded.

Singing and dancing was, for the most part, what this body did onstage. The instruments included the very new banjo, advertised as an African and southern slave invention; but it was always accompanied by the tambourine (more like the Irish folk *bourrin*), and the "bones," a variation on the "spoons" or castanets. These three core instruments emphasized percussion, improvisation, and unusual, syncopated rhythmic variations; they were played, by all accounts, with a whole-body passion, the blacked-up masked figures frenetically jerking and adopting unusual stances as if barely able to keep their seats, interrupting these with sudden and quite artificially slow and stately rhythm and movement. To this core "beat" were added, typically, a fiddle and (less often, but surprisingly) the accordion as melodic instruments. The common image of the historical minstrel show that persists today begins and ends with the performance of a number of dialect standards—"Buffalo Gals," "Camptown Races," and "Oh Susanna" among them. These songs were certainly standard features, and the sheet music for them was a source of income; but we might better think of them as the stimuli for a highly energized, possibly exhausting evening of near chaos. With the performers seated (barely) in a rough semicircle, the entertainment ranged from jokes based on the bad pun, through parodies of classical operatic music and dance styles, burlesques of well-known plots (often from Shakespeare or the opera), and "stump speeches," parodying contemporary events, trends, entertainments, and politics through a mock-stentorian declamation in a malapropism-prone dialect.

Popular street culture has always been mined for profit; but the commercial performance industry—the "show" business—also abhors chaos. Commercial performance will always, even as it imitates, do what it must to reproduce and disseminate its product as widely as possible geographically, and to as broad an audience as possible. The commercial needs of the early minstrel show altered its most immediate roots in folk tradition and popular street performance, increasingly emphasizing the exhibition of that "other" culture being represented, over confronting one's own. It controlled and curtailed those elements that would have driven away the middle classes, women, and children, all potential paying customers. This conflict, between the street culture of the trickster fool and the commodity culture of the minstrel show, established an irresolvably contested figure in the blackface performer, the legacy of which can be read throughout this volume.[12]

W. T. Lhamon Jr., whose work on blackface minstrel tradition has been so influential to its study through his books *Raising Cain: Blackface Performance from Jim Crow to Hip Hop* and *Jump Jim Crow: Lost Plays, Lyrics, and Street Prose of the First Atlantic Popular Culture,* begins this volume by updating and adding to his already prodigious work with "Turning around Jim Crow." Beginning with an image provided by Herman Melville, Lhamon revisits the character of Jim Crow that has been so prevalent in the American cultural argument since the early nineteenth century, reminding us that this figure's most influential incarnation, in the performances of T. D. Rice, were aggressively integrationist and markedly abolitionist, rooted in populist politics and the common desire for a greater inclusion in the workings of society. He was a "rogue," but he was a rogue who "figured black and white relations," writes Lhamon, an integrationist trickster taking "occupation of the troubled interzone between blacks and whites." Rice's Jim Crow presents a topsy-turvy world that, in his version of Othello, for instance, ends with a marriage and the presentation of a mixed-race child to the assembled audience. The rewriting of this character into the quintessence of suppression and segregation based on race began early in the practice of commercial minstrelsy, to be sure; but Lhamon suggests that the (troubled) integrationist complexity of this character never wholly disappeared, and that the first promise of Rice's Jim Crow, the "fantasy of merger," has something to teach us about the emotional responses of the nation (and the world) surrounding the election of Barack Obama in 2008. Lhamon has argued repeatedly and persuasively for the significance and strength of the blackface minstrel tradition, the complex and conflicting nature of the "lore" it produced, and the extent to which this lore has continued to affect American popular culture. Using the 2008 presidential election as a starting point, Lhamon revisits the "lore" of Jim Crow, and more generally the contradictions and complexities inherent in the blacked-up performing body as evidenced in its first significant American iteration, all in ways that resonate throughout this volume, making a fitting opening essay. Appended to this argument is a previously unpublished sketch by Dan Emmett (remember the name), which Lhamon suggests may have been a source for Melville's *Benito Cereno.*

Dale Cockrell has also added significantly to the body of knowledge about the performance of blackface with the publication of *Demons of Disorder: Early Blackface Minstrels and Their World,* in which he examines the folk origins of early minstrelsy from a musicologist's perspective. In "Of Soundscapes and Blackface: From Fools to Foster," he revisits that earlier study to ruminate on the great changes that can take place in a brief period through seemingly small actions. Beginning, like Lhamon, with the early character of Jim Crow, he draws a distinction between that character's song—rough, prosaic, unmemorable (as a tune), requiring the performance of the individual parodist for its significance—and the song sung by and about "Zip Coon," notably by the performer and scandal sheet editor George Washington Dixon, which was immensely popular at the time and is extant today (albeit with very different lyrics). The distinction between these two songs initiates a discussion of the shift in focus of the entertainment called "minstrelsy" during its very early years. The blackface character's complex roots in social carnival, embodied by the very political, moralistic, scandal-mongering Dixon, become obscured by the effort of early minstrelsy to appeal to a broader audience, and to imitate (and parody) the popular touring concerts of the day. Cockrell pinpoints a particular evening, around New Year's 1843, when everything changed. (I overstate the case; Cockrell is too fine a scholar to be quite so certain.) That evening Dan Emmett (serving the same pivotal function as he does for Lhamon) and Frank Brower performed an entertainment purporting to re-create the "sports" of southern plantation slaves. In an evening, blackface changed from the presentational parodic performance of the class, race, and gender politics of the audience to the representational delineation of someone else's festivals of misrule. Though Stephen Foster later takes back the form to some significant purpose, what Cockrell explores here is the small, seemingly insignificant moment when the aggressively derogatory and segregationist uses of blackface began overshadowing and finally repressing the broader complexity of the tradition. Lhamon takes the long view, Cockrell the microhistorical view, in two essays that corroborate each other's arguments.

My own essay, "Death and the Minstrel: Race, Madness, and Art in the last (W)Rites of Three Early Blackface Performers," follows up on the arguments of the first two, teasing out of specific documents a sense of the life, work, and legacy of the early blackface minstrel performers, as seen through the men who wrote about their deaths. To some extent these writers prefer to focus on the exhibition and dissemination of skill and cultural practice and the strength of human character evidenced in the camaraderie of touring. But also embedded in these documents—obituaries, brief parable-like biographies, calls for post-funeral fund-raisers, and the medical records of an asylum—is the fear of failure, the idolization of wealth, and the exhibition of madness and race. The simple common image of the blackface minstrel man depicted nostalgically, and then critically, in the twentieth century is belied by such documents.

Providing a bridge from early blackface performance and its later incarnations is "The Uncanny History of Minstrels and Machines, 1835–1923," the contribution to this volume of Louis Chude-Sokei, whose influential work *The Last "Darky": Bert Williams, Black-on-Black Minstrelsy, and the African Diaspora* is widely referenced (including by the other contributors here). This wide-ranging essay throws into relief aspects of the minstrel tradition that are easily missed, by tracing its (surprisingly) close lineage with the history of the automaton. Beginning with the purchase and exhibition of Joice Heth by P. T. Barnum, an early episode in a founding narrative of "the show business" in America, Chude-Sokei examines the exhibition of race as it becomes inextricably intertwined in popular culture with images of sexuality and technology. In what follows he traces the complex attitudes that North Americans have brought to bear on nature and an increasingly industrialized society, through depictions of the southern plantation as by turns wild and natural, or industrialized and dehumanizing. Like the previous essays in this volume, Chude-Sokei's traces this dualistic, ambivalent attitude toward the black and blackface character back to the early years of minstrelsy, with its "simple" plantation folk juxtaposed with the rebellion of the trickster clown. He then takes the argument forward to 1923, the triumphs of jazz, and the invention of the word "robot." His account articulates the fear of the dehumanizing tendencies of technology, and of the "other"-humanizing performances of minstrelsy.

Chude-Sokei establishes a strong connection between the history of blackface minstrelsy and the history of technological spectacle and entertainment in the nineteenth century, a relationship that finds its strongest outlet through film. Blackface has been present in film from its inception, though until recently it was primarily addressed in scholarship as an embarrassing stage archaism. Linda Williams has addressed this challenge in other work, notably *Playing the Race Card: Melodramas of Black and White from Uncle Tom to O. J. Simpson*, in which she discusses the uses (and abuses) of the performance of race on page, stage, screen, and television. In her essay here, she revisits the work of D. W. Griffith, whose radical depiction of race (much of it through blackface) in *Birth of a Nation* has been persistently incendiary throughout the twentieth century and beyond. In "Surprised by Blackface: D. W. Griffith and *One Exciting Night*," she examines a little-known late work that, though clearly created by a master craftsman, has been commonly dismissed as a throwback and a failure because of its treatment of blackface. In *One Exciting Night*, based on the stage hit *The Bat*, a work that includes no blackface component, Griffith adds two significant blackface plots. Williams asks why, and in her answer explores the possible uses of blackface as a formal narrative element of melodrama and farce. *One Exciting Night* becomes not an easily dismissed work that includes blackface performance through habit, but an intentional examination of race. The twinned blackface characters are an amalgam of attitudes from race melodrama and minstrel parody, over which are laid references to military service and heroism in the recent war, and the moral force of loyalty to family. The resulting imagery and tone are decidedly strange: characters are by turns noble and bestial, apparent sexual predators and comically fearful, endearing and disconcerting. By exploring a late Griffith work that did not, as *Birth of a Nation* did, gloss over its use of blackface with technical prowess, and that has not had that more famous film's continuous cultural presence and critical baggage—in other words, it is a film that did not "age well"—Williams sets into relief the continued complexity of the tradition. Taken on its own, Griffith's use of this form can be dismissed as merely inappropriate, a thoughtlessly imposed archaism. But in the context of the film as a whole, and the times in which it was made, blackface performance is never "simply" anything.

Nicholas Sammond's writing on the use of blackface minstrelsy in early sound animation has brought a new appreciation to a body of creative work long dismissed for its demeaning reinforcement of racial stereotypes and its grotesque comic violence. In " 'Gentlemen, Please Be Seated': Racial Masquerade and Sadomasochism in 1930s Animation," Sammond pays careful attention to the chaotic semiotics of one very strange, surrealist film in which Mickey Mouse—a "vestigial minstrel" who had not quite yet been sanitized as part of Walt Disney's changing vision of his legacy—meets, is nearly eaten by, plays jazz with, and battles into submission an animated tribe of "Africans." Sammond seeks to understand this complex work, most particularly by placing it in the historical tradition of minstrelsy. He notes that as blackface waned in vaudeville and seemed merely archaic in film, it continued unabated, and to some degree unnoticed, in animation. In this example, a very American minstrel character (Jim Crow again?) is set in opposition to the savage and uncivilized African character. Mickey/Crow shows ingenuity, an appealing energy, and an aggressive diminution of the other "other" in the film. There is no question to whom our loyalties and identification should be directed, and this illustrates the distinction that can be drawn between the minstrel character and the racist caricature. On the one hand, in this respect the essay points back to those of Lhamon and Cockrell, suggesting that early minstrelsy passed along to us both the trickster character and the passive-aggressive, primitive character that equated the "Old South" and Africa. On the other hand—in this regard resonating with Chude-Sokei's essay tying together minstrelsy and the machine—Sammond invokes the roots of the minstrel tradition in the industrial working class, who looked upon Jim Crow as a fellow "slave" (literalizing the "wage slaves" they considered themselves). That relationship was personal: the trade of animation at the time had quickly become industrialized, with animators assigned piecework that gave them no personal creative control or sense of accomplishment. The explosion of minstrelsy, the musical playing of everything and everyone (including the dead: note that the "jaw bone" was an instrument in minstrelsy), the rebellion of jazz over all, the general loss of control in a chaos of imagery—all this Sammond sees as a creative outlet for the animators, as much as it was for performers and audiences at the beginnings of blackface minstrelsy.

Like Williams and Sammond, Alice Maurice takes on just one film, exploring its use of blackface from every conceivable angle, in the process engaging with many of the roots and branches of the minstrel tradition, along with its legacy in places where (as with Sammond's Mickey) it appears not to be. The film is Spike Lee's *Bamboozled.* Maurice points out that critical response, surprisingly similar to the attitude taken toward Griffith's films, labeled Lee's use of blackface in this film too narrow, dated, and therefore disengaged with contemporary issues. On the contrary, in "From New Deal to No Deal: Blackface Minstrelsy, *Bamboozled,* and Reality Television," Maurice argues persuasively that Lee uses all the tools of the formalist filmmaker he is, to explore the persistence of the tradition in contemporary cultural practice. The use of blackface as a narrative device exposes all similar practice satirically. (The film makes no secret of this, defining the word "satire" in its opening voiceover.) We are taken through a series of examples of Lee's use of composition, editing, set decoration, and acting style, all of which manipulate and complicate our attitudes toward the use of blackface. Maurice draws comparisons between Lee's deployment of blackface and the origins of the Virginia Minstrels, the career of the great Bert Williams, and the notable use of "automaton" collectibles as figures of dehumanization and commodification (resonating clearly with—and illustrating—Chude-Sokei's contribution in this volume). Maurice argues that, far from being "irrelevant," the film is prescient. Drawing from the rich tradition of audience participation and identification in popular culture—and, as we see in this volume's earlier essays, important to the minstrel tradition—Lee's film looks forward to the explosion of "reality" television, with its own variations on the "consumable identity" so explicitly exemplified by "blacking up." Maurice ends with the dissection of an episode of *Deal or No Deal* in which the "models" (arranged not unlike the performers in the larger nineteenth-century minstrel concerts) all don wigs resembling the black contestant's, to troubling effect. Maurice identifies what she calls a "soft racism" that Lee exposes through his use of "archaic" blackface. The racist past of blackface—by extrapolation its entire chaotic, contradictory tradition—is "forgotten but not gone."

Catherine Cole's "American Ghetto Parties and Ghanaian Concert Parties: A Transnational Perspective on Blackface," like Maurice's chapter, takes two distinct events that, on the face of it, have little in common, and connects them through the minstrel tradition. She first of all revisits her earlier research on the "concert party" theatrical tradition in Ghana, discussed in her important work *Ghana's Concert Party Theatre*. In that popular form, a colonized society co-opted the entertainment traditions of the colonizer, using variations on blackface minstrel characters to speak back to the desires and disappointments of their lives. Drawing parallels to the early years of minstrelsy, in particular the parodic, political figure of Jim Crow (him again!), Cole provides a much-needed (and, she points out, not sufficiently explored) reference to the dissemination of blackface minstrelsy internationally, and its translations and permutations when confronted by other cultures. In some ways the Ghanaian concert party might provide us with a window onto the uses (and abuses) of those earlier traditions; and in some ways it is something quite different. In this essay most particularly, Cole reminds us just how aggressively a local culture can rewrite the "lore" of a performance idiom, and how easily it can forget that idiom's origins and disparate readings. Cole notes, for example, the difficulty Ghanaian performers have had understanding why *their* blackface would be treated with such antagonism by Americans.[13]

The second part of Cole's discussion brings the investigations in this volume full circle. In the first essay, as we have seen, W. T. Lhamon explores the persistence of T. D. Rice's integrationist Jim Crow in as recent and as seemingly disconnected an event as the election of Barack Obama. *In fine* Cole, invoking Lhamon's ideas about the "lore" of blackface, explores the persistence of a very different strain of the idiom in American "ghetto parties"—troubling semi-private events in which (mostly middle-class) white college students attend a theme party dressed (and sometimes blacked up) as American ghetto stereotypes. Her discussion of this recent phenomenon—illustrated particularly in the "Compton Cookout"—resonates back through all of the essays in this volume. The private and amateur status of the ghetto party speaks to my discussion earlier in this introduction concerning the persistence and ubiquity of the minstrel tradition. This is not a "figure" that disappeared and then reemerged; it has always been present and accounted for, but only recently widely disseminated through YouTube and, in the case of the ghetto party, through Facebook. The early integrationist and populist complexity of minstrelsy revisited by Lhamon, Cockrell, and myself, and which we all maintain persists in contemporary popular culture in some measure, appears from Cole's description to be missing from the Compton Cookout. If Obama's election, to Lhamon, resonates with one strain of minstrelsy, the ghetto party continues another strain, promulgated by Dan Emmett and others in those early years of minstrelsy: the objectification and dehumanization of the black American that was one project of mainstream commercial minstrelsy. That more derogatory strain is strongly evident in the ghetto party; and yet its organizers insist that there is no harm intended, or even unintentionally possible, in effect (though not with any kind of historical knowledge) invoking that early integrationist trickster as a defense. The often unintentional complexities unleashed by blackface are discussed by Chude-Sokei, Sammond, and Maurice, all of which are echoed in the ghetto party: the acts of misrule and dreams of escape from repressed, "civilized" behavior allowed through blackface minstrel characters; and conversely the caricaturing and dehumanizing of targeted cultural groups. Most troubling of all for Cole is the collective amnesia concerning traditions that are nevertheless co-opted, resurrected, and recycled. Without any understanding of history, in Ghana as in California, the "performers" have no idea how others will read their actions. By way of antidote, Cole provides us with an afterword, in an image and description of a "Blackout," a public demonstration against the recent resurgence of racism represented by the Compton Cookout, in which hundreds of African American students silently protested with obscured faces, in another way both invoking the mask of minstrelsy and making it signify to a wholly different purpose.

I end this introduction, then, with two disparate images from contemporary American culture—the inauguration of Barack Obama and the Compton Cookout. The contributors to this volume argue that events such as these, representing as they so clearly do two divergent attitudes toward race, are also both informed by a long-standing, significant performance of race on stage, screen, and in public event. Like so much else about the past, blackface never really disappeared. What we hope is that this volume assists in the understanding of contemporary manipulations and negotiations with race (and class, and gender) by providing a critical-historical context for its most persistent and influential image, the performing body in blackface.

NOTES

1. Supplementary materials related to all the chapters in this volume can be found through the publisher's website and at www.utm.utoronto.ca/~w3minstr/burntcork. There you will find further imagery, film footage, a database, an annotated list of links to pertinent sites on the Web, and a bibliography, to assist the reader in learning more about blackface performance. See this site also for citations and online material related to the examples in this introduction. Information on print sources is provided in the notes only for historical and local examples that may not be easily located on the Web.

2. Although this may seem something of a stretch with respect to the blackface tradition, its link on YouTube has been sent to me repeatedly by colleagues and students as an instance of the tradition. See Alice Maurice's discussion of *Deal or No Deal* in chapter 7 for more on this idea. There are other examples of blackface, modeling, and advertising. See the website associated with this volume.

3. When this company used blackface in 1981 in *Route One & Nine*, it was met with scorn and protest. See Mel Gussow, "The Stage: Route 1 & 9," *New York Times*, October 29, 1981. This use of blackface affected the group's government funding. See also David Savran, *Breaking the Rules: The Wooster Group* (New York: TCG, 1986). Used again more recently by the Wooster Group, in *The Emperor Jones* (2006), it met with acclaim—a shift that reinforces the argument in this introduction. See Charles Isherwood, "An Emperor Who Tops What O'Neill Imagined," *New York Times*, March 14, 2006.

4. For a sample citation of the newspaper parody, see Tianna Dowie-Chin, "A Black Voice on Blackface," *The Varsity* (University of Toronto), January 21, 2008. For the Halloween controversy, see Denise Balkissoon, "How a Halloween Getup Went Badly Wrong," *Toronto Star*, November 12, 2009. There is a substantial Web presence for this incident. Concerning the imagery, note that there was also a black contestant in whiteface playing John Candy. This is not the only recent reappearance of blackface at Halloween, suggesting its persistence in traditions of carnival, misrule, and charivari. See Dale Cockrell's essay in this volume, and his work in *Demons of Disorder: Early Blackface Minstrels and Their World* (New York: Cambridge University Press, 1997).

5. Clips from YouTube come and go with alarming speed. All examples mentioned were viewed within the previous five years as of May 2011. Similar clips to those mentioned can still be found in some incarnation there by using the keyword search.

6. See www.youtube.com/watch?v=owDUPtBuY78.

7. See www.youtube.com/watch?v=KoYOraDt1_k.

8. Here is a list of further references to blackface performance that came to my attention while writing this introduction: a historical novel described how the "Luddites" of the 1830s, in their attacks on the textile mills that were putting them out of work, disguised themselves in blackface and in drag for their nighttime raids (Sten Nadolny, *The Discovery of Slowness*, trans. Ralph Freedman [Harmondsworth: Penguin, 1997]); a dissertation about arctic exploration noted the common occurrence and importance of performance of all kinds on ships, including a strong element of blackface minstrelsy, and described an Inuit ritual involving a religious use of "blacking up" (Heather Davis-Fisch, "Lost Ships: Performance and the Disappearance of the Franklin Expedition" [Ph.D. diss., University of Guelph, 2009]); an archive at the University of Western Ontario of 8 mm film, shot by a minister during the 1940s, recorded a significant range of cultural events from that time and place, including a local amateur minstrel show; a sound technician for a recording session I attended remembered in conversation that he was in a minstrel show when he was a lad in the 1940s, organized through his local Sunday school; a student showed me a photograph of her husband's great-grandfather, a German dancer, in full minstrel dress in the late 1940s; a "Fun Fact" in the program of an Elvis Presley festival I attended in Collingwood, Ontario, noted that Elvis first sang onstage in his high school's annual minstrel show; a student, in passing, described a Nicaraguan festival in which men black up for performance using petroleum grease; and finally, in a further international example, I have recently been told that there are tribute bands in Japan that play soul music in blackface. If I put all of these examples together randomly, without a clearly articulated context, or further research—

something I should not do—I might get the impression that the use of black makeup to cover the face while enacting some organized, at least partly theatricalized performance was until recently a near-ubiquitous occurrence.

9. Notwithstanding this statement, the history of early minstrelsy has been written about with enthusiasm almost from its inception. T. Allston Brown published what amounts to a (surprisingly accurate) documentary history in the *New York Clipper* in an 1876 series, revised and expanded in 1912. An abundance of newspaper articles can be found in files and scrapbooks in the New York Public Library and the Harvard Theatre Collection, among other archives; by their existence and content it appears that minstrelsy had a strongly loyal and long-lived fan base, which was keenly interested in the original of the genre and its change over time. For earlier narrative histories, see Carl Wittke, *Tambo and Bones: A History of the American Minstrel Stage* (Durham: Duke University Press, 1930); Harry Reynolds, *Minstrel Memories: The Story of Burnt Cork Minstrelsy in Great Britain from 1836 to 1927* (London: A. Rivers, 1928); Edward Leroy Rice, *Monarchs of Minstrelsy, from "Daddy" Rice to Date* (New York: Kenny Publishing Co., [ca. 1911]); Charles H. Day, *Fun in Black; with The Origin of Minstrelsy by Col. T. Allston Brown* (New York: DeWitt Publishing, 1893); and especially Hans Nathan, *Dan Emmett and the Rise of Early Negro Minstrelsy* (Norman: University of Oklahoma Press, 1962; reprinted 1977); and Robert Toll, *Blacking Up: The Minstrel Show in Nineteenth-Century America* (New York: Oxford University Press, 1974).

10. Dale Cockrell's *Demons of Disorder* and William Mahar's *Behind the Burnt Cork Mask: Early Blackface Minstrelsy and Antebellum American Popular Culture* (Urbana: University of Illinois Press, 1999) examine the roots of blackface minstrelsy in folk and popular tradition and its transition into a commercial form; W. T. Lhamon's *Raising Cain: Blackface Performance from Jim Crow to Hip Hop* (Cambridge: Harvard University Press, 1998) explores the genre's long-term legacy; and Lhamon's *Jump Jim Crow: Lost Plays, Lyrics, and Street Prose of the First Atlantic Popular Culture* (Cambridge: Harvard University Press, 2003) examines the legacy in southern folk ritual. A range of periodical literature also exists in what has been a rich field of research since the mid-1990s (see the online bibliography). For reference to Harlequin and minstrelsy, see George F. Rehin, "Harlequin Jim Crow: Continuity and Convergence in Blackface Clowning," *Journal of Popular Culture* 9 (1975): 682–701. For a more wide-ranging discussion of Atlantic culture, see Joseph R. Roach, *Cities of the Dead: Circum-Atlantic Performances* (New York: Columbia University Press, 1996).

11. Eric Lott, *Love and Theft: Blackface Minstrelsy and the American Working Class* (New York: Oxford University Press, 1993). This volume was the first of a number of serious scholarly studies of blackface beginning in the early 1990s; generally credited with helping to revive interest in the subject, it examines the complex psychology and politics of those first audiences.

12. This description of early minstrelsy has been adapted from material published, to different purpose, in "Testimonials in Silk: Juba and the Legitimization of American Blackface Minstrelsy in Britain," in *Testimonials in the American Marketplace: Emulation, Identity, Community*, ed. Marlis Schweitzer and Marina Moskowitz (Basingstoke: Palgrave Macmillan, 2009), 23–49. See that article for a more elaborate discussion of the effect of commodity or consumer culture—the "show business"—on folk and popular performance as experienced in early blackface minstrelsy.

13. Documentary film of these performances and performers accompanies this volume on the Web, available through the publisher's website and at www.utm.utoronto.ca/~w3minstr/burntcork.

1

Turning around Jim Crow

W. T. LHAMON JR.

I am convinced that we shall overcome because the arc of the universe is long but it bends toward justice.

—Martin Luther King Jr., Addresses to the AFL-CIO, 1961

"If you pass Hepzibah's cent-shop," wrote Herman Melville to Nathaniel Hawthorne after reading *The House of the Seven Gables,* "buy me a Jim Crow (fresh) and send it to me by Ned Higgins."[1] In 1851, when Melville asked his friend Hawthorne for a Jim Crow cookie, the phrase, figure, and behavior had a different sense than they do today. My subject is that difference, how it came about, and its implications. I begin with Melville's enthusiasm for Jim Crow tokens not because they return us to an origin for Jim Crow. That origin is a process begun long ago in Africa (where blackface very like the American version is still performed) and continually adapted since crossing the Atlantic in chains. I begin with Melville's note because it returns us to a specific phase in the flip-flopping rites of faux blackness in the United States that, despite our present-day meaning of the phrase "Jim Crow," in this case is positive. Melville's postscript inserts us into a different feeling about Jim Crow that we have forgotten, if we ever knew it, but that Melville could well remember and that his friend Hawthorne had first noticed a decade and a half before in Williamstown, Massachusetts. On the Fourth of July, 1838, Hawthorne saw gingersnaps stamped out in the shape of a dancing Jim Crow for sale during the local celebration of freedom. Was this an early inkling of the radioactive kitsch—lawn jockeys and handkerchief-headed Jemimas, spittoons and coin banks—that would become black memorabilia? Yes, and more. It also encodes a cluster of counter-meanings that pivot on Jim Crow.

These compounded meanings are already responding to and, in turn, exciting the other sides' positions. These included the urge of white people (and, in the case of Hawthorne's Ned Higgins, Irish) to take in, digest, black gestural charisma. Jim Crow promoted this cross-racial affiliation among the ragged low majority. That constitutionally disfranchised connection threatened privileges ensconced in the representative democracy of the mid-nineteenth-century United States. Melville was quick to see the provocative irresolvability of this issue that has, indeed, grown all the more intractable as time has passed. It was a perfect topic for a novelist, as for all cultural expression in a country trying to understand its emerging amalgam, and he would increasingly fasten on it almost as tightly as American popular culture has through the intervening years.

Melville's request to Hawthorne reflects processes of cultural history and social change that intervening activists make taboo at considerable cost. That's because top-down prohibition does not quickly, and may never, change the country's consciousness. If the question is whether it takes formal sanction, including law and social taboo, on the one hand, or practice, on the other hand, to make change, the one-syllable answer is: both. They are both necessary. But outlawing Jim Crow is not an easy intervention, because the racism that people of goodwill wish to purge is knotted up in social processes that we must sustain if we hope to bring emotions in line with intentions. What's at stake is how to admit, then narrate, the relationship between intervention and inflection of deep social rehearsal. Getting that right was what Martin Luther King Jr. had in mind when he told the labor movement that the arc of the universe bends toward justice. How to bend it—that's the question.

The year after Melville's letter, Hawthorne would write the campaign biography for Franklin Pierce. There he tried to explain how, if elected president, Pierce would hold the line on slavery. While they were neighbors in the Berkshires, perhaps Hawthorne and Melville discussed how slavery could not be legislated out of existence, how it had to "vanish like a dream." That is what Hawthorne wrote that Pierce believed, and it is also what Hawthorne's own fatalism seemed to accept.

Melville himself held a more robust attitude toward this change. He understood that cultural rehearsal could work on that dream. Melville would soon finish *Moby-Dick,* and then "Benito Cereno," increasingly pushing readers toward racial interpretation. Americans, however, didn't need Melville or Hawthorne to tell them that figuring out race would be important to their country's consciousness. In addition to laws that might change that consciousness, what they needed—and are still improvising—was a thoroughgoing process for trying out their racial attitudes. Laws would not hold in the United States, would not even occur to citizens, if they did not first imagine, then desire, the change.

The struggle over Jim Crow remains the central American issue. It tells us what has most obsessed Americans for the longest time. Imperial hubris and gluttonous markets may drive misbegotten adventures abroad, but at home the continued failure to include ragged citizens in public decision making is what mocks both the premise of self-evident equality in the Declaration of Independence and the more perfect union promised in the preamble to the Constitution. The contradiction persists because rogues and rags are not politically franchised, so the culture obsesses over them. They have dominated American popular culture since May 1830, when the white actor T. D. Rice first performed the song about Jim Crow in Louisville, giving William Leggett's story "The Rifle" a rejuvenating makeover as "The Kentucky Rifle."[2] A white frontier story immediately turned into a tale whose most charismatic character was a black rogue in rags. When Rice blacked up to sing "Jump Jim Crow" that first time, he changed the complexion of American cultural performance. He brought blackness into the house in a way that started some Americans, white and black, to consider identifying with it. We are still rolling with the implications (Figure 1.1).

The paradox of Jim Crow is that buying him fresh all these years focused Americans on a fictive blackness that brought us our first African American president. This realization drives us to probe the rich backstory of "Jim Crow," to wonder about *delivery* beyond the usual suspects, and to reassess the gravity and persistence of popular culture.

How people deliver social change depends on desires funneling actions that history habitually documents. The way these desires determine plots is the backstory. Its underlying history is as organized as legislation and as disruptive as war—just to name two topics that obviously count as history. Rather than blaming the dark sky, the backstory animates the weather that brought on the front, showing more of its process. For example, when asked how modern democracies change, historians usually turn away from the backstory to finger electoral activism and the responses from the policy administrators who contain change. The sovereign account of American segregation provides a textbook case of this sort of front-story blame. C. Vann Woodward in *The Strange Career of Jim Crow* lists "many sources" for the emergent disapproval, and eventual outlawing, of segregation. These sources include "the United States Supreme Court and its succession of dramatic decisions down to 1954," along with pressure from civil rights organizations, as well as, Woodward goes on, "executive orders of Presidents, acts of Congress, policy decisions of federal agencies, actions by labor unions, professional organizations, churches, corporation executives, and educational leaders . . . the officers of the army, navy, and air force [and] acting orders of both Democratic and Republican administrations. . . . Behind these conscious and deliberate agencies of change were such

Figure 1.1. T. D. Rice dancing and singing "Jump Jim Crow" on New York's Bowery Theatre stage, Evacuation Day, November 26, 1832. The holiday celebrated the withdrawal of British troops from the city in 1783. Earlier on this night, Junius Brutus Booth had reprised illegitimate sovereignty in *Richard III.* Three hundred jubilant audience members jammed the stage to encourage the action, making it "indescribably ludicrous." When Rice came on to sing special verses of his "celebrated song," an "avalanche of spectators . . . made him repeat it some twenty times [but] hemmed him in so that he actually had no room to perform the . . . turning about" (*Morning Courier and New York Examiner*, November 28, 1832). From its outset, crowds both cheered and confined the playing out of Jim Crow's meaning. Museum of the City of New York, Gift of Carl F. Grieshaber. For another image of Rice as "Jim Crow," see Figure 2.1.

great impersonal forces of history as . . . economic revolution, rapid urbanization, and war."[3] But his account makes no mention of desire, hope, or shame.

These lists dissatisfy because they paper over the conflicted moods—the weather—that push citizens to conceive alternatives. If policies seem to prove that people have believed whites superior to blacks, how could citizens now come to vote for integration, intermarriage, and equality? How did these integrative ideas ultimately reorient behavior, then laws, to become self-evident truths in fact? After a while, historians have to track the tears that flow below, and often against, conscious agency. That flow of desire is where the clues are.

If we record only the realm of policy and legislation, change will blindside us. It will seem to come out of nowhere, as we often say, even though there is always an emotional history we should have been watching. That backstory is an archive of unrealized ambitions lurking effaced but not erased. Indeed, the more it is disdained, the more it sustains. Totemic figures carry and compress this archive.

Jim Crow is one of those totems—a palimpsest of accreted meanings, new layers often contradicting and inverting the layer written before, as when a hound lays its scent over a coyote's scat as the two keep contesting their ownership of the increasingly fetishized spot. And vice versa. Or Melville gives us Benito Cereno after Hawthorne gives us Ned Higgins. The instrumentation accompanying early Jim Crow performances, the moves and patter of his danced songs, the momentum of his attractions all persist in forms that his performance has bequeathed. They now are a structure of complex meanings compressed into the words "Jim Crow" that would have provided William Empson an ideal opportunity for an additional chapter in his last book, *The Structure of Complex Words* (1951). Empson pointed toward a history of conflicted codes that key words convey. His loaded words point toward the gestural markers that cultural anthropologists now decode even at home. These include steps and tunes, syncopations and dialects. They especially include tears.

Jesse Jackson's Tears at Grant Park

What Barack Obama calls his "improbable story" was truly already scripted in *Otello,* a blackface play that T. D. "Jim Crow" Rice wrote and first performed on October 28, 1844. Rice swapped out the dignified sonority of Shakespeare's Othello for the twisting cackles of the Jim Crow rogue he had been reinventing for a decade and a half. Rice inserted this rogue into the plot Shakespeare had made canonical, but pronounced him "Otello" to cue on Rossini's 1816 opera. Certainly there were costs for this exchange, but also gains. Rice's Otello spoke and sang the emergent blackface dialect, interspersed with b'hoy coinages that working white youths were rallying round on New York's Lower East Side in the 1840s. Otello was a spry b'hoy, not an import to admire, patronize, or kill off. His blackness in this incarnation of the old story made him local, not exotic, marked him as an insurgent American. And his play had a stunning supplement and conclusion.

The conclusion: unlike in Shakespeare's version of the ancient Mediterranean folktale, Rossini's opera, or the extant blackface mockeries of Shakespeare ("Dars de Money," playing off Desdemona's elite caste), Rice made sure that both Otello and Desdemona survive. He has them appealing across the footlights at the end, asking the audience to "dance and sing / 'Till the whole house ring. . . . And, if all right tomorrow night, / We'll have this wedding over."[4] If *Otello* had its way, this marriage would thrive.

The supplement: two decades before U.S. Emancipation and contrary to every other version of the Othello plot in all its centuries of performance—during which their marriage remained barren—Rice's *Otello* delivered the interracial couple their child. We realize after experiencing this variant that generating this problem child had always been the story's untold reason for being. But for centuries that possibility was too taboo to materialize. Players could not deliver this repressed desire until after Atlantic cultures had played out blackness in the form of Jim Crow. He who could deliver viable interracial progeny and have that offspring applauded would not be an "extravagant . . . stranger" like Shakespeare's Othello (1.3.135). Instead, he would be a local champion, talking as Rice's low audience did. Embodying their home charisma intensely for more than a decade, Jim Crow filled theaters with audiences learning his lyrics so they could whistle them later, recollected in tranquillity. Here's a little of what they learned:

Now my brodder niggars,
I do not think it right,
Dat you should laugh at dem
Who happen to be white.

Kase its dar misfortune
An dey'd spend every dollar
If dey only could be
Gentlemen ob colour.[5]

Only after this culture-wide experimentation could the latent attraction repressed in the conventional Othello plot turn toward its next phase. Now audiences would need to accommodate themselves to its living pressure.

Played by a child actor, graphically African American, the boy who is the product of Otello and Desdemona appears onstage half dark, half light, split right down the middle of his face.[6] (Do not think black gloss or grotesque white lips, not yet; others apply those signs later.) Arriving on Cyprus with young Master Otello (who was born in transit), Desdemona lifts their son to his father: "Behold this pledge—your image here is seen. / Not this side love, the other side I mean [points to child's face]." Kissing his son, Otello breaks into celebratory song that ends, "De longer den de family grows / More stronger am de Union."[7] Philadelphia first heard this verse. That city was of course the place where the members of the Constitutional Convention coined the phrase that continually reminds everyone that Americans systematically struggle with inequality and disunion. And Philadelphia was where Barack Obama delivered his speech on race, March 18, 2008, titling it with the same idea, "A More Perfect Union."

The daily practice of the lore is what binds, confirms, and channels the correspondences embodying them. This blackface lore comprises American winks so sublimated that even the many racist and antidemocratic Americans who are mocked within it cannot or will not read its contrarian content. Nevertheless, this lore practiced from 1830 in Louisville to the present in Philadelphia focuses citizens on a struggle to move toward full union. That is to say, this lore has continually played out the problem of incorporating roguery, black and otherwise. This is the cultural process that Melville's enthusiastic call for Jim Crow cookies suggests he meant to inflect, not censure.

Jim Crow is the earliest popular construction of blackness that Americans provided themselves. The performance of Jim Crow as staged song, inserted in popular dramas, danced and sung in parlors and saloons and on street corners across the country, became the dominant image of blackness. Accuracy has almost nothing to do with this dominance. Its power derives from a fantasy of merger across gulfs of difference: race, class, circumstance, and region. Because these meanings were piled on Jim Crow's totem, they came to undergird both the politics of segregation and the politics of inclusion.

Jim Crow is the fetish figure that tangles these American oppositions, demanding that we untie them. To learn that knot is to understand the contrarieties in American life—something beyond the disgust and shame and horror at the cruel facts. It is to acknowledge the intense waves of emotional release, manifest in tears, that coursed through the country on election day, November 4, 2008, and again on inauguration day, January 20, 2009. Down the tracks of those tears, Americans were releasing pent-up shame and longing tamped tight for centuries. Those tracks reenact and retell a story running from Jim Crow through Barack Obama. After calling attention to his improbable story, a little later in his memoir Obama writes—speaking about the Kenyan father he hardly knew, although he might just as well have been writing about "Daddy" Rice's Jim Crow—"I was living out a preordained script, as if I were following him into error, a captive in his tragedy."[8] In fact the Jim Crow story has become incrementally probable but slow to fulfill itself.

For her parallel reasons, the novelist Zadie Smith has called attention to Obama's mixed family. She notes that interraciality was a failed dream for the president's parents, and that he concludes his first chapter saying, "I occupied the place where their dreams had been." Smith hijacks that profoundly American statement into a comparison of Barack Obama with the Bristolian Englishman Archibald Leach, whom Hollywood transformed into Cary Grant. He "came from nowhere," she says. "Grant seemed the product of a collective dream, dreamed up by moviegoers in hard times, as it sometimes feels voters have dreamed up Obama in hard times."[9]

There is no denying the hard times. But it is a characteristic wrong to imply that Barack Obama's story came from nowhere or is recent. The particular blackness Obama has worked out for himself, fitted into, and repeatedly affirmed could not be more real or rooted in American cultural history. Obama has lighted it up and recharged its possibility. He certainly occupies the place where American dreams and nightmares have long played out a distinctive, indeed the *diagnostic*, American trauma. During and after the 1830s, Jim Crow moved beyond his role as a black trickster. He took occupation of the troubled interzone between blacks and whites. Once there, he figured white and black relations, particularly their overlapping problems within a country that promised self-evident equality but withheld it from poor people, whether or not they were or had ever been enslaved.

Black and More than Black

The candidate's speech on race which arguably propelled him into the White House was important not just for its alignment with constitutional struggle and with the submerged lore of black-white relations at the center of American racial rehearsals. It also reprised a passage Obama had published thirteen years earlier in *Dreams from My Father*—and that passage, too, was of a piece with the lore. Obama had written then that Jeremiah Wright's Chicago church gave him a hope that was "black and more than black." His parlance points out the emotions all Americans have been heaping on "blackness." Obama applied it to his pastor's sermons, confessing that they prompted his own tears of relief and discovery. But Obama's phrase works equally well, perhaps even better, to explain how Jim Crow has evoked a super-blackness for Americans since the mid-1830s. Obama's words, repeated in his memoir and his speech, allow us to mesh the political means that his electorate intended with the disdained legacy that enabled his victory and underwrote what he could achieve. The phrase is clarifyingly solid, but is it new? In fact it is old and also scripted throughout America's blackface rites. For instance, a playbill for Daddy Rice's *Otello*, from Cincinnati on May 9, 1846, notes that the Moor to be performed that night was "born in Orange Street" (in New York's Five Points neighborhood) and is "a Nigger . . . as good as a White Man, and a little gooderer."[10]

My claim is not that Rice's Jim Crow and his play *Otello* luckily anticipated the way Obama appropriated the language of the Constitutional Convention ("more perfect union"). I am not making or disagreeing with the argument that the Constitution overplayed its commitment to equality while licensing slavery and a disfranchised majority. I am certainly not claiming that Obama's "more than black" phrase consciously steals from or alludes to its blackface antecedent. Obama was not consciously engaging in either love or theft of blackface. The point to insist on here is rather that the sort of intentional discourse that people use in memoirs and campaign speeches—whenever they try to make history—bobs willy-nilly on those tides of popular imagery that move a people. Obama's candidacy was successful because he echoed a positive counterlegacy that Jim Crow conveys along with its radioactive patrimony of hatred and segregation. The default accounts we have of "Jim Crow" as a political term hide how very strange Jim Crow's career has really been.

They hide the doubleness of Jim Crow as a persistent American performance. We know Jim Crow's horror. But what a history that chronicles the level of legislation and institutional behavior cannot realize is that Jim Crow entered the American lists by registering the very opposite of the segregation he came to signify. When he first entered popular American consciousness, well before other parts of him entered history, Jim Crow figured freedom, integration, and unity. He did not merely represent desire for those qualities but also embodied them insistently, querulously, while much of the world practiced their opposite. Here, for example, are some consecutive stanzas from the earliest published lyrics of "Jump Jim Crow":

Should dey get to fighting,
Perhaps de blacks will rise,
For deir wish for freedom,
Is shining in deir eyes.

An if de blacks should get free,
I guess dey'll fee some bigger,
An I shall concider it,
A bold stroke for de niggar.

I'm for freedom,
An for Union altogether,
Aldough I'm a black man,
De white is call'd my broder.[11]

These lyrics (performed 1830, published 1832) show how radical Jim Crow originally was. He was wheeling out of bounds while he was singing these verses. Jeering at propriety, he was wearing his tatters into all the spaces designed to exclude him. Despite its residual racist tics, this rehearsed behavior produced a figure whose charisma played toward the full human value of its ragged audience. Jim Crow demanded inclusion. He lambasted a culture that could declare all men are created equal but leave multitudes in chains, disfranchised and disdained.

"Black and more than black," Jim Crow exceeded the categories, spilling dangerously over into the consciousness of disaffected whites. That's why empowered Americans black and white came to outlaw him as soon as they could. But they could not erase or eradicate him. He lived on, hiding in the shadows, coming out the more strongly, the more diversely, each time protocols disdained or policy disciplined him.

By 1835, T. D. Rice, the white man who blacked up as Jim Crow, had extended his song into hundred-verse extravaganzas. He was wheeling through them from New Orleans to New York. He had written three plays capacious enough to house his jumps, his "Yah! Yah!" cackle, and his backtalk: *Oh Hush!* (1832), *The Virginia Mummy* (1835), and *Bone Squash Diavolo* (1835). Their wild performance (mummies coming to life, chimneysweeps bursting Faustian pacts) organized a cross-class and cross-racial public that had never before seen itself figured so provocatively. Yes, blacks attended in the usually segregated audiences, North and South, as the advertised theater ticket prices make clear. This lumpen trickster figure, the lowest of the low, charismatically represented for disaffected white clerks and artisans, along with the white and black underclass, all their mutual resentment at exclusion. His performance diagnosed their dilemma and demonstrated one way to spin free of it.

By 1843 the minstrel show had started to pick up on Jim Crow's clues. Dan Emmett's Virginia Minstrels and Ned Christy's Minstrels had scandalized the black image with their circus conventions yoked to disjunctive stuttering of stump speeches and mock sermons. Rice responded the next year with *Otello.* Emmett and Rice indicate differing proportions among the values contending for attention in the American quarrel about race. That quarrel also measures the issue of democratic inclusion, for which racial segregation was the diagnostic case. While Emmett's stump speeches remain surprisingly radical and inventive in close examination, they often played up exaggeration of black malapropisms for their own, surreal sake. Rice's scripts pushed black fecklessness as a strategy to fend off American political hypocrisy.

By moving the African-Venetian general to the streets of New York, Rice inserted Otello into a blackface dialect community whose ambiguous signification enabled the black hero to resist Brabantio's patriarchy and withstand Iago's racist ploys. Instead of Emmett's salacious double entendre ("take your time, Miss Lucy") with nothing to show for it—which is how minstrel shows often titillated their audiences—Otello instead produced a problem child. In this play, as in its public, the problem with young Otello's interraciality is not his existence, but how to sustain what he stands for through the future. During these culminating years of Atlantic slavery, *Otello* played across the States—in Philadelphia, New York, Cincinnati, and Chicago—provoking both warped variants of itself and twisted opposition. It shows us that the sympathies that Obama reawakened have a history older than, and partly responsible for, Emancipation.

When Jesse Jackson cried at Grant Park, when mixed crowds cried for joy on the Mall for days around January 20, 2009, they were crying not *for* Jim Crow but because of him. They cried not for any of his polar meanings but because a black person was achieving the highest office in the nation.

What none has recognized, however, is that subversive rehearsal of Jim Crow's original modes, usually under other guises, has sustained hope that democracy would finally include all citizens. Barack Obama's biography does not show him admiring many cultural figures in the Jim Crow line—unless Reverend Wright's progressive activism counts—although Obama does evince familiarity with hip hop performers and can quote their lyrics. He is a politician who tends to read and avow the view of history that Woodward typifies in his analysis—namely, that we achieve change by passing laws that force governmental action. But when we track the tears in Grant Park and among the Mall's elated crowds at the inauguration, we have to recognize that their source was a shadow figure that has been hiding in plain sight, not even at the margins of the wider culture. He is a rogue who is black and more than black because many blacks and whites have responded to his position as representing their hopes. Rogue, because he was not approved or included in systems of sovereign governance. Black, because everyone could see that of all the forms of inequality folded into the American experience, poor blacks and slaves suffered the most. Thus people enlisted the black rogue to represent their worst fears of perplexing exclusion.

Jim Crow, then, began and has continually refigured the most radical cultural force known in America. He acted out the full franchise promised, but never yet achieved, in the Declaration of Independence. He held up to view the failed promise of the Constitution to move toward union. What happened? How did this imagined rendition of intimate integration turn into the metonym for segregation?

Abolitionists and slaveholders, patrons of propriety all, turned upon—as in turned *against*—the frightening figure of lumpen energy that was Jim Crow; they outlawed his message. In 1828 newspapers used "Jim Crow" to talk about unracialized vernacular energy. Just a dozen or so years later, by 1842, in newspapers North and South, the phrase had become an adjective for segregation, entirely in our contemporary sense: "Jim Crow America." I conclude that burying Jim Crow's original threat compounded its meaning and ensured its troubling reiteration over the intervening years. By burying it, opponents locked in Jim Crow as America's token for an argument that could play out only in infra dig popular culture.

Through Thick and Thin

Jim Crow has persisted despite continual attempts to erase him. His morphs reappear in irregular continuity. The current that delivers him is syncopated but strong, even when it goes thin, seeming to fade out. He persists through thin years because his gestation was thick. Around 1830, when the black rogue first came inside the theatrical house, T. D. Rice was the most popular of those who danced Jim Crow, but there were others, black and white: Sam Cowell, George Nichols, and George Washington Dixon (white), Old Corn Meal, William Henry Lane, and Picayune Butler (black), from New York to New Orleans. By 1844, when Rice started performing *Otello,* he had written (and had written for him) over a dozen plays to display the rogue figure. The black figures associated with Rice were rude and saucy. A decade in, however, variants appeared that were based on his fame but intended opposing effects, some even verging on saintliness, like Stowe's Uncle Tom. And eventually Rice inhabited that role, too, complicating it further.

We can sense the thick gestation of black charisma by following one strand as it tangles around the first staging of *Otello* in 1844 at Philadelphia's Chesnut Street Theater. This moment occurs more than a dozen years into the burgeoning craze for Jim Crow performance. Rice had sung his song, jumped his dance, expanded both to hundred-verse extravaganzas, and created some of the earliest plays with distinctively American content to house his roguery. The form had momentum abroad and at home. But Rice was losing control of it, too, as other performers gave his characters varied interpretations, both hostile and sympathetic.

During their initial run of *Otello,* many of the actors in Rice's newest play were rehearsing by day the scripted version of George Lippard's novel *The Quaker City,* then serialized in Philadelphia papers and contracted to open immediately after *Otello*'s run. But Lippard's scandalous story of cross-class sex, race mixing, and teeming low life would in fact never be staged. Scandalized local businessmen, whose intimate capers Lippard had transparently disguised in the plot, threatened to provoke riots. The Philadelphia police intervened on their behalf to close the play the afternoon before it was to open. There remains but one surviving playbill at the Historical Society of Pennsylvania. It shows the drama's significant planned alterations in the novel's characterization.

The biggest change is in the grotesque character Devil Bug, white in the novel. In the play he would be in blackface, personated by the actor doing Iago in *Otello.* Blackening the white character was probably intended to make him conform to the tightening convention that black was the color of the ragged low in America. Among the panoply of characters with whom Lippard asked his audience to relate, Devil Bug was their toughest investment. Turning him black in that attitudinal climate was to ensure that the sympathy audiences were asked to extend would feel more transgressive. The gap to be bridged would be broader, the payoff greater. Blackfacing funneled audience investment down the groove that Jim Crow pioneered: rogue chic. Swarthy is the color of early blackface, not the shiny caked makeup with white lips and gloves that Al Jolson made most famous. That differentiating *contrast* came later, in the turnaround that C. Vann Woodward so thoroughly documents at the end of the nineteenth century. In the antebellum era, at least sometimes, the intent was instead merger: *commonality.* This commonality clued the political danger in the form.

Meanwhile, at the rival Arch Street Theater, William Burton was performing the English blackface play that T. D. Rice had significantly altered—Maurice Dowling's *Othello Travestie* (1834).[12] Hindsight gives us a chance to see this play as the rejected antagonist of *Otello.* Dowling scorned the title character. He looked at Othello from Brabantio's insider angle, scraping away the sympathy the senator's daughter extended to the stranger. Dowling's view played at one theater, while Rice's played at another nearby. Both interpretations fed upon certain audience knowledge of Shakespeare's canonical model. Both struggled to alter the attraction and repulsion in relation to black charisma. Dowling scoffed at that attraction; Rice's more popular play celebrated it. But this argument had already become acceptably conventional. The authorities significantly allowed these ritual rehearsals of race to continue when they closed down Lippard's pointed attacks on the city's scions. Thus the cultural work of Americans performing race and inflecting dreams eluded surveillance in Rice's *Otello* and Dowling's *Othello* while Lippard's scandal triggered shutdown. *Otello* simply continued at the Chesnut, filling in Lippard's gaps.

If we broaden *Otello*'s juncture a bit, we find more thickening. Rice was playing the title part in *Otello* eight years later in New York City at Purdy's National Theater, where it was alternating with the first staged version of *Uncle Tom's Cabin,* by Charles W. Taylor (1852). In fact, Taylor himself played Brabantio in *Otello* while the two plays shared the house. This theater fostered many of the earliest American blackface plays, beginning with Dixon's *Coal Black Rose* (October 28, 1829), back when the building was named the Chatham Theater. After an interval in the early 1830s, during which abolitionists converted the theater into an evangelical chapel, Dan Emmett's Virginia Minstrels gave their first performance at the Chatham in January 1843. Also on Chatham Square, at the Franklin Theater, Emmett's play *The Barber Shop in an Uproar* (Figure 1.2) had some of its early performances, featuring Eph Horn, who had been scheduled to play minor black characters in the stage version of *The Quaker City.*[13]

Herman Melville would appropriate Emmett's shaving scene from *Barber Shop* for his quintessential novella about misinterpreting racial masquerade, "Benito Cereno," and Robert Lowell would employ it again a century later for his play with the same title (performed 1964, published 1965). When Melville lifted Emmett, he was developing the premises delivered in the Jim Crow cookie that he had requested from his friend Nathaniel Hawthorne in 1851. Everyone notes Melville's judgment, in his famous letter of April 16, that Hawthorne's prose confronted mid-century velleities with a firm "NO! in thunder." But everyone has been too embarrassed to register Melville's postscript: "If you pass Hepzibah's cent-shop, buy me a Jim Crow (fresh) and send it to me by Ned Higgins." This chain of references had begun on Independence Day, 1838, when Hawthorne's journal recorded "gingerbread figures, in the shape of Jim Crow" at the Williamstown fair. The figure brooded for eleven years in his imagination until he wrote *The House of the Seven Gables.* Then he punctuated the novel with repeated scenes of the Irish urchin Ned Higgins helplessly buying such cookies from the impoverished spinster Hepzibah Pyncheon, now supporting herself by opening a cent shop in a corner of her mansion. These scenes play out Hawthorne's meditations on democratic leveling and inclusion. His deft irony makes these thoughts material in the clustering of Jim Crow's meaning as the culture casually commodified him: the youth's addiction to the dancing figure, the disdain of the prominent woman even as the boy's investment in the stamped-out tokens saves her.

Already "cookie" is an agent of delivery almost precisely in the mode we now assign the word in our digital era—agents of stealth and invasion, inevitably carrying meaning that reveals values of the citizenry through their daily commercial choices. Their presence in our sensorium, as on our hard drives, tells others who we are by the small choices we make even when—most significantly when—we do not realize it. But the recipe for this cookie did not remain fixed in 1851. Melville reworked it more quickly, violently, scathingly when he wrote out Babo's doubleness and the fatal politics of racial misreading in "Benito Cereno" (1855). Here was, truly, the thunder in fact that Hawthorne deftly muffled. Melville's brilliant story developed all the doubleness of effect and impotence implicit in the performance of black roguery, and he did it largely by repeating Dan Emmett's scene of a black barber bloodying a white customer. It is no wonder, then, that when Robert Lowell reanimated this core scene, his puzzled American captain noted that "even shaving here is like a High Mass."[14]

FRANKLIN MUSEUM,
175 CHATHAM SQUARE. GEORGE LEA, Proprietor.
Coolest place of Amusement in the City !!
PRICES OF ADMISSION.
Seats in Private Boxes.......................50 Cents
Stage Seats, with Cushioned Arm Chairs......37½ Cents
Boxes............25 Cents | Gallery........12½ Cents
Doors open at 7, Performance to commence at 8 o'clock precisely.
Children not admitted. No money or tickets returned. Tickets not Transferable.

ANNIVERSARY WEEK !
GREAT TIMES FOR THE CLERGY.
Wonder and Amusement Combined!!
Greatest Place of Entertainment in the United States.
Variety to please all Classes !!

MAD'LLE CAZINET'S TROUPE OF
MODEL ARTISTES
IN SEVERAL NEW TABLEAUX

Signor Joski !!
IN HIS BEAUTIFUL FEATS OF
LIGHT & HEAVY BALANCING !

THE CELEBRATED ANTIPODEAN PEDESTRIAN
Who will without the aid of any Secret Process
WALK HEAD DOWNWARDS !
ON A
FLOOR CEILING,
27 feet in Length, at an Elevation of 18 feet from the Ground

PROGRAMME.—PART I.
LEA'S FEMALE MINSTRELS
Will appear in the following selection of Songs, Choruses, &c.

Overture	Full Band	Dutch Song	Mr. Waddee
Opening Chorus—Let's be Gay	Company	Going to Run all Night	Mr. Smith
Alabama Again	Mr. Smith	Sly Young Coon	T. Waddee
Days of 76	T. Waddee	Dearest May	Miss Louisa
Oh Lud Gals	P. H. Keenan	Angelina Baker	Mr. Mulligan
Nelly Bly	Mr. Mulligan	Going over the Mountains	Mr. Keenan

Intermission of TEN MINUTES to obtain Refreshments at the Bar.

PART II
Burlesque and Miscellaneous Variety.
Tamborine..............Miss Lea
A Grand Musical Fantasia, performing several popular Melodies on a new and peculiar Instrument lately introduced by the Hungarian..............CZARWENKI JOSKI
Sailor's Hornpipe..............M'lle Cataline
Tamborine Solo..............Mr. Smith
The Barber's Shop in an Uproar,
Characters by Messrs Mulligan, Smith, Keenan & Waddee.
Feats of Light & Heavy Balancing....Signor Joski
Sylphide..............M'lle Cataline
Banjo Solo..............Mr. Keenan
Cracovienne..............Miss Lea
Comic Song..............Mr Smith

PART III.
The Antipodean Pedestrian will now appear and walk Head Downwards on the Ceiling without any assistance or secret contrivance whatever.

Intermission of Ten minutes to arrange the Stage for the Tableaux Vivants.

MAD'LLE CAZINET'S TROUPE OF
Model Artistes
Numbering some of the FINEST FORMED WOMEN in the WORLD, will appear in the following
Selection of Beautiful Statuary !!

Sappho	Canova's Studio
Faith, Hope and Charity	May and Morning Star
Maypole Dance	Amazonian Triumph
The Three Graces	Sleeping Beauty
The Thunder Storm	St. John preaching in the wilderness
Worship of Mars	Young Warriors Dream
Innocence	Grand Tableaux in honor of the U. S.

An Afternoon Performance takes place every day at 3 o'clock, for the accommodation of Strangers and others visiting the City, when an entire CHANGE OF PROGRAMME will be given.

Figure 1.2. Playbill for an early performance of *The German Farmer; or, The Barber Shop in an Uproar,* Franklin Museum (bpf TCS 65), Harvard Theatre Collection, Houghton Library, Harvard University. Note the radical mixture of events on display in one evening, ranging from "antipodean pedestrians" to "model artistes" to violent shaving.

While following this chain of connections, I have leapfrogged past the actor T. D. Rice's own changed involvement in the process he had brought to the fore. After performing *Otello* in Philadelphia, and after sharing the bill in New York with the first production of *Uncle Tom's Cabin,* Rice also played the lead in an 1854 Tom show, this one by H. E. Stevens, stage manager at the Bowery Theatre. The timing of this production might have made it available to Melville as he composed "Benito Cereno." In any case, two extant reviews of the play indicate its importance. The *Spirit of the Times* said that Rice impersonated Tom "more successfully than any of his competitors."[15] "Successful" can mean many things, so it is fortunate the other review specifies that, in this case, Rice's Uncle Tom roused

> a gross, robust unreasoning sentiment of hatred to slavery in the very ground tier of society, that may be the germ of a tremendous social explosion. Do slave-holders count upon the steady support of the masses whose seething, throbbing pulses, inconstant purposes, and unchained and reckless impulses, there rocked the brains of thousands? Let them as well reckon upon the quiet of the rumbling volcano. If slavery shall persist in her blind purpose of defying the philanthropic sentiment of the age, and contemning the explosive forces of an outraged humanity, let it beware of the deep sentiment of human brotherhood that lies beneath the brittle transparencies of all political ties.[16]

If this writer in the *New York Tribune* seems to practice political stem-winding himself, then he secures my point. Progressive blackface lore was clustering thickly around Jim Crow. It was also spinning off into surrogates like Uncle Tom, and when it did so, its core sentiment spun with it, at least when the Jim Crow actor inhabited the role. That sentiment was "human brotherhood."

So far we can see that deliverance of cultural work starts with a material thickening, as when a cluster of attempts occurs in a culture trying to think through troubling problems, pondering their complexity. The material thickening—songs, plays, jokes, and fad behavior noticed in cartoons, speeches, stories, novels, reviews—accompanies, furthers, and ultimately documents strata of compound emotions that groups generate about their mutual involvements. Involvement is not necessarily agreement. But it is the working past *dis*agreement, and it leaves a tested residue that survives related rehearsals of issues. Social thickening also discovers the "stratified hierarchy of meaningful structures [that silently sort out] twitches, winks, fake-winks, parodies, rehearsals of parodies" in the way Clifford Geertz used Gilbert Ryle's distinction between twitches and winks to raise the bar for ethnography.[17] Geertz and his adherents argued that an unspoken awareness of mutual meanings, shown in small signs, coalesces to sustain local cultures and to differentiate one from another.

Geertz's formulation allows us to access the history of a people's self-understanding. It also brings into view many people whose consciousness can enter the historical record in almost no other way. These consciousnesses surge beneath laws and administrative policy. They tell a story that may well be quite different from, or even opposed to, the laws ordained to manage the surge. Governments fight wars and pass laws to police the flow of community desires. That's the history of administrative intent, which may or may not enable the desire it manages. It often exists to choke off popular aspirations. Sometimes it achieves both, choking and encouraging desire at once in varying proportion. The history of American democracy, following this principle, has been the gradual incorporation of Jim Crow's roguery.

How to explain the persistence? Why do social movements not dissipate once lawmakers deny them? How do they keep re-forming in guises that keep their core? Persistent morphing occurs because historical thickenings inevitably accumulate contraries. Because they represent and contain arguments, these thickenings around fetish figures include codes sufficiently complex on all sides to reproduce cantankerous meaning over time and through changing scenes. Piling on contraries that draw different crowds to the totem is a tactic that sustains it through slack periods that might have erased anything less often layered and transformed.

The inclusiveness that sustains the symbol also stokes fights over it. Thus the parties who believe they can control the issue will try to bury the fractious meanings they oppose. In practice, that means empowered publics try to outlaw blackface while disfranchised publics deploy it to broadcast their anger and remind everyone else of their existence. If we can achieve an observational stance, suspending moral or self-interested takes, the lore cycle can teach a lot just at this juncture. At least three core groups organize themselves around signs of blackface.

One group deploys its codes to scandalize blacks, believing that the stereotypes they have imputed to blacks deserve scornful laughter. This is the cohort that conventional analysis of blackface luridly emphasizes. This is the audience that guffaws at big lips, checkered costumes, purported black idiocies.

Another group, opponents of the first, appropriate those negative codes to invert them. They scoff at and exaggerate the bigoted condescension of their disdainers. These activists play in a performance zone that their opponents have marked off. They dramatize their incapacity to change laws and attitudes quickly. They display, at least to their own members, their oppressive conditions. This is the group that sophisticated black minstrels organize, in and out of blackface. Their agents have ranged from Billy Kersands to Bert Williams to Chris Rock. They are joined by sympathetic white minstrel performers from T.

D. Rice to Elvis Presley, Mick Jagger to Marshall Mathers (playing Eminem). They perform their disfranchisement as part of their oppression.

A third group, sick of the whole turmoil, including successful blacks who align themselves with progressive allies in the dominant culture, work to outlaw the scandalized sign of blackness—burnt cork and its gestural surrogates. This cohort does not use performers as its agents. Instead, it mobilizes activists and concerned citizens to outlaw performance. (I return to the efforts of this group at the end of this essay.)

All these struggles continually deposit strata of their residue on the American blackface fetish. That's why thick and heavily heaped totems sustain effaced meanings. Lore cycles tend to manage properties without erasing them. They narrow or knead attitudes rather than stopping or starting them. Social and cultural history is therefore not a pattern of clean beginnings or sudden ends but is full of returning repressions. Sometimes the return is as similar as Otello to Othello, or as the white impersonation of Jim Crow was to the previous black trickster. Practiced participants and their publics recognize and take what delight they can in the layering of the palimpsest. Sometimes the returns come in guises as different as rock 'n' roll is from the minstrel show's banjo and bones, as different as standup comedy is from Dan Emmett's stump speeches. Here the connections are tenuous enough that players and audiences in their midst may not recognize them, although the pattern is apparent in the long view. Then the forms rehearse the function of their predecessors even when the recipients are not aware of the burden of history borne in their delivery.

"The 'Refuse' or 'Jim Crow' Car"

I can ground these abstractions in specific cases that demonstrate both the intention to bury blackface metaphysics and the certainty that what is repressed will return. My account so far, in which Jim Crow struts a ratio of antebellum desires and distress, is hardly what we usually think when we hear the phrase "Jim Crow." People of goodwill all over the English-speaking world now use the phrase "Jim Crow America" to put daylight between themselves and the racist history of the United States. We talk of Jim Crow America to scorn the segregated lavatories and schools, the outlawed love and marriages, the enforced ghettos and dashed hopes that slavery and recoil from it produced in the United States. Well past Reconstruction, that now conventional Jim Crow poisoned America's experience right up until . . . until what? Bert Williams and George Walker started laughing at Jim Crow America by billing themselves as "Two Real Coons" in 1899? Until ragtime, then jazz, then rock 'n' roll, then hip hop became the soundtrack of national life? Until Thurgood Marshall started challenging Jim Crow schooling in the 1930s and 1940s? Until the civil rights movement of the 1950s? Until Martin Luther King's "I Have a Dream" speech in the summer of 1963 and the Civil Rights Act of 1964? Until African Americans ran for the presidency in 1972 (Shirley Chisholm), 1984, and 1988 (Jesse Jackson)? Until 2008, when Americans elected President Barack Obama? The list will surely continue because living Jim Crow still constitutes the distinctive trauma of American life and because many events will be required to turn around the momentum of Jim Crow America. Bumper stickers have recently proliferated: "Obummer" and "Uncle Barack," as well as "We Did It." Websites have suggested the advisability of yet another political assassination. But so has confidence gradually increased that our national rites of dehydration—vividly enacted in Jesse Jackson's tears at Grant Park—may have nudged the ratio's proportions away from disdain and toward inclusion for America's untouchables. Just a bit.

It is not enough to say that race is the American theme and Jim Crow its name. If we ever close out that agony, however, it will not be by any fiat that makes the messenger taboo. Laws will not suffice. We will first have to realize *how* Americans themed and fetishized their racism. Understanding its varied intentions, facing it all, perhaps we might work it through. That's why I have attempted here to evoke not the origin, not the statutes, not the oppressive protocol alone, but all the Jim Crow that nineteenth-century social conflict thickened. I have described the way blacks and whites working together and apart made Jim Crow a powerful lever to objectify as well as mask their trauma.

The first general publics to applaud Jim Crow used him to express their anger at their own continuing disfranchisement. Those feelings spawned plays that hosted biracial overlay at stage center, displaced and mocked inherited plots, tamed new agonies as jokes, excited the first Atlantic-wide popular culture, and certainly touched off an unaccommodated spasm in American style. This was a radical delivery system of democratic images: white working youths, an excited segment of disaffected clerks and *calicots,* aligning themselves as black in order to talk back to overweening authorities, wheeling about in concerted affiliation as they have done ever since.

A full analysis of the American-ness of Jim Crow, however, must go beyond this early recovery. It must do more than display its persistence into the present. Full analysis must explain how conventional authority took advantage of enabling features in the presentation of Jim Crow to turn the phrase inside out. Franchised publics were able to turn Jim Crow from a vernacular sign embodying radical integration into its opposite, the very figure of segregation. Some intervening activists acted so ardently that their eagerness suggests they saw a chance to kill two birds with one fervor. Certainly they were eager to help blacks avoid demeaning accommodations. But they hoped also to obliterate the multiform modes that represented blackness. Trying to replace popular integrative activism with more pointed propaganda, they waged a turf battle under cover of morality. They tried to replace frayed rogues with madonnas and children. They intended to produce propriety.

A full analysis must note the partial success and ultimate failure of that strategy. It must illustrate the integrative impulse in the early popular success of Jim Crow persisting despite apparent effacement. The repressed modes hang on to haunt the three fundamental groups of antagonists that still circle racism, on the one hand, and believe they are beyond it, on the other. Jim Crow lore, now proceeding under pseudonyms and conveying morphed codes, still excites diffuse anxieties. My working assumption is that the power of Jim Crow's provocations triggers the continuing depth of his censure. Therefore Jim Crow's history now both conveys and blocks delivery of democratic hope. The reversals in the history of Jim Crow follow from this unacknowledged double history. They are no more natural or magical than card tricks. But behavioral momentum combines with metaphor and media to force emerging meanings so completely switched that the victims seldom realize the sleight.

Here's a concrete example. The usage history of "Jim Crow" reveals an early reversal, an unfortunate force that took and then stuck. Two years before the young actor first sang "Jump Jim Crow" in Louisville that spring of 1830, a Hagerstown, Maryland, newspaper was using "Jim Crow" as an adjective for the vernacular energy that Rice would bring onstage. Their usage was unracialized. A defender of John Quincy Adams attacked a previous letter to the editor supporting Andrew Jackson for president by calling its author a "Jim Crow poet."[18] This vernacularity, as the unbridled jaspers leaping beyond themselves practiced it, is what its antagonists would later outlaw. Jim Crow still remained transracial a year after Rice took on the role, when the *Richmond Enquirer* explained that when a politician had "jump'd Jim Crow," he had "gone over to the opposition."[19] Many were the cartoons that reinforced this meaning over the years by drawing tubby guys in suits making fools of themselves twisting and turning, arms akimbo (Figure 1.3).[20] The papers were picking up on the trickster's shape-shifting instability—and white youths in blackface must have seemed to have abandoned their birthright. The usage was beginning to turn.

In 1833 a Charleston arts reporter noted that "'Jim Crow,' Major Downing, and Davy Crockett are decidedly the most important personages at present in the land of the living."[21] This correspondent signed himself "Oh Hush" after T. D. Rice's play first performed that year, including a week in Charleston. He exactly anticipated Constance Rourke, who wrote ninety-eight years later in *American Humor* (1931) that these same three images constituted the nation's "comic trio."[22]

APRIL 21, 1860.] VANITY FAIR.

DANCING FOR EELS IN THE CHARLESTON MARKET.

DOUGLAS IN HIS CELEBRATED BREAKDOWN.

RIVAL CHAMPIONS.

Figure 1.3. Stephen Douglas "Dancing for Eels in the Charleston Market," from *Vanity Fair,* April 21, 1860. This cartoon spoofs the deals Douglas was making at the Charleston spin-off of the Baltimore Democratic convention. It shows the common currency of Jim Crow imagery.

This widespread and long-lasting meaning showed its troubling diffusion when a *Baltimore Sun* commentator pretended puzzlement at "the unexplainable attractions of [Jim Crow's] sooty face and garments of rags and tatters."[23] This was one of the couplings that transformed Jim Crow into a racial figure, or brought out its unspoken racial dimension. Tom Rice was then on a packet returning from London, so the Baltimore comment was not specifically about him. Rather, it was about the cultural style that Jim Crow's representation encouraged. By then, the popular appeal had gone beyond Rice—or returned—to the charisma of race for parts of his public. The target was not the actor but the public who cheered what he portrayed. The *Sun* commentator registered the divide in the land between the included, who controlled the press, and the excluded, who expressed their feelings in general tatters the others professed not to understand.

By October 1838, the "Jim Crow" category could no longer contain whites. A conductor found two drunken white sailors, abusive and profane, entering his train in East Boston, Massachusetts. Because the sailors were behaving improperly, the conductor forced them to "the 'refuse' or 'Jim Crow' car." Their obscene objection offended others in that car, so the conductor put the sailors off the train, and they began sabotaging the tracks with stones and iron scraps. They were tried and fined steeply, and of course they had no counsel.[24] The "refuse car" on this railroad became increasingly famous because William Lloyd Garrison's magazine *The Liberator* tried to shame the company's superintendent, a Quaker, for enforcing segregation.[25] By the spring of 1842 *The Liberator* was urging readers to boycott the line (or, if white, to join blacks in the Jim Crow car). Garrison's reporters repeatedly told stories of the abuse blacks suffered in its cars and wondered who could stomach such injustice "in sight of Bunker Hill?"[26] By evoking Bunker Hill to remind readers that their founders had fought for self-evident equality, Garrisonians invoked the same index for blame that the Jim Crow songs themselves deployed—and that Barack Obama would much later evoke in his campaign speech on race.

By the autumn of 1842, *The Liberator* was using "Jim Crow" wholly as we do still into the twenty-first century. The magazine published a resolution unanimously passed by its Essex County Anti-Slavery Society: "*Resolved*, that the churches of this land, who retain the Negro Pew, are responsible for all the negro hatred which exists among us, and all its effects manifested in the expulsion of colored people from cars, stages, omnibuses, schools, seminaries—from mechanic, mercantile, and professional employments—manifested in the Jim Crow car."[27] In this resolution, *The Liberator* achieved the categorical rejection that our era shows when it uses "Jim Crow" adjectivally to refer to oppression by segregation.

Both blackface performers and abolitionists fought exclusions that delayed democracy. Whites and blacks doing Jim Crow routines were impersonating a complex image of blackness for various reasons, at least some of which included members of both races joining to that image. In their moral appeal against segregated railcars, however, the abolitionists prepared for the coming attack on performances that were "black, and more than black." In the spirit of the Massachusetts abolitionists, such subsequent censors as the NAACP in the 1950s attacked any manifestation of overt blackface performance, staged, broadcast, or filmed. They hounded the mark, the mask, in order to abolish its content, no matter its effect. Thus they made taboo the convention that had indicated the process was a ritual building on its trickster origins and translating them into a mass drama of cultural identity. They knocked Jim Crow and drove the conversation underground. The landmark analyses by Hans Nathan and Robert Toll in the 1960s and 1970s shamed scholars off their fond chuckling at romantic racism and enlisted them to join the attack.[28] These allied crusaders tried to purge the process by which American culture had long agreed to think through its deferred democracy.

One can sympathize with the good intention, as I do, and still judge the crusade to suppress Jim Crow both misguided and an inevitable failure. Declaring Jim Crow taboo highlighted his position as the representative of the refused. Censuring Jim Crow performance continues to disperse it into spin-off modes of rebellious spectacle, from standup comedy to the parade of black musics, on to rag trade attire and end-zone dancing. Blackface surrogation is astonishingly fecund. Its wide spectrum now includes a presidential campaign premised on the candidate's professed post-raciality. Until he won: then it was clear to everyone that he was black and as proud of it as were the people of all races who voted, campaigned, and cried for him. This was the flip side, the first side of Jim Crow, confirmed. It has been a long time coming, and the inversions are not yet over. The grotesque makeup is now gone, but the pledge across genealogies to nurture their combined offspring, neither side forgotten and both maintained, became manifest in the Obama victory.

The combined parentage in our national makeup is now resurfacing, as it did at the popular outset of Jim Crow in the 1830s, and explicitly so in *Otello,* Rice's last play. We have turned one more twist around Jim Crow. Will it hold? Surely the old buried argument is still out there, lurking and working to come back in. If it does, the true American compound will again be obscured, the cultural work of Jim Crow will again be diluted, the racism prolonged. Democratic inclusion will thin out.

The ultimate solution is the one that politically correct conscience impedes. We must bear with the agonized deliberation of "masked and anonymous" public rites.[29] They began in minstrelsy and continue in its surrogates. They discomfort us. They formed not to ease life but to figure out trauma. As he bloodied his white customer, Dan Emmett's black barber gave solid advice: "Hold still I tell you! Twill feel good when it gits done hurtin." The long persistence of this ritual irrigates national tears. After we have passed all the way through these rites, we might make the union whole and achieve democracy. It is likely, however, that some unforeseen barrier will emerge. We will be blindsided yet again.

Afterword

The German Farmer; or, The Barber Shop in an Uproar
an original Ethiopian Burletta in 1 act
by DAN D. EMMIT

In February 1992 I found and transcribed this play at the Ohio Historical Archives in Columbus, which house the Dan Emmett papers. It was handwritten on crumbling brown paper, tossed in a cardboard packing box with Emmett's songs and skits, many of which remain unknown. If they have not now totally decomposed, these papers remain a rich trove for research. The format and spellings remain as I found them, including Emmett's rendering of dialect, how he spelled his surname, and the extra characters in the cast list—except I have italicized Emmett's underlining.

The Play: Extreme Fun

"I'm de Nigger dat do de whitewashing," sang a white man wearing blackface in the early American play *Bone Squash* (1835). Actors sang it all over North America, England, and Ireland from the mid-1830s past Reconstruction. "We are niggers . . . as it's commonly called; that is, negro melodists," said a blackened white man, explaining his calling to Henry Mayhew in London in the late 1840s—just when Herman Melville was there seeking material.[30] None of this was at all unusual: ragged runaway blacks outsmart and bedevil pretentious white men in all the plays of T. D. Rice, the player who became famous, as we have seen, by activating the black folkdance "Jump Jim Crow" in 1830. In Rice's scenes of a robust and quickly growing Atlantic popular culture, rogue blackness is licensed to speak truth to power. Just as important, the audience cheers on Jim Crow and Bone Squash and applauds the London street singers in blackface as they make rough music.

Sometimes the fun is more extreme. The largely white audience claps when Ginger Blue in *The Virginia Mummy* bites and head-butts and kicks whites who poke or probe him. That is the vein that nourishes Dan Emmett's play. That is the vein that Pompey Smash nicks when he gives the German Farmer a rough shave. That vein and that action underwrite Babo's cunning performance as Cereno's barber in Herman Melville's "Benito Cereno" (1855). The editors of Melville's *Journals* remark that during these years he was "inveterately going to theaters at all levels." Melville probably derived his scene from performances of *The Barber Shop in an Uproar* in New York around 1850.[31] Was it the gore or the thrill of black threat against white disdain that gave this skit legs and life?

Whatever the answer, Emmett's play certainly had wide popularity. Blackface troupers took it west to San Francisco, on to Hawaii, and even played it in South Africa.[32]

Shaving was a significant rite for nineteenth-century men. Robert Lowell caught this role a century later when his adaptation of the scene Emmett and Melville had pioneered has Captain Delano remark, "Even shaving here is like a High Mass." Harriet Beecher Stowe attached similar significance from a different angle when she called shaving the "anti-patriarchal operation."[33] Add race to the mix and everything cuts deeper. The black barber was a common role in blackface theater. He acted as a kind of emcee for male bonding, and, more important, he was a male counterpart to the black nursemaid. Barber and nursemaid were both low roles vested with mortal power. When they rehearsed their intimacies without hitch, barber and nursemaid confirmed protocols of power. When they harmed the child or cut the patron's throat, they dramatized furies of oppression. That is the point of Charles W. Chesnutt's story "The Doll" (1912), which revolves like Melville's story around the scene of a black man shaving a white racist. And of course black rogues with razors appear in threatening cartoons throughout U.S. popular culture, perhaps most memorably rendered in Walker Evans's photograph of an Alabama minstrel show bill (1936).[34]

Certainly there is much that was racist about early Atlantic blackface performance. But *Barber Shop* emphasizes that there was also much more. There was transracial and cross-class identification. There was indelible marking of blackness as authenticity; in some productions, the farmer's ethnicity changed, for example, to French, and blackness would make fun of that dialect, too, but black wit always won against every European contender. There were working youths calling and marking themselves black in order to indicate their difference from their employers. Always there was the tricking—and sometimes the cutting—of stupid white authority.

What does it mean, then, when Dan Emmett's Pompey Smash teaches his novitiate, Slippery Joe, to gore the German farmer? The text is unfinished. It never brings all its characters onstage. And it breaks off at the moment of maximum pain for the rube come to the city. Such encounters are really always unfinished, the way the Punch and Judy show is ongoing, the way we can never compensate or consummate consequences of disdain. Still, Emmett's skit achieved its point. It bootlegged aggression onto the stage against a stiff bigot who presumed to judge rapscallions and laughed at the misfortunes of Pompey. The skit makes its white target writhe in the name of "de old walkarounds style."

Dan Emmett is famous for writing "Dixie's Land" (1859) as a walkaround, the climactic moment in the fundamental social rite that was the minstrel show. Emmett taught drumming, played stringed instruments, and from the early 1840s wrote performance notes toward some of America's most complex expressive culture—songs, stump speeches, and sermons that scarified pretense. All Emmett's work nested in a supple lore that remembers the integrated life of poor people on the frontier he fled at age sixteen. But the way Emmett's work is quick, sly, and surreal also shows him working the mediated urbanity of popular culture. Employing volatile irony, Emmett's wit bucks and nips nearly everything, cutting against black people, surely, and against white people as well, and certainly against powerful people. It simultaneously celebrates rich black dialect and the filiations that smudge social hues. Pompey Smash is the most sympathetic character in a play named for someone else's stereotype. Just so, Babo is the most sympathetic character in Melville's story named after the captain of the slave ship. Emmett and Melville knew what the German farmer and Captain Delano did not: it is dangerous to take popular rites at face value, especially when the face is masked. And when is it not? The real fool is he who pays a stereotype for a shave.

Characters

Hans Nitrelhammer	*A German Farmer*
Pompey Smash	*a negro Barber*
Slippery Joe	*apprentice to Pompey*
Walberena	*a fashionable lady of color*
Jack Ballagher	*a traveling musician*

Scene 1st. Inside of Pompey's barber shop—table in the centre a few old chairs in appropriate places, a pair of large wooden scisors [sic], *one large wooden razor, one large wooden comb, towels, two buckets of lather, one white and the other black, a newspaper, etc. to complete a barber shop. A hair trunk in one corner of the shop. All things in their place. Pompey discovered in his chair, sharpening his razor.*

Pompey. Well, well: who de debble eber thot dat dis child would ebber come to de 'cefsity ob settin up 'Broker shop; but what's de use o'taukin? caze de white folks hab got to be shaved any how an as dat great africum author Mr. Jerolima Ceasar Mark Hannibal says, "Dars jist good meat under brack, as dey're is under white wool." Den, why aint a niggars money jis as good as a white mans? In course it is (*takes up paper*). I'll read de news a little while jis to pass off de time till some body comes in (*reads*). Lost, strayed, or stolen, an empty bag wid a cheese in 'em, marked J. M. wid de letters tore off (*laughs*). I guess I won't look arter dat. What's dis I see: "Strayed away from his amiable mudder, a little boy about four years old, he wasn't missed till he was lost, nor won't be fotch back till he's found: whoebber will return de said boy to his discomsumlate mudder shall hab four shillin took't away from dem." (*knock outside*) Dar's a customer: walk in, sir! (*enter Slippery Joe*) What does you want here child?

Joe. Nuffin.

Pompey. Who's your mudder?

Joe. Pompey de barber.

Pompey. (*aside*) Ha, ha! somebody told im to say dat. What you come here for?

Joe. I wants to larn to shabe folks.

Pompey. Den I tooks you for my 'prentice an ebry ting you see me do to de customers, I want you to do to dat hair trunk, but don't you speak fore de white folks, but tend to your work.

Joe. Yes Hoss! (*sets down on the trunk.*) (*enter Farmer*)

Farmer. (*looking around*) Dunder wedder! if dish Ny Yorg doesnt peat all de under downs I never seen areatty. What! 'ter tyful—de house all shingled over mit glotts! Dish musht pe de parpers shop house. I wonder whar de plack rashcal can pe, tat musht pe him tat tied my hoss loose agin outside teyre. (*rapps* [sic] *on the floor with cane*) Hello! Hello! ish te parpers shop in de house?

Pompey. (*rising*) Look here, Mr. Dutchman, I keeps order in my shop.

Joe. Yes we keep order in our shop.

Farmer. Are you te parpers? [Figure 1.4]

Pompey. I is dat.

Farmer. I gum town to Ny York all te way any more, to set on top o'te chury, we've chuste cot thro' mit de gase aretty; so I wants you to shave me pefore I coes home, and I want my hair cut.

Pompey. Took a seat an I'll cut your harr for you in less dan no time (*Farmer attempts to set down. Barber pulls the seat from under him*)

Farmer. Was for you too tat, Mr. Parper?

Pompey. (*wiping chair*) Only cleanin' de charr. Dat boy ob mine is so lazy, when I got him he hadn't a rag to his back; now he's full ob 'em. Took a seat.

Figure 1.4. Dan Bryant and Eph Horn in Dan Emmett's play *The Barber Shop in an Uproar:* "Are you te parpers?" Courtesy of the Laurence Senelick Collection.

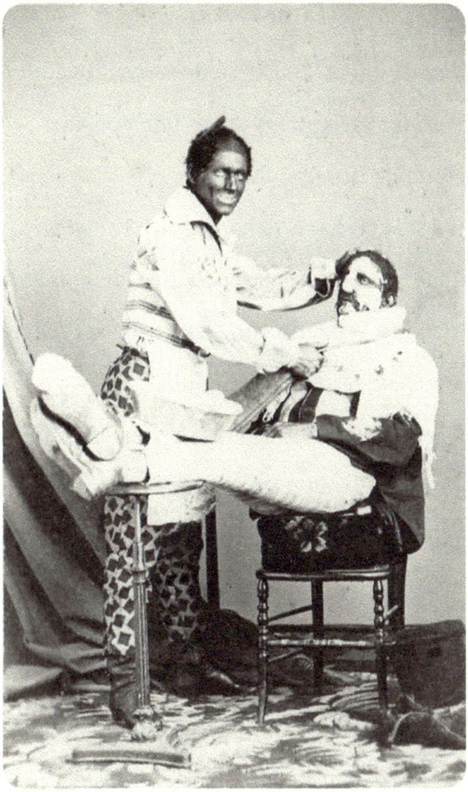

Farmer. (sets down and begins to sing while Pompey fixes towel)

Tune: "Old Dog Tray"
De morn of life is pasht
Lasht night has coom'd at lasht,
It prings me a tream I was trunk te udder tay.

(*Pompey chokes him with the towel*)

(*speaks*) Parpers you dickels me!

(*sings*) Und happy times I've seen
Along mit Honnas Green
While gittin trunk mit Yockup Gray

(*Pompey gets the shears and accidentally gets them around Farmer's neck [business]. Joe puts wig on the trunk and imitates Pompey*)

Pompey. Dar, Mr. Dutchman your harr is cut; don't you want to get shaved?

Farmer. What do you charge to make shave in dis shop, heh?

Pompey. Dat 'pends on de style altogedder.

Farmer. How many styles hab you got?

Pompey. Three styles.

Farmer. What is te name funn te styles?

Pompey. Darrs de French, de Garmon and de old Warginny styles.

Farmer. What do you charge for te French Style?

Pompey. A quarter of a dollar.

Farmer. O tass is too mush! how much for te Charman style?

Pompey. Twenty fibe cents.

Farmer. Tass is sheaper te under one, but what y'e charge for te furchinny style?

Pompey. Two shillin—

Farmer. Dunder und Blixum, tass is de style—go on mit te shave (*aside*) I always peats em town a little.

Pompey. Took your choice an I'll shabe dat bale ob oakum off your face in less dan no time. (*Joe imitates Pompey in all that follows) Pompey gets the lather and stirs it up near the foot lights. Farmer retreats to the other side of stage. tableau*) Now Mr. Dutchman, I'll gib you de best shave what I got in de shop.

Farmer. Was is tas?

Pompey. Dis is ladder. You didn't tink you was gwine to git all dis for Quarter did ye? Sit down, I say. (*Farmer sits down*) It pears to me I have seen you fore—

Farmer. Yesh, I've peen tare areatty when I was foreman settin on top o'te chury.

Pompey. When did ye come down?

Farmer. Last night pefore yesterday.

Pompey. How is de roads?

Farmer. First rate. I makes travel like ter tyful all day, und come four miles from sundown. (*Pompey dabs him with the lather*) You's a verry coot parper—was is your name?

Pompey. Pompey Smash.

Figure 1.5. Dan Bryant and Eph Horn in Dan Emmett's play *The Barber Shop in an Uproar*: "Te Furchinny style makes tam pad hurt on mine face." Courtesy of the Laurence Senelick Collection.

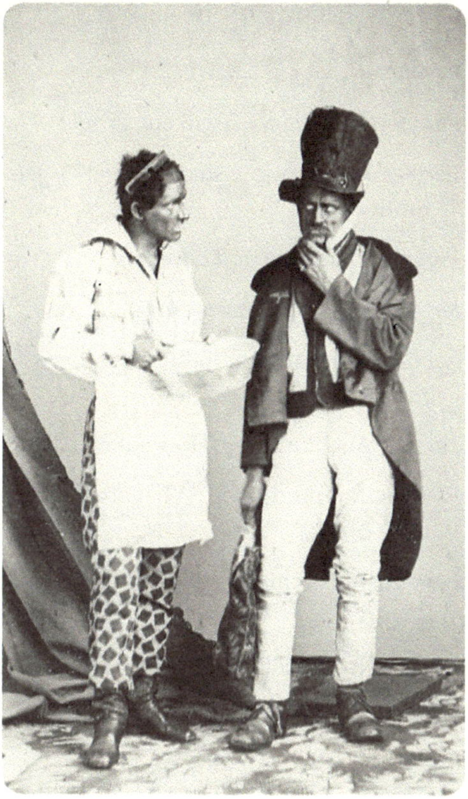

Farmer. Ha, hah! yous ter nager was cot from the church turned out, (*dabs*) how was tas Mr. Parpers.

Pompey. Why I tole you. You see, when I fust set up shop, my razors was sharp den, an ob course I hab a good many customers; den I gib de church $10. Ebry body call me *Bruder Smash.* De next year my razor got dull an I didn't hab so much custom, an I couldn't ford to gib but $5.00. Den dey call me *Mr. Smash.* Den somebody stole my razor, an ob course I got berry poor an couldn't gib any ting, and arter dat dey call me *Old Niggar Smash* so den I leff um! (*Pompey lathers him during the foregoing speech. At the end of speech he puts the strop on Farmer's shoulder and strops razor in a rough manner*).

Farmer. How many razors hab you cot, Mr. Parpers?

Pompey. Three! One shaves alone. Tother you hab to hold back. And de last one shabes half a mile 'fore de edge. (*He strops razor on floor and cuts a hair*)

Farmer. Was is tass?

Pompey. Dis de beardum pullum out by de rootum.

Farmer. Will it cut a hair?

Pompey. (*cuts table*) 'Twill cut a rope!

Farmer. Go on mit te shave. (*Pompey gets on his back*) Pe careful, I peen cot te tooth ache.

Pompey. Dats easy nuff cured.

Farmer. How you makes cure?

Pompey. Fill your mouth full ob sour-crout an set on de fire till it's cooked (*wipes razor on Farmer's clothes*).

Farmer. Auch! murter! How dat razor pulls.

Pompey. It pulls does it? What ob dat. De beard am bound to come if de handle don't break.

Farmer. Te Furchinny style makes tam pad hurt on mine face (*writhes*) [Figure 1.5]

Pompey. Hold still I tell you! Twill feel good when it gits done hurtin.

NOTES

1. Herman Melville to Nathaniel Hawthorne, postscript, April 16, 1851, in, for instance, Herman Melville, *Moby-Dick* (1851), ed. Harrison Hayford and Herschel Parker (New York: W. W. Norton, 1976), 556.

2. See W. T. Lhamon Jr., "21 May 1830: Rogue Blackness Comes in the House," in *A New Literary History of America* (Cambridge: Harvard University Press, 2009), 201–5.

3. C. Vann Woodward, *The Strange Career of Jim Crow* (1955), commemorative ed., afterword by William S. McFeely (New York: Oxford University Press, 2002), 9.

4. T. D. Rice, *Otello,* reprinted in W. T. Lhamon Jr., *Jump Jim Crow: Plays, Lyrics, and Street Prose of the First Atlantic Popular Culture* (Cambridge: Harvard University Press, 2003), 383. All citations of Jim Crow songs and quotes throughout this essay are available in this volume.

5. Stanzas 21 and 22 in "The Original Jim Crow" published first probably in 1832, ibid., 98–99.

6. Playbill for *Otello* in Cincinnati, May 1846, reprinted ibid., 82.

7. Ibid., 362–63.

8. Barack Obama, *Dreams from My Father: A Story of Race and Inheritance* (1995; reprint, New York: Three Rivers Press, 2004), 277.

9. *New York Review of Books,* February 26, 2009, 42.

10. Lhamon, *Jump Jim Crow,* 82.

11. Ibid., 101.

12. For a full account of Dowling's play and the changes Rice made in it when he wrote *Otello,* see ibid., 73–86.

13. *The Barber Shop in an Uproar* is published for the first time in this volume, at the end of this essay.

14. Robert Lowell, *The Old Glory* (New York: Farrar, Straus and Giroux, 1965), 167.

15. *Spirit of the Times* (New York), January 21, 1854.

16. *New York Tribune,* January 17, 1854.

17. Clifford Geertz, "Thick Description: Toward an Interpretive Theory of Culture," in *The Interpretation of Cultures* (New York: Basic Books, 1973), 7; Gilbert Ryle, "The Thinking of Thoughts: What Is 'Le Penseur' Doing?" in *Collected Papers: Collected Essays, 1929–1968* (Bristol: Thoemmes Antiquarian Books, 1990), 480–96.

18. *The Torch Light and Public Advertiser* 14, no. 42, August 14, 1828, 3. This antagonism between Jackson and Adams embodies enduring problems both on American ground and in American historiography. Almost two centuries on, historians are still taking one side or the other; see Daniel Howe's review essay "Goodbye to the 'Age of Jackson,'" *New York Review of Books* 61, no. 9, May 28, 2009, 35–37.

19. *Richmond Enquirer,* June 13, 1831.

20. A later example is the cartoon of Stephen Douglas "Dancing for Eels in the Charleston Market," *Vanity Fair,* April 21, 1860, 265. See Figure 1.3.

21. *Southern Patriot* (Charleston, S.C.), February 27 and December 14, 1833. Rice's play *Oh! Hush!* is anthologized in Lhamon, *Jump Jim Crow,* 148–58.

22. Constance Rourke, *American Humor* (1931), ed. W. T. Lhamon Jr. (Tallahassee: Florida State University Press, 1985), 98.

23. *Baltimore Sun,* August 25, 1837.

24. *Salem Gazette,* October 12, 1838.

25. This Jim Crow car is the one, on the same railroad line, into which Frederick Douglass describes being violently deposited in *My Bondage and My Freedom* (1855; reprint, Chicago: Johnson Publishing Company, 1970), 309. Another account of the struggle over railroad segregation in Massachusetts is Louis Ruchames, "Jim Crow Railroads in Massachusetts," *American Quarterly* 8, no. 1 (Spring 1956): 61–75.

26. *The Liberator,* November 5, 1841, March 3, 1842.

27. *The Liberator,* October 7, 1842.

28. Hans Nathan, *Dan Emmett and the Rise of Early Negro Minstrelsy* (Norman: University of Oklahoma Press, 1962); Robert C. Toll, *Blacking Up: The Minstrel Show in Nineteenth-Century America* (New York: Oxford University Press, 1974).

29. *Masked and Anonymous* is the title of Bob Dylan's underrecognized movie (2003), with its crucial blackface scene, and its insistent singing of Emmett's "Dixie." As Scott Warmuth discovered in 2009 and posted on his blog, Dylan lifted the phrase for the title from Dale Cockrell's analysis of blackface, *Demons of Disorder: Early Blackface Minstrels and Their World* (New York: Cambridge University Press, 1997), 122.

30. Lhamon, *Jump Jim Crow,* 179. See Henry Mayhew, *London Labour and the London Poor,* vol. 2, *1861–62* (New York: Dover, 1968).

31. Herman Melville, *Journals,* ed. Howard C. Horsford and Lynn Horth (Evanston: Northwestern University Press, 1989), 173. The Harvard Theatre Collection has two playbills from New York City's Franklin Museum that give details of *The Barber Shop in an Uproar.* The first is dated June 12 [1848, penciled]. The second is likely from 1851; it shares actors and skits with other playbills securely dated to that year. See Figure 1.2.

32. On San Francisco and Hawaii, Matthew Wittmann reports in his dissertation, "Empire of Culture: U.S. Entertainers and the Making of the Pacific Circuit, 1850–1890" (Ph.D diss., University of Michigan, 2010), that on Tuesday, January 14, 1851, Rowe's Olympic Circus concluded their evening's show with "the laughable afterpiece entitled The Barber Shop in an Uproar." The playbill is in the Hawaii State Archives, Broadside Collection, M-485. Rowe's base was San Francisco. On South Africa, Chinua Thelwell reports in his dissertation, "Nothing Now Goes Down but Burnt Cork": Black Face Minstrelsy and Ethnic Impersonation in South Africa, 1862–1968" (Ph.D. diss., New York University, 2010), that the Juvenile Christy Minstrels performed *The Barber Shop in an Uproar* in Port Elizabeth, according to the *Port Elizabeth Telegraph*, August 29, 1863.

33. Lowell, *The Old Glory*, 167; Harriet Beecher Stowe, *Three Novels*, ed. Kathryn Kish Sklar (New York: Library of America, 1982), 169.

34. For Chesnutt, see *The Crisis: A Record of the Darker Races* 3, no. 6 (April 1912): 248–51, reprinted in *The Short Fiction of Charles W. Chesnutt*, ed. Sylvia Lyons Render (Washington, D.C.: Howard University Press, 1981), 405–12. For Walker Evans, see his *American Photographs*, pt. 1 (1938; reprint, New York: Museum of Modern Art, 1988), 34.

2

Of Soundscapes and Blackface

From Fools to Foster

DALE COCKRELL

The song "Jim Crow," first made famous by Thomas D. Rice in 1830, was a lot of theater and dance, and not much music. One critic observed that it "has a feature that belongs to few songs—it is mostly made up of dancing."[1] Another said of "Jim Crow" that it was "a dramatic song, depending for its success, perhaps more than any play ever written for the stage, upon the action and mimetic powers of the performer."[2] Tom Rice himself came from the theater and always remained a part of it, never laying claim to being a musician.[3] All first-person accounts of his art suggest that he was especially sensitive to the visual and theatrical aspects of blackface minstrelsy: the costumes, the ways in which the body moves, gesture, physical attitude, and even the black mask itself—a quintessentially theatrical statement (Figures 2.1, 2.2, 2.3).

And without Rice to "wheel about, an' turn about, an' do jis so," "Jim Crow" quickly fell from popularity. Known then to millions around the world, the song today is virtually extinct. The online database *Folk Music—An Index to Recorded Resources* lists only four recordings of "Jump Jim Crow" in the twentieth century: two by the old-time fiddler Melvin Wine in the 1970s, one recorded in 1943 as a number in a set titled *Early American Songs*, and one by Taj Mahal and Michelle Shocked that was released in 1992.[4] "Jim Crow" exists today as a social and political icon, but without Rice's theatrical presence and genius it is dead as music. Because this tune is melodically awkward, disjointed, and thus musically "noisy," it encourages us to forgive the sound and embrace the action. The "reality" of the song "Jim Crow" is not the music; it is, rather, the theater, dance, and declamation.[5]

Figure 2.1. T. D. Rice as "Jim Crow." Sheet music cover (New York, n.d.). Courtesy Lester S. Levy Collection of Sheet Music, Department of Rare Books and Manuscripts, Sheridan Libraries, Johns Hopkins University.

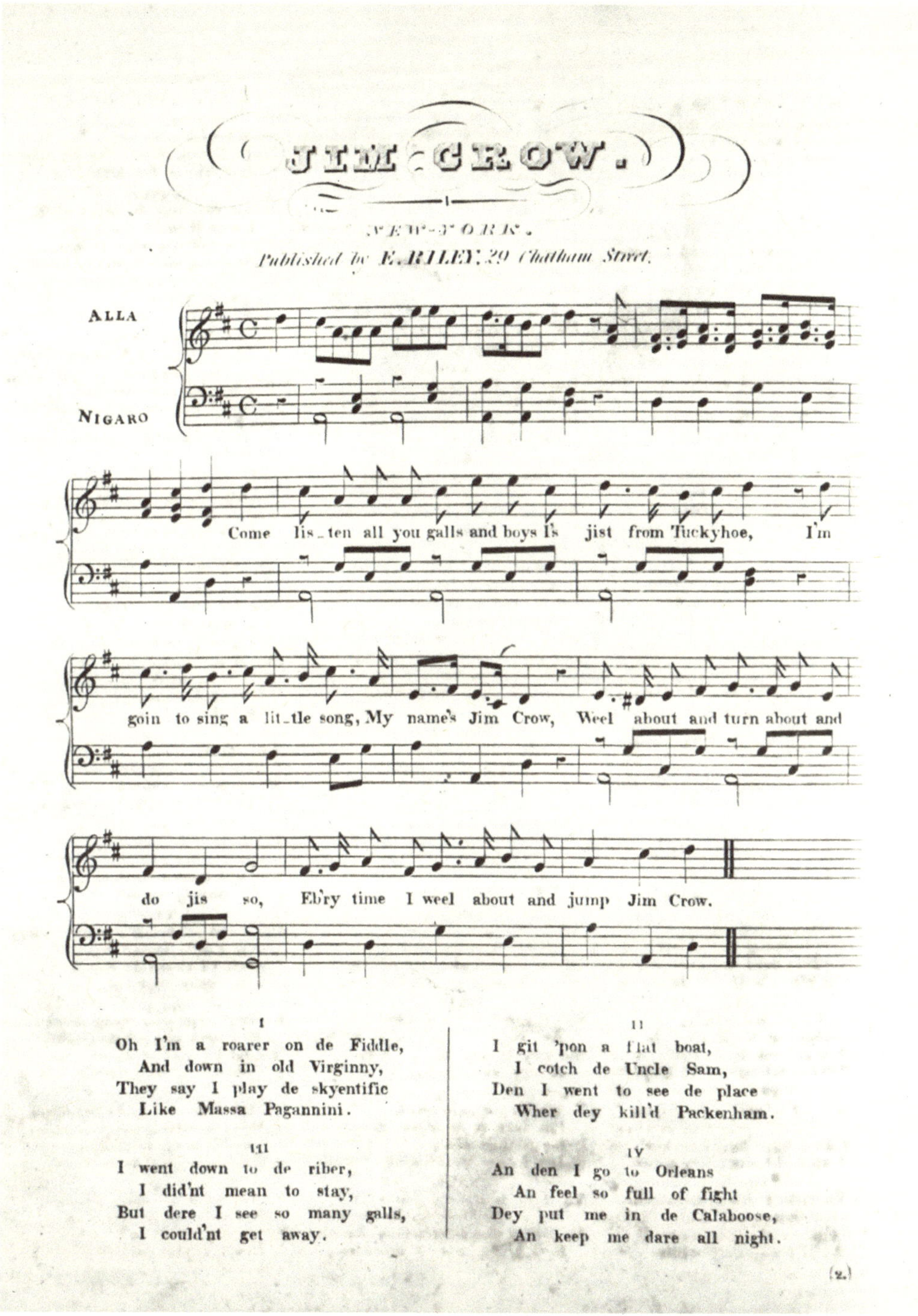

Figure 2.2. "Jim Crow." Sheet music, first page (New York, n.d.). Courtesy Lester S. Levy Collection of Sheet Music, Department of Rare Books and Manuscripts, Sheridan Libraries, Johns Hopkins University.

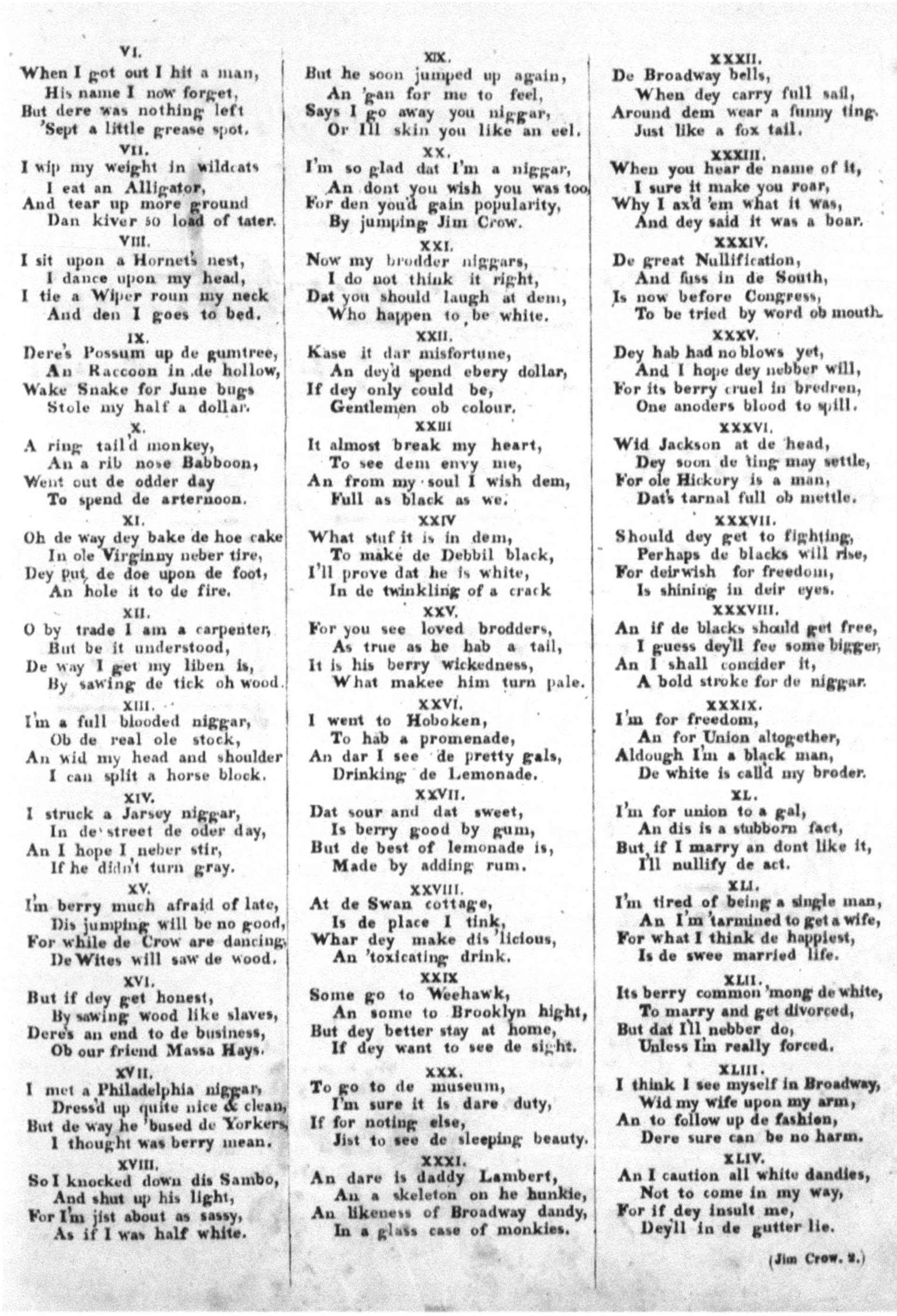

VI.
When I got out I hit a man,
His name I now forget,
But dere was nothing left
'Sept a little grease spot.

VII.
I wip my weight in wildcats
I eat an Alligator,
And tear up more ground
Dan kiver 50 load of tater.

VIII.
I sit upon a Hornet's nest,
I dance upon my head,
I tie a Wiper roun my neck
And den I goes to bed.

IX.
Dere's Possum up de gumtree,
An Raccoon in de hollow,
Wake Snake for June bugs
Stole my half a dollar.

X.
A ring tail'd monkey,
An a rib nose Babboon,
Went out de odder day
To spend de arternoon.

XI.
Oh de way dey bake de hoe cake
In ole Virginny neber tire,
Dey put de doe upon de foot,
An hole it to de fire.

XII.
O by trade I am a carpenter,
But be it understood,
De way I get my liben is,
By sawing de tick oh wood.

XIII.
I'm a full blooded niggar,
Ob de real ole stock,
An wid my head and shoulder
I can split a horse block.

XIV.
I struck a Jarsey niggar,
In de street de oder day,
An I hope I neber stir,
If he didn't turn gray.

XV.
I'm berry much afraid of late,
Dis jumping will be no good,
For while de Crow are dancing,
De Wites will saw de wood.

XVI.
But if dey get honest,
By sawing wood like slaves,
Dere's an end to de business,
Ob our friend Massa Hays.

XVII.
I met a Philadelphia niggar,
Dress'd up quite nice & clean,
But de way he 'bused de Yorkers,
I thought was berry mean.

XVIII.
So I knocked down dis Sambo,
And shut up his light,
For I'm jist about as sassy,
As if I was half white.

XIX.
But he soon jumped up again,
An 'gan for me to feel,
Says I go away you niggar,
Or I'll skin you like an eel.

XX.
I'm so glad dat I'm a niggar,
An dont you wish you was too,
For den you'd gain popularity,
By jumping Jim Crow.

XXI.
Now my brodder niggars,
I do not think it right,
Dat you should laugh at dem,
Who happen to be white.

XXII.
Kase it dar misfortune,
An dey'd spend ebery dollar,
If dey only could be,
Gentlemen ob colour.

XXIII
It almost break my heart,
To see dem envy me,
An from my soul I wish dem,
Full as black as we.

XXIV
What stuf it is in dem,
To make de Debbil black,
I'll prove dat he is white,
In de twinkling of a crack

XXV.
For you see loved brodders,
As true as he hab a tail,
It is his berry wickedness,
What makee him turn pale.

XXVI.
I went to Hoboken,
To hab a promenade,
An dar I see de pretty gals,
Drinking de Lemonade.

XXVII.
Dat sour and dat sweet,
Is berry good by gum,
But de best of lemonade is,
Made by adding rum.

XXVIII.
At de Swan cottage,
Is de place I tink,
Whar dey make dis 'licious,
An 'toxicating drink.

XXIX
Some go to Weehawk,
An some to Brooklyn hight,
But dey better stay at home,
If dey want to see de sight.

XXX.
To go to de museum,
I'm sure it is dare duty,
If for noting else,
Jist to see de sleeping beauty.

XXXI.
An dare is daddy Lambert,
An a skeleton on he hunkie,
An likeness of Broadway dandy,
In a glass case of monkies.

XXXII.
De Broadway bells,
When dey carry full sail,
Around dem wear a funny ting,
Just like a fox tail.

XXXIII.
When you hear de name of it,
I sure it make you roar,
Why I ax'd 'em what it was,
And dey said it was a boar.

XXXIV.
De great Nullification,
And fuss in de South,
Is now before Congress,
To be tried by word ob mouth.

XXXV.
Dey hab had no blows yet,
And I hope dey nebber will,
For its berry cruel in bredren,
One anoders blood to spill.

XXXVI.
Wid Jackson at de head,
Dey soon de ting may settle,
For ole Hickory is a man,
Dat's tarnal full ob mettle.

XXXVII.
Should dey get to fighting,
Perhaps de blacks will rise,
For deir wish for freedom,
Is shining in deir eyes.

XXXVIII.
An if de blacks should get free,
I guess dey'll fee some bigger,
An I shall concider it,
A bold stroke for de niggar.

XXXIX.
I'm for freedom,
An for Union altogether,
Aldough I'm a black man,
De white is call'd my broder.

XL.
I'm for union to a gal,
An dis is a stubborn fact,
But if I marry an dont like it,
I'll nullify de act.

XLI.
I'm tired of being a single man,
An I'm 'tarmined to get a wife,
For what I think de happiest,
Is de swee married life.

XLII.
Its berry common 'mong de white,
To marry and get divorced,
But dat I'll nebber do,
Unless I'm really forced.

XLIII.
I think I see myself in Broadway,
Wid my wife upon my arm,
An to follow up de fashion,
Dere sure can be no harm.

XLIV.
An I caution all white dandies,
Not to come in my way,
For if dey insult me,
Dey'll in de gutter lie.

(Jim Crow. 2.)

Figure 2.3. "Jim Crow." Sheet music, second page (New York, n.d.). Lester S. Levy Collection of Sheet Music, Department of Rare Books and Manuscripts, Sheridan Libraries, Johns Hopkins University.

"Zip Coon" and George Washington Dixon

Such is not the case for "Jim Crow's" complementary Other—"Zip Coon." Also a comedic fool like Jim, Zip was in so many ways different from him. He was northern, urban, a freedman, and a sartorially splendid dandy (Figures 2.4, 2.5, 2.6).

And, I'd suggest, a musician. "Zip Coon," as a song, is still much with us today, whether loved as the tune "Turkey in the Straw," "Natchez Under the Hill," or "Zip Coon." The same database I referred to earlier lists 137 recordings of it, not including those released under the myriad alternate names by which it is known.[6]

"Zip Coon's" musical aptitude is not, I believe, happenstance. As it is useful to know something of the man of the theater who fashioned "Jim Crow," so is it doubly instructive to unmask the man of music who sang most persuasively through "Zip Coon's" blackface, one George Washington Dixon.

Dixon, unlike Rice, was a southerner, likely of humble birth, born in Richmond, Virginia, in 1801. When he was fifteen, "his voice attracted the notice of old [James] West, who attached him forthwith to his itinerant circus company, in the capacity of ostler and errand boy."[7] He spent ten more years learning the business and made his New York debut in July 1827 as a singer.[8] By 1829, the year in which he sang "Coal Black Rose" (arguably the first widely popular minstrel song), he was being prominently billed as "The American Buffo Singer," a tag that would remain with him the rest of his life and one that Dixon welcomed.[9] A charismatic star, he appeared to "crowded galleries and scantily filled boxes."[10] (Since the galleries contained the cheap seats and the boxes were expensive, here is some indication of the lower-class nature of his audience.) He performed what came to be his signature song, "Zip Coon," first in 1834, to enormous acclaim from his plebeian audience. Dixon almost never acted onstage, and I have found no record at all of any skill at dancing; his stage career was as a singer, one who occasionally performed in character blackface. He must have been good, too, for the press exclaimed about his singing: "His voice seems formed of music itself—'*it thrills* it animates' ";[11] "a voice which *all* unite in pronouncing to be of remarkable richness and compass."[12]

By 1836, though, Dixon was trying to shed his image as a stage singer for the masses. He began featuring operatic selections from Rossini, Bellini, and Donizetti, and his bills trumpeted that he was accompanied by performers from "the Academy of Music, London," with various "Professor" and "Signor" credentials.[13] Dixon advertised that his performance space had been fitted up "after the manner of the Operatic Saloon in Paris," and advised: "Ladies are respectfully informed that this will be a 'Dress Concert.' To prevent confu-

Figure 2.4. The character "Zip Coon." Sheet music, cover (New York: Thomas Birch, 1834). Library of Congress.

Figure 2.5. "Zip Coon." Sheet music, first page (New York: Thomas Birch, 1834). Library of Congress.

Figure 2.6. "Zip Coon." Sheet music, second page (New York: Thomas Birch, 1834). Library of Congress.

sion, carriages will set down their company, horses [*sic*] heads turned towards Milk street."[14] That this was to be a "Concert" provides us with a key to Dixon's strategy. Concerts at this time were coming much into favor, in implied opposition to "Theater." The latter had a long history aligning it with the sybaritic, the overwhelming of reason by emotion, the visceral, the body, the popular, blackface, and more: all things anathematic to then-developing family-based systems of value. Concerts were, instead, more cerebral, exclusive, and from a somewhat "higher" European tradition; they were also thought to be uplifting, even moral. This was in addition where the money was to be found, for the very ones who patronized concerts were the ones then building the American business class. Quite simply, Dixon, ever the opportunist, saw an opening and made a dash for it. He hoped to remold himself into an American idol of the white middle class by espousing its values and respecting its traditions (new and fluid as they often were).[15] The next several years would present one ludicrous scene after another as Dixon/Zip Coon tried to leave his blackface behind him (and

Figure 2.7. George Washington Dixon as himself, circa 1836. By permission of the American Antiquarian Society.

all that suggests) and show his fresh white face to fresh white paying audiences (Figure 2.7).

George Washington Dixon was not just a singer, though, for he had a particularly significant shadow career. In 1833 in Stonington, Connecticut, he edited his first newspaper, called *The Cannon,* which apparently folded quickly, leaving no trace. By April 1835 he was back at the trade in Lowell, Massachusetts, and had opened *Dixon's Daily Review,* with its banner "Knowledge—Liberty—Utility—Representation—Responsibility." In 1836 he moved to Boston and started up yet another paper, the *Bostonian, or Dixon's Saturday Night Express.* And after relocating to New York City in 1838, he announced the founding of *The Polyanthos and Fire Department Album,* which turned out to be the most successful and influential of his publishing ventures.

By this time Dixon was writing and publishing for working-class readers (the second part of the title—*Fire Department Album*—signals this). *The Polyanthos* came to specialize in exposing upper-class "libertines," especially those with a taste for the seduction of lower-class women. Toward "moral reform," Dixon, perhaps in the first issue of *The Polyanthos,* published an explosive piece on the (likely) relationship that Thomas Hamblin, noted womanizer and famed manager of the Bowery Theatre, was having with one of his brightest young stars, who also happened to be sixteen years old. A few weeks later he reported that Rowland R. Minturn, a middle-aged, unmarried merchant from one of New York's most powerful commercial families, was enjoying a dalliance with the wife of a leading Gotham citizen.[16] Dixon also around this time charged the Reverend Francis L. Hawks, Episcopalian rector of Saint Thomas's Church in New York City, with sexual adventure, and provided the illicit details.[17] With these published revelations (and many more such), Dixon was following in a fresh line of self-appointed moral reformers who turned to print to regulate community mores.

The few historians who have noticed Dixon's newspaper career have generally cast it as yellow sheet journalism—titillation for the sake of sales. But the record is overwhelmingly clear that Dixon meant passionately what he was about. He led the charge against the famed abortionist Madame Restell after his publishing career had ended, thus with no opportunity to benefit financially from his crusade. And it took physical courage to take his stands. Dixon was severely beaten by Hamblin as a result of the exposé,[18] and on another occasion he was "assailed by a man named Johnson, who undertook to castigate him with a cowhide."[19] Other accounts include an anonymous assault by "a rowdy" in the street, after which Dixon was reported to be "lying with his head split open, and his interesting locks all gory—the effects of a blow from an axe."[20] He may also at least once have been the object of a charivari.[21] He was no coward.

He got results, too, often dramatic, and sometimes unexpected, even unfortunate. Hamblin's mistress, for example, long frail, died ten days after Dixon's article appeared, precipitating a nasty scandal. A coroner's jury found that she had died as a result of "inflammation of the brain caused by great mental excitement, induced jointly by the violent conduct of [her] mother and the publication of an abusive article in *The Polyanthos.*"[22] Minturn, shortly after being exposed, threw himself to his death from the roof of his house "while in a state of mental depression."[23] Minturn's brothers sued Dixon, and the subsequent trial in April 1839 lasted three full days. It was the biggest news of the day; the *New York Express,* just by way of example, printed more than seventy column inches of proceedings. The *New York Herald* proclaimed it the biggest trial since the Helen Jewett murder case of 1836.[24] Dixon was effective in showing that Minturn did in fact consort with lower-class women and introduced graphic, shocking, even sensational evidence to that effect. The result, a hung jury, led the prosecution to abandon the case.

Reverend Hawks had also sued Dixon, and his case was docketed for May 1839, a month after the Minturn suit. Hawks had seen Dixon's legal strategies at work, though, and surely perceived that he was not in a winning position: he could not withdraw the suit, for that would be interpreted as an admission of guilt; and if he brought the case to trial, Dixon would use the popular media to sully Hawks's reputation, irrespective of guilt or innocence. There then unfolded a most curious development wherein a defiant, resolute, and (most uncharacteristically) silent Dixon appeared before the court in May 1839 and changed his plea to guilty. He claimed for years afterward that Hawks paid him $1,000 to change his plea, in return for which Dixon was sentenced to barbering in the state penitentiary for six months, room and board included. A thousand dollars was not bad pay for taking the rap and letting Hawks salvage what he could of his reputation. In the final, telling turn, Hawks, shortly after Dixon's sentencing, was expelled from the pulpit by his congregation and exiled from Manhattan to the hinterlands of Mississippi, by all appearances a most guilty man.

What Dixon was about was mediating for the masses the functions traditionally assumed by charivari—moving, as it were, from the black and white of tar and feathers to that of ink and paper. In fact *The Flash*—a direct spinoff of *The Polyanthos*—made the connection itself when it claimed to "walk invisible and intangible; yet . . . stick to [its] enemies like tar and [be] as impalpable to . . . attacks as feathers."[25] As those who engage in charivari are masked and unidentified, so were the editors of *The Flash,* who identified themselves publicly only as "Scorpion, Startle & Sly," and as with charivari, their intention was to shape through transgressive entertainment a carnivalesque engagement with the humanly compelling.

Let me pursue only one strand of this here, though, for there is an overlay with the development of blackface entertainment. I have argued elsewhere that popular nineteenth-century blackface entertainment was rooted in ancient social masquerade rituals conducted by white people masked in soot or blackface, such as carnival, mumming, Christmas, Lord of Misrule—and charivari. It is not just blackface that makes its way from folk traditions to the popular stage, but the way in which blackface is used—as a transgressive mask enabling comment, criticism, or advocacy of social and political change. In such a light, songs like "Jim Crow" and "Zip Coon," among many others, make sense, for they are at base political songs that comment on social conditions.[26]

In order to understand Dixon as "Zip Coon," one had to grasp the folk traditions that gave him shape; and to understand Dixon the "scandal sheet" editor, one had to grasp the folk traditions that gave *him* shape. In both cases, mediation follows from real people trying to preserve traditional values while confronting real social problems—which is why Dixon as concert singer is so noteworthy. He was seeking a new audience, roughly what we would call the middle class, composed of citizens who did not share his background, his concerns, or his problems. Dixon was in it for their money. "Reality" was not the issue: it was all about the "representation" of values and meanings, a word, I remind, that he had used in his newspaper banner from 1835. Dixon seemed to grasp, however dimly, that the future lay in an elision of traditional modes of body-based expression (a form of the real) with that of middle-class mediation (or representation).

The Virginia Minstrels

This, then, brings us around to the Virginia Minstrels, and the development of the minstrel show, for social rituals and their representation were manifestly of the moment here. Two of the four performers who would shortly constitute the Virginia Minstrels, Dan Emmett and Frank Brower, teamed for a New Year's 1843 entertainment at New York's Bowery Amphitheatre Circus titled "Negro Holiday Sports, in Carolina and Virginia."[27] Emmett and Brower could very well have known firsthand about "Negro Holiday Sports, in Carolina and Virginia," for the year before they had jointly toured through the Carolinas and (likely) Virginia with a "Circus and Caravan," right at the season of slave Christmas misrule festivities. Their "Sports" included representations of slave misrule rituals, which they named "Corn Huskings, Slave Weddings and Junketings,"[28] the last term probably linguistic slippage from "Jonkonnuings," a slave Christmas ritual special to the Carolinas and Virginia, derived in part from Anglo-American mumming. I employ the term "representation" carefully and deliberately here, for in this concept is the original and critical difference between minstrelsy before and after the Virginia Minstrels. The most important earlier developments concerned that which was "real" enough to the audience—politics, class, gender, race. But representation is "that which exhibits by resemblance."[29] Minstrel representation is a phenomenon in which "Others" (African Americans) are held up in resemblance only. Despite the currency of "representation" in postmodern theoretical studies, it is not a word of our time only, for it belonged also to Emmett and Brower (and, of course, to Dixon). In late November 1842, at the Franklin Theatre in New York, the bill read, "Mr. EMMET [*sic*], the great Southern Banjo Melodist, [and] FRANK BROWER, the perfect representation of the Southern Negro characters."[30] The genius of what the Virginia Minstrels were about needed only the melding of falsifying representation to the forces of music, economics, and advertising to change forever the direction taken by blackface entertainment (Figure 2.8).

The Virginia Minstrels were different not in that they banded together and presented a show; it was that they banded together and presented a concert (there's that word again). They were thus in direct emulation of another band, this time of three brothers and a sister—the Hutchinson Family Singers—who began to fill concert halls in late 1842 with a format that represented the values of

Figure 2.8. Virginia Minstrels in performance, from the cover of Th. Comer (arr.), *The Celebrated Negro Melodies, as Sung by the Virginia Minstrels* (Boston, 1843). Notice the extremes of caricature in this image and the sense of movement in the positioning of the bodies.

Figure 2.9. "The Old Granite State." Sheet music showing the Hutchinson Family Singers, circa 1843. This popular group typifies the kind of performance parodied by early minstrelsy. Courtesy of the Center for Popular Music, Middle Tennessee State University.

family and middle-class community through music accessible to "respectables" (Figure 2.9). The idea was not original to the Hutchinsons—who sometimes referred to themselves as "The Granite State Minstrels"—for they were developing a performance modality learned from a European singing family who toured the United States from 1839 to 1842, the Rainer Family, who were also known as "The Tyrolese Minstrels."[31] It is thus not surprising that Dan Emmett and friends would get the idea to establish "The Virginia Minstrels" at precisely this time, and to advertise themselves as "Chaste, Pleasing . . . Elegant . . . and refined."[32] Why emulate a group of clean respectables like the Hutchinsons or the Rainers, even to the extent of troping ironically on their name? The answer was simple economics. Blackface performers at that time (with the exception of the venerable Thomas D. Rice) could expect to earn about $10 per week at their trade.[33] While theaters still foundered under the lasting effects of the Panic of 1837, concerts were building a quite different economic model. It was surely not lost on Emmett and friends that the Hutchinsons—four performers and an agent—had gates of $100 for two concerts in Portsmouth, New Hampshire, in October 1842 and $75 in late November in Lowell, Massachusetts. By the end of May 1843 the Hutchinsons were taking in up to $130 per concert, per night.[34] This degree of success was achieved by control of their image and its successful marketing, and followed their turn to a professional manager, an agent of representation. Blackface performers learned from this model, and by 1844 the century's best-known troupe of blackface minstrels was abroad in the land (and around the world), known by the name of its manager alone: E. P. Christy's Minstrels. But among the blackface crowd the Virginia Minstrels discovered it first, and they turned in search of a manager. They eventually hired a friend of theirs, a journalist who had lauded the Virginia Minstrels in the pages of a sporting weekly he had once edited and a ne'er-do-well who lived parasitically off New York's Tenderloin, a person experienced in mediating traditions. Not George Washington Dixon, although the description would fit, but perhaps his closest friend and colleague, one of the former editors of *The Flash:* George B. Wooldridge.[35]

I am attempting here to document and describe a moment when musical representation became a popular commodity—a time when "resemblance" was advertised as the real and was sold through the power of music to unite in manufactured community a class that was itself manufactured. Some of the long-term results have been especially pernicious, as in the power developed by media and advertising to convey notions of authenticity in the face of contradictory realities. Much was lost in this process; nuance, ambiguity, paradox, transgressive possibilities were all defeated. Minstrelsy came to be what historians (another class of agents of representation) told themselves it was—that it was simply about the unfortunate and laughable black, and that the power of its expression had to be contained and controlled, as its audience had to be denied its traditional social license.

Stephen Foster

At the nexus between the career of George Washington Dixon and the growing power of representation, the image of songwriter Stephen Collins Foster (1826–1864) begins to appear (Figure 2.10). As a boy in Pittsburgh, Foster donned blackface and participated in minstrelsy. He was seventeen when minstrelsy became big business, and he too noticed the vast amounts of money that could be made and that one did not have "to come from Alabamy" or even know anything about the real "Alabamy" in order to tap into it. Music for the people no longer had to be based in experience. In fact, beguiling melodic contours, polished surfaces of sound, and grace and lilt were virtues, characteristics we still associate with musical "quality." Foster possessed a form of the new genius, and already by 1848 he was delivering musical products that were snapped up by a hungry populace: representation commodified. His "Oh Susanna" of that year was the first huge hit—indeed, the seminal hit—in the history of American popular music. The second verse, almost never performed anymore (and for good reason) is:

I jump'd aboard the telegraph and trabbled down de ribber,
De lectrick fluid magnified, and kill'd five hundred Nigga.
De bulgine bust and de hoss ran off,
I really though I'd die;
I shut my eyes to hold my bref,
Susanna don't you cry.

And the third verse is just about as bald in its racist representation.

The greater genius of Foster, though, is that he managed effectively to deconstruct himself in the early 1850s. He revealed his own myth to his own man—and acted on his discovery. For several critical years in the tragic run-up to the Civil War, Foster used the language of representation—the language of his audience—to force on them confrontation with the real.

"Old Folks at Home" ("Way Down upon the Swanee River"), a song from 1851, serves well as an example. In its text there are no real surprises:

Way down upon de Swanee ribber,
Far, far away;
Dere's where my heart is turning ebber,
Dere's where de old folks stay.

All up and down de whole creation,
Sadly I roam,
Still longing for de old plantation,
And for de old folks at home.

Standard "darkey-wants-to-be-on-de-happy-ole-plantation" song. But the music (as opposed to the text) is taken straight from the sentiment-filled, white middle-class parlor. This is real music for real (middle-class) people, intended for consumers with real money and real parlors, not music in a style traditionally associated with the blackface stage. At the level of musical understanding—surely what this song is *really* about—it is hard to imagine a white, probably northern, antebellum amateur singer performing the song and *not* feeling in her sentimental bones that the yearning for home is somehow real, more than just representation, for those feelings were hers, too, expressed by a musical language that was also hers. According to a posthumous tribute to Foster in the *Atlantic Monthly,* an extended article that addressed the note of authenticity and truth perceived in his expression and its derivation:

> [Foster's] verses are distinguished by a *naiveté* characteristic and appropriate, but consistent at the same time with common sense. Enough of the negro dialect is retained to preserve distinction, but not to offend. The sentiment is given in plain phrase and under homely illustration; but it is a sentiment nevertheless. The melodies are of twin birth literally with the verses, for Foster thought in tune as he traced in rhyme, and traced in rhyme as he thought in tune. Of easy modulation, severely simple in their structure, his airs have yet the graceful proportions, animated with the fervor, unostentatious but all-subduing, of certain of the old hymns . . . derived from our fathers of a hundred years ago.[36]

Then, in 1853, came "My Old Kentucky Home," a song that Foster first titled "Poor Uncle Tom, Goodnight." The song is in fact the story of Harriet Beecher Stowe's Uncle Tom being sold downriver from his "Old Kentucky Home."

The sun shines bright in the old Kentucky home,
'Tis summer, the darkies are gay,
The corn top's ripe and the meadow's in the bloom,
While the birds make music all the day.
The young folks roll on the little cabin floor,
All merry, all happy and bright;
By 'n' by Hard Times comes a knocking at the door,
Then my old Kentucky Home, goodnight!

No dialect here, but white, middle-class American English. (Foster shortly afterwards attempted to pull his dialect songs and replace them with verses in standard English, for he came to find the dialect demeaning to the race.)

Figure 2.10. Stephen Foster, circa 1859. Courtesy Foster Hall Collection, Center for American Music, University of Pittsburgh Library System.

And what wonderful music—probably Foster's finest song—wedded to a text about a slave sold away from home to misery and death, which Foster termed so poetically "a shadow o'er the heart."

The head must bow and the back will have to bend,
Wherever the darkey may go;
A few more days, and the trouble all will end
In the field where the sugarcanes grow.
A few more days for to tote the weary load,
No matter, 'twill never be light,
A few more days 'till we totter on the road,
Then my old Kentucky Home, good night!
Weep no more, my lady,
Oh! weep no more today!
We will sing one song for the old Kentucky Home,
For the old Kentucky Home far away.

If, as Lincoln suggested, *Uncle Tom's Cabin* was the cause of the Civil War, it was Stephen Foster who got everyone singing, in chorus, a strongly voiced refrain of support for that cause. The *Atlantic Monthly* again:

> In the true estimate of genius, its achievements only approximate the highest standard of excellence as they are representative, or illustrative, of important truth. They are only great as they are good. If Mr. Foster's art embodied no higher

> idea than the vulgar notion of the negro as a man-monkey—a thing of tricks and antics—a funny specimen of superior gorilla—then it might have proved a tolerable catch-penny affair, and commanded an admiration among boys of various growths until its novelty wore off. But the art in his hands teemed with a nobler significance. It dealt, in its simplicity, with universal sympathies, and taught us all to feel with the slaves the lowly joys and sorrows it celebrated. . . . [M]ay we who owe him so much preserve gratefully the memory of the master, STEPHEN COLLINS FOSTER.[37]

Taught by Dixon the father, Foster the son, now all grown up, instructed Americans on how to sing songs critical of representation, songs that sang transgressively and compellingly of a terrible reality.

I offer no single bright, illuminating flash of understanding that follows from my two-decades-plus study of blackface minstrelsy. Ambiguity, even equivocation, is essential to masquerade, irony, evanescence, and the subliminal, and meanings are always slippery and multivalent—for things must never be what they seem. That's the beauty and the frustration of chasing Dixon's story, for example, for one always ends up in a blind alley, scratching one's head and wondering where the ghost went, and then realizing that perhaps that's not such a bad thing after all. It's the chase that's the main thing, kinetic on the one hand, yet also filled with potential for something that *almost* starts to look like understanding. Dixon was above all a performer in what he attempted: he was always literally "acting out." Minstrelsy too is quintessentially performative. And Foster's music must be performed to be understood. These artistic moments are filled with the motions and dimensionalities implicit in kinesis, as history must also be about motion, dimensionality, and kinesis. To read the dead texts of blackface minstrelsy and look at the two-dimensional images is to comprehend things in potential but to be necessarily limited by the chiaroscuro of bold black and timid white, the path from which to the ahistoric polemic is well trodden. But to imagine T. D. Rice's vital dance and feel the electricity of his stage, to be challenged by Dixon's outrageous and de-centering foolishness over serious matters of representation and reality, and to be moved to express almost unwittingly the prospect of a different world by Foster's music is to prize open the window of the mind and exercise the limb and lift the voice. By so doing one admits to the prospect of change wrought by transgressive ambiguity—at the very least a kind of uncertainty that leaves us open to meaningful dialogue about and between our common complicated and troubled past and our common complicated and troubled present.

NOTES

1. *Cork Herald* (Ireland), quoted in *The Spirit of the Times* (New York), May 13, 1837.

2. [Y. S. Nathanson], "Negro Minstrelsy—Ancient and Modern," *Putnam's Monthly: A Magazine of American Literature, Science, and Art* 25 (January): 72.

3. I argue in my *Demons of Disorder: Early Blackface Minstrels and Their World* (Cambridge: Cambridge University Press, 1997) that the "minstrel show" form is much more about music-making than about "showing."

4. See www.ibiblio.org/folkindex/index.htm.

5. See Cockrell, *Demons of Disorder*, chap. 3 ("Jim Crow"), for more on the song and what it signifies.

6. See www.ibiblio.org/folkindex/index.htm.

7. I base his age and place of birth on the admission information gathered by the New Orleans Charity Hospital, February 27, 1861, which stated that the patient was sixty years old and a native of Richmond, Virginia. The remainder of his biography is compounded from an article in the *Sunday Mercury* (New York) of September 19, 1841, and another in *The Flash* (New York), December 11, 1841. Neither source is in agreement on all points (the *Mercury* claims that Dixon was born in Baltimore, while *The Flash* insists on Alexandria, Virginia). Neither source is a paragon of virtue, for they were both "sporting" weeklies much given to satire, irony, innuendo, distortion, and misrepresentation. See Cockrell, *Demons of Disorder;* and Patricia Cline Cohen, Timothy J. Gilfoyle, and Helen Lefkowitz Horowitz, *The Flash Press: Sporting Male Weeklies in 1840s New York* (Chicago: University of Chicago Press, 2008), for more on the sporting culture.

8. George C. D. Odell, *Annals of the New York Stage*, vol. 3 (New York: Columbia University Press, 1927–48), 354.

9. *Virginia Herald*, issues throughout February 1929; Stuart Thayer, *Annals of the American Circus* (Manchester, Mich.: Stuart Thayer, 1976), 221.

10. Odell, *Annals of the New York Stage*, 3:400, 413, 421; *The Flash*, December 11, 1841. Dixon is sometimes given credit for performing "Coal Black Rose" as early as 1827. See, e.g., Isaac J. Greenwood, *The Circus: Its Origin and Growth Prior to 1835: With a Sketch of Negro Minstrelsy* (New York: William Abbatt, 1909), 124.

11. *Bedford (Pa.) Enquirer*, quoted in the *Harrisburg Telegraph*, January 18, 1834.

12. *Portland (Me.) Eastern Argus*, August 5, 1837.

13. *Boston Post*, April 12 and 29, 1836, and February 4, 1837.

14. *Boston Post*, December 6, 1837.

15. Thus I tend to agree with Stuart Blumin, who, in *The Emergence of the Middle Class: Social Experience in the American City, 1760–1900* (Cambridge: Cambridge University Press, 1989), argues against the neo-Marxist perspective, and claims that there was both the concept and the fact of an urban American middle class during this period. It was ill-defined and sometimes amorphous to be sure. But Dixon (and the others in his cohort whom we will meet later in this chapter) was quite obviously and consciously trying to move "up" to something, and it surely was not the elite class, which was far out of his reach. With the proper education, discerning sensibilities, and refinement, however, one could hope for improvements in one's living conditions and status by social elevation.

16. *The Polyanthos*, December 8, 1838. This issue appears not to be extant; I date the article from its listing among "People's Evidence," New York City Municipal Archives and Record Center, New York City Court of General Sessions, Minute Books, April 15, 1839.

17. In making this kind of charge Dixon was one of a string of editors at this time who fixated on exposing the illicit sexual doings of the clergy. For many more details, see Daniel A. Cohen, *Pillars of Salt, Monuments of Grace: New England Crime Literature and the Origins of American Popular Culture, 1674–1860* (New York: Oxford University Press, 1993); and Cohen, Gilfoyle, and Horowitz, *The Flash Press.*

18. *Boston Post,* July 31, 1838.

19. Quoted in *The Spirit of the Times,* September 1, 1838.

20. *Sunday Mercury,* September 12, 1841.

21. Also variously called a shivaree, skimmington, or rough music, charivari was a centuries-old folk ritual, somewhat like tarring and feathering, intended to regulate social behavior by subjecting a person to ridicule, fright, fear, or ostracism in a manner entertaining to the larger community.

22. *Boston Post,* June 20, 1838. The mother of Hamblin's mistress apparently ran a brothel.

23. *New York Herald,* December 21, 1838.

24. *New York Herald,* April 19, 1839. See Patricia Cline Cohen, *The Murder of Helen Jewett: The Life and Death of a Prostitute in Nineteenth-Century New York* (New York: Alfred A. Knopf, 1998).

25. *The Flash,* October 31, 1841. The editors of *The Flash* had—familiar story—just been indicted for publishing an obscene newspaper.

26. For more details on this line of argument, see Cockrell, *Demons of Disorder.*

27. *New York Herald,* January 1, 1843; it appears that the duo had presented the show two days earlier as well.

28. Quoted in Jon W. Finson, *The Voices That Are Gone: Themes in Nineteenth-Century American Popular Song* (New York: Oxford University Press, 1994), 178.

29. Noah Webster, *An American Dictionary of the English Language* (Springfield, Mass.: George and Charles Merriam, 1855), 939.

30. *New York Herald,* November 28, 1842. It is significant, too, that as "Others" came to represent "Others" on the minstrel stage, representation was politicized. The second generation of minstrel performers and composers—Emmett, Sweeney, George Christy, Dan Bryant, Stephen Foster, and many others—were Irish Americans. They were part of the development whereby minstrel shows became, to a certain extent, a product by and for Irish Americans. The Irish, who occupied a "low Other" social niche with black Americans, claimed a triumph over blacks in issues of power and control—representation again—on the stage and in the streets, with the draft riots of 1863 being only the bloodiest instance. See Eric Lott, *Love and Theft: Blackface Minstrelsy and the American Working Class* (New York: Oxford University Press, 1993), 94–96. Irishness was not a significant part of minstrelsy during the first generation, so the point was then moot. Rice had an Irish name, but he and his family had been in the United States long before the immigration waves of the 1820s and 1840s, and he never drew attention to his roots. There is even evidence that Dixon was virulently anti-Irish; a report from the end of 1843 had it that Dixon shot someone in the thigh over an argument about the Native American Party (the Know-Nothings), "of which George is a leading member," this in the first year of the movement's existence. *Lowell (Mass.) Courier,* December 21, 1843.

31. I trace this development in greater depth in my *Excelsior: Journals of the Hutchinson Family Singers, 1842–1846,* Sociology of Music no. 5 (Stuyvesant, N.Y.: Pendragon Press, 1989).

32. *Worcester (Mass.) National Aegis,* March 22, 1843. The word "minstrel" had a polite connotation before the Virginia Minstrels co-opted and subverted it. Webster's *American Dictionary* was still defining the term in 1855 as "an order of men, in the middle ages, who subsisted by the arts of poetry and music, and sang to the harp verses composed by themselves or others," with no mention at all of the much wider popular notion of the word then in worldwide currency.

33. See the reminiscence on the Virginia Minstrels in the *New York Clipper,* May 19, 1877.

34. Cockrell, *Excelsior,* 86, 88, 140.

35. Cockrell, *Demons of Disorder,* 154.

36. Robert Peebles Nevin, "Stephen C. Foster and Negro Minstrelsy," *Atlantic Monthly* 20, no. 121 (November 1867): 614.

37. Ibid., 616.

3

Death and the Minstrel

Race, Madness, and Art in the Last (W)Rites of Three Early Blackface Performers

STEPHEN JOHNSON

The work of historians of popular culture demands that we make much of little, the more so the further back in time we wish to travel, and the further down we descend in the hierarchy of personal celebrity and generic respectability. For those of us who make this journey, our research is measured in lines of text, not pages, and in partial itineraries, not scrapbooks of press clippings. And yet there is a virtue to studying such nearly invisible brute events, in part (counterintuitively) because there is so little intervening and interfering historical record. Significant personalities who are acknowledged as groundbreaking innovators in their profession or art tend to generate, and have generated for them, a self-serving narrative that obscures events or details that may be, shall we say, distracting. The showmen of the nineteenth century who were not remembered, or who were remembered only briefly, were not rewritten with the passing years, their lives not shaped, the material detritus of their careers not intentionally archived. What we find is accidentally preserved for reasons that do not have to do with the individual. This can be valuable by two measures. First of all, the accident of preservation—in this essay the passing reference, the medical report, the local tribute—speaks to the larger societal relationships negotiated by individuals. They were not in a position to control their own legacy, leaving the institution to report on their behalf; this can be interesting to "read through." But also, the accidental preservation of a document can lead to discoveries that do not suit the standard history, that are troublesome to our present understanding, and that, finally, can cause us to complicate and reinterpret what we thought we knew about that time and place. These are the documents that the individuals themselves may not have wanted to preserve; they are what has been called in microhistory parlance "the exceptional normal"—the joke we don't get (as Robert Darnton has put it), that which appears strange to us but passed without notice at the time. With so few records to assist historians in this cause, we look for these kinds of documents, reading into them what we can—making "much of little." "If only," writes Thomas Postlewait in his discussion of microhistory in theater studies, "we could write history in the Chekhovian mode," where "documentary study and cultural speculation are two aspects of a complex yet united understanding."[1] At its best, I would certainly hope that such history is possible. The three particular documents negotiated here, for example—relating to the deaths of "Boz's Juba," G. W. Pell, and Tom Briggs—might provide insight in microcosm into the complex relationships in the early minstrel show among and between mask, performer, and audience member, discussed on a broader (macrohistorical) scale by a range of fine scholars in recent years, among them the authors represented in this volume. Whatever we historians can *make* of the documents we accumulate (with all of the complexities that word *make* should invoke, causing me to italicize it), in this case it allows us access to the workaday world of the itinerant performer who was not a celebrity. Or not for long.

This essay avoids the more expansive narratives of blackface minstrelsy, which have been rehearsed elsewhere (see the introduction to this volume).[2]

Figure 3.1. The Ethiopian Serenaders in 1848, with Pell, Briggs, and Juba performing together. They later appeared as a trio touring Scotland. From an advertisement for Vauxhall Gardens. Harvard Theatre Collection, Houghton Library, Harvard University.

It focuses on three single documents, one each related to the deaths of three early minstrel performers, for what they might reveal about the culture of early blackface, and with the hope that they might tell us something about its legacy as well. Gilbert Pell, William Lane ("Juba"), and Thomas Briggs all lived around the same time, were well known (even famous) in their day, but soon forgotten. They traveled and performed together for a period of time (Figure 3.1), including as a trio in Scotland late in 1849 (during a cholera epidemic, no less). Together they embody the range of performance that blackface minstrelsy displayed; Juba was a dancer, Pell a clown, Briggs a musician. The documents examined here provide distinct entry points into what was (is?) peculiar to minstrelsy: from an insane asylum outside Liverpool, a medical report on a disgraced, dissolute, and out-of-control body; from the comfort of the offices of the *New York Clipper*, a brief report on the final resting place of the only black performer in early minstrelsy; and from the goldfields of California, a toast to a master craftsman. Each document is quite different from the others, each in its own way revealing disparate attitudes toward the blacked-up body—as the embodiment of race, madness, and skill.

Case 1: The Mastering of Juba

Looking back in 1876, Colonel T. Allston Brown, writing for the *New York Clipper*, reflected: "[Juba] married too late (and a white woman besides), and died early and miserably. In a note addressed to Charley White, Juba informed him that, when next he should be seen by Charley, he would be riding in his own carriage. It has been said that in 1852 his skeleton, without the carriage, was on exhibition at the Surrey Music Hall, Sheffield, England."[3]

In the late spring of 1848 a young American dancer of African descent arrived in London, advertised as "Boz's Juba"—Boz a reference to Charles Dickens, in whose *American Notes* there is a description of a young black dancer in New York. He appeared as part of a blackface minstrel troupe (including Gilbert Pell and Tom Briggs) at Vauxhall Gardens and throughout Britain in the better-class concert halls. Juba received an unusual amount of press. Descriptions of him in performance ran from rubber-legged clown to sublime artist, a "genius of the heel"—his dance compared to everything from clog, jig, and fling through whirling dervish and the wilis (Figure 3.2). He performed a particularly wide range of dances, from the drag wench dance common to the early minstrel stage, to "the dances of his own simple people on festive occasions." This Juba shone like a bright star in the firmament—of the press—for nearly two years; then, leaving the minstrel troupe, he danced in working-class concert saloons and as a theatrical entr'acte hired for the "gallery crowd." Then he disappeared.[4]

Figure 3.2. Juba dancing at Vauxhall Gardens, London, from the *Illustrated London News,* August 5, 1848.

This is the brief chronicle of Juba's career.[5] That career raises a variety of questions worth exploring, because he is an example of the microhistorical "exceptional normal" mentioned earlier—that is, the circumstance that goes unnoticed at the time but seems exceptional to our contemporary view. He was a performer of color in an aggressively racist and, by definition and mask, a segregated performance idiom. His presence is loaded with contradiction and complexity—for proof of which I only have to invoke the image of a young, openly black male (that is, in my opinion, without blackface), in drag, dancing in front of a semicircle of young white men in blackface, who are singing a comic-grotesque and erotic love song to him, all in front of a mixed-gender English middle-class audience, under the guise of authentic slave culture.[6] If we could understand this body's presence in this environment, we would surely complicate our understanding of the culture of blackface minstrelsy.

The microhistorian indulges in the close reading of a quite limited number of documents, arranging them into a significant structure, and extrapolating to some more general purpose. Two examples of making "much of little" concerning Juba illustrate the results. In 1947 Marian Hannah Winter's close reading of the documents at her disposal (a total of six, none of which mentions his skeleton or his performance in drag) resulted in an article that *made* Juba—at the time a completely forgotten figure—the originator of a distinctly American dance idiom, tap, through his authentic infusion of (so-called) African into (also so-called) western European forms.[7] To Winter, he was an aesthetically righteous figure by virtue of the triumph of his talent over prejudice, dancing because, Jackie Robinson–like, he was too good to keep off the stage (a position he holds, thanks to her, in all subsequent histories of dance). By contrast, there is the brief nano-history quoted earlier, written in 1876 by T. Allston Brown as part of a series of articles on minstrelsy in the *New York Clipper,* the most influential show business trade paper of its day. Brown constructs a very different tale—he's writing after a very different war—of a talented man who falls from the grace of the white race's permission to dance, because he rose above his station.

The microhistorian's Chekhovian intentions notwithstanding, when documents are this scarce, each carries a more than usual potential importance. The temptation is great, as in earlier, biblical exegesis, to read too much into each word, and to extrapolate too much from it. Vigilance is the watchword—but how much is too much? I wish to explore that question as it relates just to Brown's last statement, that Juba's skeleton was on display.[8]

Perhaps we should suspect the factual value of Brown's construction because of its blatantly racist message. Nevertheless, it is no more nor less a construction than Winter's was—or than my own will be—and my skepticism concerning the shape of the narrative here does not negate the potential value of the individual statements. So I should follow the lead. Is it possible that Juba's skeleton was on display in a Sheffield music hall in 1852? In general terms, yes. Skeletons were displayed in a variety of venues, from the fairground to the museum, as exhibitions of the exotic, the notorious, the abnormal, or the pedagogical.[9] As to this specific event, Juba danced in Sheffield on at least three occasions, once at the upmarket Music Hall on Surrey Street, where, for several months in 1852, J. T. Woodhead booked rooms to exhibit his "Anatomical Museum and Gallery of All Nations," which included the display of skeletons.[10]

I am skeptical of Brown's document; or I should say that I *wish* to be skeptical of Brown's document. Nevertheless, it is given some credence for three reasons. First of all, it is only the second posthumous reference to Juba, coming twenty-six years after the (proposed) event.[11] That carries some weight. Second, there is the circumstantial (to use the parlance of the detective) motive and opportunity. What are the odds—if I wanted to argue the case—that Brown would use the words "skeleton," "Sheffield," "Surrey," and "1852" in a sentence, and that I would find just the time, the place, and the venue in the local papers? The conclusion is tempting, though I know it is no proof. There is no advertisement for the "bones" of Juba. There is just an "Anatomical Museum," and documentary silence. And that is the third circumstance that gives extra weight to this claim—the absence of other documentation for Juba's life after 1851, or for his death and burial. I can assure the reader that I have searched diligently. This document carries such potential in any structure—any closure—I wish to give to Juba's life that again it becomes tempting to make it a part of his story, however much I repeat the historian's mantra, "Absence of evidence is not evidence of absence." In the world of the microhistorian, this statement becomes most troublesome.

The next question concerning this document—and the most important for our purpose—is this: What can be learned from it, whether or not this statement is true? What can the mere threat of the anatomical museum tell me about the way "that world then" perceived Juba and his dance?

The kind of museum represented by Woodhead's had a particular set of goals. Arising out of the scandals involving grave robbery and antipathy toward the science and business of surgery, anatomical museums proliferated at this time, always advertising themselves as educational in purpose, always particularly advocating the attendance of the laboring classes. A knowledge of the parts of the body, the advertisements promised, would lead to a greater understanding of modern healing and a greater control over oneself.

The typical museum contained skeletons, as well as wet and dry preparations, and wax and *papier-mâché* models, the most complex of which were the "Anatomical Venus and Adonis," which were taken apart during an illustrated lecture. Many displays were purely instructional—the operation of the senses and the circulatory system, the growth of the fetus. But many illustrated what could go anatomically wrong—invariably presented as avoidable through individual self-control. So patrons saw the terrible effects of syphilis, onanism, and the tight lacing of women's dresses. Even seemingly unavoidable physical aberrations—hydrocephalus, Siamese twins, or the giant and the dwarf—were presented as somehow avoidable through lifestyle. "Know thyself," said the advertisements for these museums. But as Michael Sappol admirably outlines in his book on the subject, *The Traffic in Dead Bodies,* knowledge was not so much power here for the laboring classes as it was the responsibility to take control over one's body. In what Sappol describes as the "anatomical worldview," the individual was instructed to think of the body in its parts, and then to reconstruct it, anatomized and categorized, into a manageable whole. At least that was the "party line." The gut-wrenching, grotesque, and voyeuristic responses to the dissected body on display—that later, and today, link anatomical museums to chambers of horrors—could never be completely suppressed by the talk of science and self-control. There was a sense in such museums of patrons being "scared straight" by displays of the body "punished" whenever it goes out of control.

Sappol usefully locates the cultural antithesis of the anatomical worldview in the minstrel show. Invoking Eric Lott's analysis in *Love and Theft,* he considers the minstrel's manic movements and outrageous freedom of expression as the mid-nineteenth-century quintessence of the body "out of control," to which the anatomical museum acted as antidote, the body under *extreme* control. Of course this is not quite true; in the minstrel show the body was only *shown* "out of control." The character of the blackface minstrel was played by—and therefore under the control of—a white performer.

If I accept this proposed relationship, then where does it leave Juba—that is, a person of color presented in the minstrel show as "out of control," but without the blackface mask to defend his actions after the fact? How, then, to control him?

The anatomical museum is an example in extremis of the battle waged in mid-nineteenth-century English culture over the body with respect to race and class. The two are clearly tied together by the presence in many anatomical museums of a "Gallery of All Nations," which presented in diorama form examples of all the "races" of the world, categorized according to the new science of anthropology into a hierarchy that descended from humanity's highest form, the Caucasian, through to its lowest, the African—not surprisingly, arranged according to the degree to which each species could control itself and its environment. Such a hierarchy was entirely consistent with the rest of the museum's message—and complemented that of the minstrel show down the street, displaying the American slave as a naturally uncontrollable body.[12] This would certainly leave Juba in a very uncomfortable position.

Quite aside from its actual occurrence, Brown's mere mention of skeletal display, on reflection, resonates throughout the documents pertaining to Juba. I have researched the nature of his performance at length, and written about his dance elsewhere.[13] This one piece of information—that someone placed his skeleton on display (or believed it should have been)—resonates throughout that other research in several ways that help me better understand how he was seen and, perhaps, how he himself "coped."

First, Juba is habitually advertised and reviewed separately from the rest of the troupe, and extant playbills can be read as creating a segregated space for his performances onstage. He is praised for his authenticity, for *being* black, and described in an unusually precise, almost ethnological manner at times.[14] The other minstrels are praised for different reasons: musicianship, humor, *acting*. Not so Juba. What is set into relief by a consideration of the museum is the degree to which Juba is both contained by the rest of the troupe and on exhibition within it (Figure 3.3). Certainly there is conflicting evidence; but in some measure I suspect Juba was perceived by this audience as an ethnological display, not *acting* but *being*, in precisely the same way as the Kaffir Zulus and Bedouin Arabs touring at the same time to the same venues, also exhibiting "the dances of their own simple people on festive occasions."[15] In this way the racial body, dancing out of control, could be made safe for viewing. It makes the idea that Juba might simply continue "on exhibition" even after death more defensible—unless I make too much of too little.

Second, I note that when Juba left the minstrel troupe and changed his audience, negative comments concerning his dance begin to appear. A reviewer in Manchester says he's jumping "too fast" and advises him to slow down. Unspoken is the phrase "or else." When he dances in the theater for the "gallery crowd," the notice says he is "rough" and "unrefined," and I infer a sense that the "thunderous" reaction of the gallery is altogether *too* noisy. As Juba begins to disappear from the eyes and ears of the *writing* class, its perception of his dance changes. No longer encircled and exhibited by the minstrel troupe, no longer on exhibition, he became, I suspect, a racial body out of control, encouraging a class body that was also perceived, just after the revolutions of 1848, as dangerously out of control. Juba, so the friendly advice said, would do better to slow down. Or stop—dead.[16]

Finally, there is a portrait of Juba in an advertisement extant from 1848. The presentation of a portrait in the iconography of minstrelsy was very much tied to the presentation of whiteness. Minstrels were near-obsessive about showing the audience that they were in fact white, which explains the other portrait published on the same page, of G. W. Pell. But why Juba? Because he was a featured performer? Yes, perhaps. But I note that the two portraits are quite different. Pell's is generic, hardly a likeness at all, sufficient to emphasize that he is white, but nothing more. The portrait of Juba, by contrast, is clearly taken from a daguerreotype, and is thus probably the first photograph of a performer of color (or a minstrel) that we have. Why take a photograph? And why of Juba and not of Pell? (Figures 3.4, 3.5)

If I am to make much of little, I might consider the portrait of Pell as generic proof of whiteness but the portrait of Juba as a clinical, ethnological proof of blackness. It is important that Pell is a fake—but it is just as important that Juba is not.

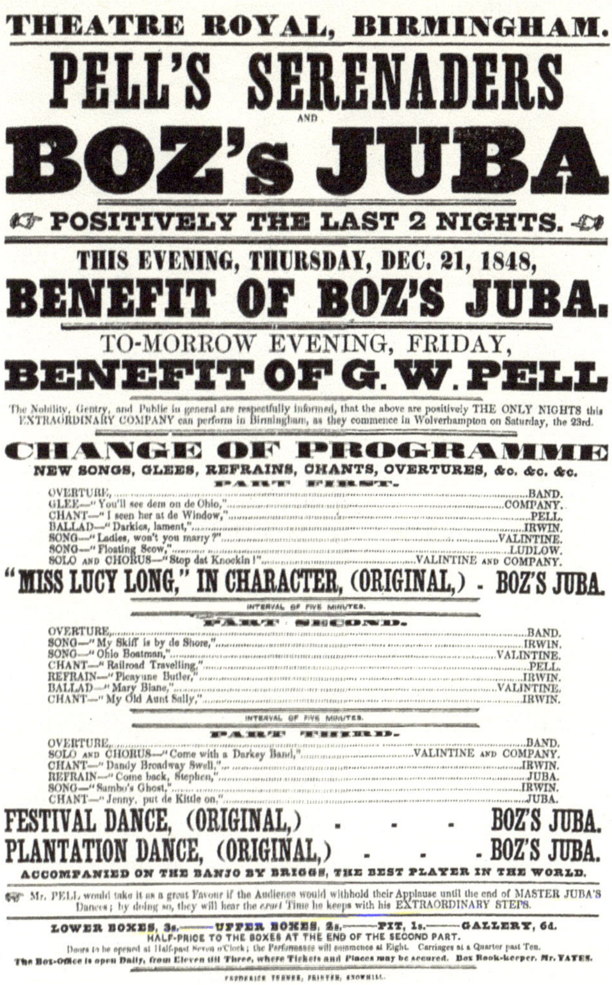

THEATRE ROYAL, BIRMINGHAM.

PELL'S SERENADERS

AND

BOZ's JUBA

POSITIVELY THE LAST 2 NIGHTS.

THIS EVENING, THURSDAY, DEC. 21, 1848,

BENEFIT OF BOZ'S JUBA.

TO-MORROW EVENING, FRIDAY,

BENEFIT OF G. W. PELL

The Nobility, Gentry, and Public in general are respectfully informed, that the above are positively THE ONLY NIGHTS this EXTRAORDINARY COMPANY can perform in Birmingham, as they commence in Wolverhampton on Saturday, the 23rd.

CHANGE OF PROGRAMME

NEW SONGS, GLEES, REFRAINS, CHANTS, OVERTURES, &c. &c. &c.

PART FIRST.

OVERTURE, ... BAND.
GLEE—"You'll see dem on de Ohio," .... COMPANY.
CHANT—"I seen her at de Window," .... PELL.
BALLAD—"Darkies, lament," .... IRWIN.
SONG—"Ladies, won't you marry?" .... VALINTINE.
SONG—"Floating Scow," .... LUDLOW.
SOLO AND CHORUS—"Stop dat Knockin!" .... VALINTINE AND COMPANY.

"MISS LUCY LONG," IN CHARACTER, (ORIGINAL,) - BOZ'S JUBA.

INTERVAL OF FIVE MINUTES.

PART SECOND.

OVERTURE, ... BAND.
SONG—"My Skiff is by de Shore," .... IRWIN.
SONG—"Ohio Boatman," .... VALINTINE.
CHANT—"Railroad Travelling," .... PELL.
REFRAIN—"Picayune Butler," .... IRWIN.
BALLAD—"Mary Blane," .... VALINTINE.
CHANT—"My Old Aunt Sally," .... IRWIN.

INTERVAL OF FIVE MINUTES.

PART THIRD.

OVERTURE, ... BAND.
SOLO AND CHORUS—"Come with a Darkey Band," .... VALINTINE AND COMPANY.
CHANT—"Dandy Broadway Swell," .... IRWIN.
REFRAIN—"Come back, Stephen," .... JUBA.
SONG—"Sambo's Ghost," .... IRWIN.
CHANT—"Jenny, put de Kittle on," .... JUBA.

FESTIVAL DANCE, (ORIGINAL,) - - - BOZ'S JUBA.
PLANTATION DANCE, (ORIGINAL,) - - - BOZ'S JUBA.

ACCOMPANIED ON THE BANJO BY BRIGGS, THE BEST PLAYER IN THE WORLD.

Mr. PELL would take it as a great Favour if the Audience would withhold their Applause until the end of MASTER JUBA'S Dances; by doing so, they will hear the *exact* Time he keeps with his EXTRAORDINARY STEPS.

LOWER BOXES, 3s.——UPPER BOXES, 2s.——PIT, 1s.——GALLERY, 6d.
HALF-PRICE TO THE BOXES AT THE END OF THE SECOND PART.
Doors to be opened at Half-past Seven o'Clock; the Performance will commence at Eight. Carriages at a Quarter past Ten.
The Box-Office is open Daily, from Eleven till Three, where Tickets and Places may be secured. Box Book-keeper, Mr. YATES.

FREDERICK TURNER, PRINTER, SNOWHILL.

Figure 3.3. Playbill for the Ethiopian Serenaders, 1848. Note how Juba is separated from the group typographically and as part of the bill structure, yet he is also included as part of the troupe. Birmingham Central Library.

If I were to go even further down the slippery exegetical slope, I would draw attention to the physical process of creating a daguerreotype. I quote Roland Barthes on the matter: "Photography transformed subject into object, and even, one might say, into a museum object: in order to take the first portraits . . . the subject had to assume long poses under a glass roof in bright sunlight. . . . [A] device . . . supported and maintained the body in its passage to immobility. . . . [T]his . . . was the pedestal of the statue I would become. . . . [And] . . . to become an object made one suffer as much as a surgical operation."[17]

Figures 3.4, 3.5. Portraits of G. W. Pell and Juba. Juba's portrait is taken from a daguerreotype. From an advertisement for Vauxhall Gardens. Harvard Theatre Collection, Houghton Library, Harvard University.

And so it goes in the teasing out of meaning for the microhistorian. I do believe that there is something to learn from the process. When Allston Brown made the display of Juba's bones the performer's punishment for rising above his station, he was only taking to the anatomical extreme the variety of ongoing efforts to gain control over that body—through the minstrel show, and through the daguerreotype. It was a dancer's hell to which Brown condemned Juba; and, after all this conjecture, I find the neatness of that punishment suspect. So it may not be true that Juba's skeleton was on display in Sheffield in 1852, and I may make too much of too little. Still, I now have in my mind's eye an image of an audience member seated in a theater observing the Ethiopian Serenaders in 1848, and for all intents and purposes seeing double: on the one hand, a band of entertainers by turns joking and singing, imitating another race; and on the other, an embodiment of that other race on exhibition, exotic and extraordinary, dancing in a way no one had seen before, dangerous, barely in control.

Case 2: The Madness of Gilbert Pell

A nearly indecipherable entry from the case notes for Gilbert Ward Pelham contained in the Rainhill Asylum "Male Case Book" for May 1870–December 1873 reads:

> Facts Certified: Is very childish in his ideas, dirty in his habits, won't keep his clothing on, tears his sheets, is very fond of washing himself *if* allowed. . . . Is under the impression he has money in Liverpool and is very anxious to get out to get it, in order to give to other patients. Is continually singing throughout night.

> Physical Symptoms: Is in a very weak and shaky condition. Slight contusion and abrasion of skin over the shoulders. Bed sore over cocyx. Lungs and heart healthy. Tongue indented at its edge and harnalous [*sic*] Is rather deaf. Cancer of rectum.
>
> Mental Features and Progress of the Case: This patient is advanced in General Paralysis, and has delusions about his own capabilities and wealth. Calls himself the Duke of Devonshire.
>
> Dec 1872. This man it appears from his Brother's statement has been bad for the last five years, and he attributes his disease to debauchery. Has been confined to his bed almost from his admission. Bed sores are forming over the hips, and is suffering from diarrhea. May not live many weeks
>
> Dec 19th had a paralytic seizure between 12 and 1 o'clock on the night of the 18th Dec. Panick [*sic*] affected his right side and he has not rallied, will probably die this day.
>
> Died Dec 20th from General Paralysis.
> [Followed by the autopsy report.][18]

In 1872 Gilbert W. Pell, itinerant American clown and blackface minstrel, died at the Rainhill Asylum outside Liverpool. In this document, typical of an overly bureaucratic Victorian institution, Pell's last sad, mad days are sketched out in a perfunctory but also humanizing report. The Rainhill "Male Case Book," entry 190, describes a man out of control, childish in ideas, dirty in habits, uncomfortable in clothing, singing at odd hours, talking about money he needs to access in town, mistaking himself for the duke of Devonshire. He's a disgrace to his brother, who describes Pell's condition as a result of debauchery. Indeed, that may have been true; "general paralysis," the stated cause of death, was a common euphemism for syphilis. As perfunctory as this document may be, it is unusual to have such a snapshot of the last actions and thoughts of anyone, let alone an itinerant, poor, workaday entertainer, for whom documents are always at a premium. I examine this document for what it might tell us about Gilbert Pell, whether it provides us with new information or merely corroborates what we already think we know.

What we think we know, in a necessarily truncated history, is this.[19] Gilbert Pelham was a child performer with his older brother Richard in a blackface variety and circus act, including songs, dances, and sketches, in late 1830s America (Figure 3.6). White males performing in burnt cork makeup were not uncommon in working-class venues at this time. They parodied and "delineated" the southern plantation slave in their clothing, banjo and fiddle music, dialect song, and African-influenced clog or tap dance. They were the wild racial and racist clowns of their time. There was nothing unusual about the Pelhams in this respect until 1843, when Richard, as part of the newly formed Virginia Minstrels, opened an unusual standalone, full evening's program at a New

Figure 3.6. Dick and Gilbert Pelham performing in 1841, from sheet music cover for the song "Massa Is a Stingy Man" (New York, 1841). Music Collection, Library and Museum of the Performing Arts, New York Public Library.

York venue. The Virginia Minstrels were later purported to be the first minstrel troupe (Figure 3.7). The truth of this statement is unimportant (see both Lhamon and Cockrell in this volume for related histories); what is important is that this "new" entertainment was a notable success, resulting in Pelham and the Virginia Minstrels doing what any good American entertainer did in those days: following in the footsteps of their predecessor, the great solo blackface artist T. D. "Jim Crow" Rice, they went to England. They were neither the first nor the most successful of many American blackface performers in England at this time; there is ample evidence that variety halls and concert venues commonly featured entertainments depicting American culture, in whole or in part presented in blackface. Indeed, some venues—the Nelson Street Concert Hall in Liverpool, for example—became for a time almost exclusively an "American" if not a "minstrel" house.[20]

Gilbert—now known as Mr. Pell and the bones player for a troupe called the Ethiopian Serenaders, arrived in London early in 1846. That troupe's appearance represents the high point of minstrelsy's success in early Victorian Britain (Figure 3.8). They appeared regularly for a year at the St. James's Concert Hall,

Figure 3.7. The grotesque Virginia Minstrels (from left to right): Dick Pelham, Dan Emmett, Billy Whitlock, and Frank Brower. From the cover of Th. Comer (arr.), *The Celebrated Negro Melodies, as Sung by the Virginia Minstrels* (Boston, 1843).

an upper-middle-class venue also frequented by the aristocracy. Well managed and well puffed in the press, the Serenaders were cleaned up in every way—formal wear with nice bright yellow vests, well-trained harmonic voices, and in all probability a toned-down performance overall. They appeared everywhere and for everyone: three times a week at the concert hall for mixed-gender audiences of the middle-classes-with-pretensions; morning performances for children; private gatherings for the aristocracy, including (remember the name) the duke of Devonshire; and, their final glory if celebrity is glory, a royal command performance for Queen Victoria, Prince Albert, the duke of Wellington, and their retinue at Arundel Castle, south of London. On the side, and perhaps on the sly,

Figure 3.8. The refined Ethiopian Serenaders, with G. W. Pell (Gilbert Pelham) on the left, from a clipping dated January 24, 1846, in the Theatre Collection, Victoria and Albert Museum.

Figure 3.9. G. W. Pell, circa 1846, during the height of his success, "from a lithograph by T. H. Maguire." From a clipping file in the Theatre Collection, Museum of the City of New York.

they appeared at saloons and "free-and-easies" around London, one assumes performing a somewhat different song and dance. Pell, interestingly, seems to have been both star and odd man out in this troupe; he was not the best singer, not the best dancer, not the manager. He was the clown, and the evidence suggests that he was the designated carnivalesque joker, the one whose costume was still (somewhat) exaggerated, who could lose control, make fun of the audience, tell the bad joke—and survive to perform another day. He became a star during this year, a *made* man (Figure 3.9).[21]

The Ethiopian Serenaders returned to America, advertising their triumphs in England and their royal performances, apparently to no great business. My own (unproven) belief is that they cleaned up their act a bit too much for American audiences. Whatever the reason, Pell returned to England in 1848 with a new troupe. This too was successful, though more because he had brought a novel attraction and overshadowing celebrity with him, the great dancer Juba. Pell was in charge this time, it seems, but even so soon after his triumphs, his own star was fading. By 1850 he was on his own, playing variety houses, noticed occasionally, sometimes with poor reviews—unheard of in 1846.[22] He faded from the sight of the newspaper-reading, document-creating classes—until he arrived at the Rainhill Asylum.

In light of this brief narrative, the description of Pell's last days in some ways only corroborates the obvious. He sings in the night: he was a musician. He obsesses about money: What itinerant performer wouldn't? His brother's negative attitude toward him does serve to complicate and humanize their relationship, somewhat. It is quite clear that Richard Pelham did not take well to his brother's success, going so far as to create attack advertisements for the press, promoting himself as the real originator of minstrelsy and its truest representation.[23] In a culture in which celebrity meant income, and ties to the aristocracy translated into bookings in higher-paying venues, origin mattered. The brothers appear to have had something of a falling-out; and yet in this final document we find them living in the same city, the older brother knowledgeable about Pell's condition. It's tempting to think that Richard, after a fashion, cared for Gilbert during these years.

Such are the temptations of an unusual document when one is researching a life and culture that created so few. I want to suggest, without drawing firm conclusions, a number of other ways in which this report might assist in understanding this life and death as it pertains to the culture of blackface minstrelsy.

First of all, the fact that both brothers lived and died in Liverpool signifies. Pelham was completely settled in a community there, listed in the census along with his wife and children, apparently involved in an active minstrel subculture, in a port city with strong connections to America and to New York in particular. His own death was noted in the *New York Clipper* with a full-page obituary praising his contribution to American entertainment, his place as an originator of minstrelsy, his status as a man of propriety. A benefit was organized for his widow and children.[24] Pell received no such press when he died and is only briefly mentioned in retrospective articles; still, he was living, after a fashion, within some kind of support system in Liverpool. This all speaks, I believe, to the presence of an American expatriate community in Britain with a degree of self-sufficiency, strong ongoing ties with the "homeland," but a degree of acceptance, comfort, even status in Britain. Minstrels were respectable, or at the very least wanted to be; those who were not were erased from the record early, perhaps even before death. In this Pell and Juba share a (lack of) history.

Minstrelsy was a great success in Britain, adopted and adapted by local performers to their own purpose, surviving in popular culture from then until now. (Witness *The Black and White Minstrel Show* on British television as late as the 1970s.)[25] On the one hand, Richard Pelham's obituary mentions in passing, as normal, that he never returned to the United States but was able to continue his career abroad. On the other hand, it is not suggested that success in Britain had any extraordinary appeal or credibility.

Second, the mere existence of this document speaks to a Victorian obsession with categorization and classification. Pell as a patient was classified in his madness by nationality (or race), religion, habits, "reputed character," and so on. Pell is surrounded in the asylum casebook by Swedes, Welsh, Scots, English, and other nationalities, all described in clinical terms in life and in a dissected death; this setting, it seems to me, mirrors the "setting" of American blackface minstrelsy as it was performed for the British middle classes. As we saw in the earlier examination of Juba's death and purported display, minstrelsy was one of an array of exhibitions of exotic culture, occupying the same venues as Bedouin Arabs, Chinese, Ojibway Indians, Kaffir Zulus, and Bushmen. To some degree, blackface minstrelsy was justified as an appropriate entertainment for the aristocracy and the middle classes because it was pedagogical. Clearly there was a difference; minstrels were not advertised as actual southern plantation slaves, only as authentic in their imitation. But the subtlety of that difference was sometimes lost on audiences; extant advertisements of Bushmen and minstrels do not make much of a distinction.[26] In death as in performance, Pell (like Juba) was examined with a clinical gaze.

Third, the fact that I could access this document is itself of significance. I was able to find it only because of the attention to detail paid by T. Allston Brown in his early retrospectives of minstrelsy, published in the *New York Clipper* during the 1870s. As little space as he gives to Gilbert Pell, as forgotten as he was, Brown tells us when he died and the cemetery in which he was buried.[27] This information is surprisingly accurate. It led to a death certificate, which gave the venue of death, which in turn led to the Rainhill Asylum casebooks. The presence of this first piece of information seems quite strange; but it was normal—one might say obsessive—in Brown's accounting of early minstrelsy to note the date of a minstrel's death and the exact location of interment.[28] To what end would such information be given in a newspaper retrospective: pilgrimage? There is a devotion in Brown's history, I believe, that betrays the pervasiveness of the subculture that Eric Lott argues for in his work on early minstrelsy. Minstrelsy was a closed shop, a more than usually bonded occupation, homosocial in its character, obsessed from the outset with rituals, origins, and standards. It started its own benevolent society, for example, to care for the illnesses and funerals of its members and to aid their survivors, its membership strictly limited to "real" minstrels and not the many imitators. (How "real" examples of an occupation based on imitation were to be distinguished is not clear to me.)[29] The outpouring of emotion and charity at Dick Pelham's death, by this scenario, was just a more conspicuous example of a highly structured society. I could locate the document because in this world, even debauched, syphilitic, embarrassing, forgotten Gilbert Pell would have had his pauper's grave recorded for care and keeping.

Finally, to return to the document's content one last time, I find myself wondering why Gilbert Pell "calls himself the Duke of Devonshire." He does not call *out* for him, or *to* him, but identifies himself *as* that duke. We should ask who the duke of Devonshire was, and why his name was called and no other.

The duke of Devonshire was among the most powerful, if least celebrated, aristocrats in Britain. He had vast landholdings and a number of palatial houses, and he had a profound influence on politics, serving twice as Lord Chamberlain, and providing important diversions for visiting foreign dignitaries. It also appears, though not particularly well documented, that he regularly attended minstrel performances and acted as a sometime patron. He had a home around the corner from the St. James's Concert Hall, where he certainly saw Pell and the Serenaders. He engaged them to perform for a party at his suburban London home, Chiswick House, famous at the time for its architecture, its formal gardens, and its zoo. There is some evidence that he was involved in the introduction of the dukes of Norfolk to the Serenaders; it was their castle at Arundel at which the Serenaders performed for the royal family. There is a playbill in the duke's scrapbook proving his attendance at an 1848 performance by Pell and his troupe in Brighton; and there is a newspaper account describing the duke's attendance at this performance with his entourage—his "excellent company." At its conclusion, according to the article, the duke "was pleased to express his high admiration" for their artistry, in effect giving his blessing and declaring his public approval. Not surprisingly, Pell used this support to advantage; he included in many advertisements a quotation from a letter written by the duke's personal musician, expressing the duke's pleasure at their performance.[30]

An appeal to the authority of the aristocracy as a testimonial advertisement was certainly not peculiar to blackface minstrelsy; but it may have been particularly important to this form of entertainment. Such performers were, on the one hand, one step away from the working-class saloon, the circus, and the variety house, and on the other, one step away from the "mere" exhibition of racial grotesquerie. Minstrelsy was certainly successful during these early years, but it was not by any means an easy "sell." This is illustrated in two brief references to that much-heralded royal command performance. Despite all the positive puffery to the contrary, Queen Victoria, in her personal diaries, declared the minstrels "rather tiresome." And a personal letter written by a member of her party the day after that event describes the music of the Serenaders as "odd noises" until, notes the correspondent, "at last . . . I imagine the Queen could not stand it any longer." In any event, the writer observes that "everybody talked all the time" so he "did not hear much of the singing."[31] Here is dismissal on two counts, entertainment value and aesthetic value, surely an itinerant performer's nightmare. This is a far cry from the duke of Devonshire's perception of these performers as skilled artists. We do not know—likely will never know—that the patronage or relationship was any more personal than these public comments. But it is no strain for me to imagine that the primary figure responsible for Pell's too-brief sojourn into a world of extreme opulence, wealth, and power would have made a strong impression. Pell's identification with the duke tends to corroborate such a strong relationship. It also argues for a reliance on patronage and an association with the powerful that an American in Britain could not avoid.

We should be skeptical of the record of Gilbert Pell's death; he had "lost his mind," and he might have said anything. But I tend toward the belief that his "madness" was an unguarded imaginative state. For three years, a long time before this moment, he had had a glorious career. He briefly attached himself to the British aristocracy, which even as it praised him set him adrift. He died alone, in a state of syphilitic madness, out of personal control but under institutional control. The document speaks to a life of uncertainty, an excessive dependency on one's "betters" for good report, an uncommon dependency on a closed subculture that was uncommonly devoted if one behaved. Even so, it was hardly lucrative. The "good" minstrel Dick Pelham received encomiums and a fundraiser for his family, but he died leaving them destitute. I cannot say that in life Pell or his brother, the white minstrel entertainers, had greater freedom or authority than Juba, the talented black entertainer. Minstrelsy itself, while popular across society, was nevertheless somehow odd and disreputable. This raises the follow-up question: If the life of the minstrel was this depressing, why not take off the burnt cork and sing another song?

Case 3: The Apotheosis of Thomas Briggs

On December 18, 1858, the *New York Spirit of the Times* reprinted an article from a California monthly magazine, the *Pioneer,* concerning the burial and subsequent tribute to the minstrel performer Tom Briggs (Figure 3.10). It deserves to be excerpted at length, in part because such documents don't come along often:

> Poor Tom Briggs! How well I recollect him as he used to enter between the first and second divisions of the performance, with his banjo on his shoulder, and his cheerful "Good evenin', white folks!"
>
> Black as Tom Briggs made himself, he could not help being good-looking. His fine features and his genial smile were white through the veil of cork, and it was no wonder that his brother players would group themselves at the side wings when he went in front, to gaze with affectionate admiration on him, whom they all "allowed" was the darkey Apollo.
>
> There are some persons so resolutely handsome that nothing will disfigure them; no garb entirely disguise—and of this sort was poor Tom Briggs. Wisely

appreciating his good gifts, he chose a neat outline and a quiet manner, preferring the silent favor they insured with the observer, to the spontaneous roar which follows broad exaggeration. He was the dandy nigger, bright as a dollar, clean as a race-horse, fine as a star, and when his finger struck the banjo, you felt that he was filled with the spirit of an artist. Altogether, Tom Briggs was an extraordinary person, and, had he chosen a less humble instrument, and subjected his taste to the tutelage of science, he might have had his likeness taken looking sideways, as the great tragedians do, for he would have been the master of a vast renown. As it was, he distanced rivalry by mere natural progression, elevated the banjo to the rank of the guitar, and rendered his performance not only *the* feature of the concert, but a by-word of surprise. This was triumph. Whenever any one played to ears that had once heard him, the comment invariably was: "Ah, but you should have heard poor Tom Briggs!" This was fame! And Tom Briggs knew it, and felt its inspiring influence, and day by day he played more famously because of it.

. . . Every one conceded the superiority of Tom Briggs. All minstrel managers endeavored to engage him, and it is the misfortune of us here, that death forced him to leave the band for the cemetery, the first week of his arrival on these shores.

Wonder as he was, Tom Briggs had other merits than attached to his professional pursuits. He was a model of a man. He possessed an honest nature, and a kind and gentle spirit; in manner he was shy, reserved, and almost diffident, and entirely free from the hard habits that characterized many of his class. He had a great notion, too, of being a gentleman, and, instead of hanging about taverns and passing his time with low associates in vulgar pleasures, he devoted himself to good company, elegant attire, and to that laborious practice which is the mother of improvement.

Nevertheless, Tom Briggs pursued these inclinations and thus sailed aloof without offense to his professional associates. . . . I verily believe his comrades took as much pride in his linen ruffles and straw kids, as he did himself, and perhaps felt that they were in some way associated with the dignity of the band. Certainly it is, that his unassuming excellence had made a deep impression on their minds, and when he was lowered out of sight, many a tear dropped from their eyes into the fresh sand that fell with a muffling sound upon his coffin.

The evening performance that followed the funeral ceremony was a doleful one. "For my part," said [Eph] Horn, the bone-player, "I scarcely knew what I was about. Tom and I had traveled together for years, and it seemed to me as if I had lost a brother. All my main business on the stage was done with him, and when I looked around, in the middle of my performance, and found a strange face alongside of me in place of his, and remembered that I had just helped to put him in the ground, I near a'most 'broke down.'"

As he said this, the eye of the humorist became moist, a slight tremor and huskiness was perceptible in his voice, and, turning half around, so as to look another way, he suddenly asked the crowd of listeners to drink.

"Ah! Gentlemen," said he, when they had all got their glasses, and he had cleared his throat, "you'll never see the like of poor Tom Briggs again—you'll not! He was different from most other players. They seldom take any pride in their business, they don't study, and they're generally satisfied with any cheap instrument they can get; but Tom was werry particular. He never stood upon the price of a banjo, and, when he got a good one, he was always studying some way to ornament it and improve it. He had a light one and a heavy one, for different kinds of work, and he played so strong that he had to get a piece of steel made for the end of his finger, as a sort of shield like, to prevent his tearing off his nail. He was werry fond of playing the heavy one, and, when we were coming up the coast, he would sometimes strike his strongest notes, and then turn round to me proud and say, 'Ah! Eph, what'll they think, up there, when they hear the old Cremona speak like that?'

"It did not make any difference even when he took sick. He played away all the same. But after he got here he could play only on the light one. He used to have it hanging against the wall, so as he could reach it in bed. Most any time you went in you'd hear him talking to the old Cremona, as he called it, and making it talk back to him. But by'm-by, he got so weak he could scarcely hold on to it, and I have sat by his bed and watched him till the sound became so faint that it seemed as if he and the banjo were both falling into a dream. All the while he kept a good heart, poor fellow! And we kept encouraging him along too; and every now and then he would raise himself up and say 'Ah! How I'll make 'em look around when I get strength enough, once more, to make the old banjo talk!'

"But at last he felt that he was going, and, after some straight, sensible talk, he told us that, when he died, to take the two banjos and pack them up carefully, and send them home to his father and mother. An hour before he went, he asked me to hand him the 'light Cremona.' He took a hold of it, and looked at it for a minute, as if he was a looking at a person who he was going to part with for ever, and then he tried to hit it, but he could merely drop the weight of his thin fingers on the chords. There was no stroke to his touch at all. He could just barely make a sound, and that was so fine that it appeared to vanish away like the buzz of a fly. It was so dim, that I don't believe he heard it himself, and he dropped his hand as if he gave it up. Then he looked at me as if he understood everything in the world, and, shaking his head, said, 'It's no use—hang it up, Eph—I cannot hit it any more!' These were the last words that poor Tom Briggs ever spoke."

At this the speaker wiped a tear from his eye; but it did him no discredit, for he had described the death of an artist, and given the best proof of a man.[32]

The Tom Briggs of this document was a popular performer with audiences and colleagues alike—good-looking, affable, debonair, and talented. A force for good in the world, he was intensely serious about his music and his mastery of his instrument and its elevation as a means to create art. He was so dedicated to his art, in fact, that he would not stop playing even as he deteriorated. Unlike the first two deaths examined in this essay, this was written as a "good" death, of a "good" man. There is scant evidence of his life elsewhere, but what there is does not dispute this view. He was commonly advertised as the greatest banjo player in the world; and if this is unprovable, it is at least arguable that he was the most influential of the early minstrel banjoists, largely because he produced a guide to playing the banjo, the first of its kind.[33] There may very well have been better banjoists; but Briggs brought the sound of this African folk instrument into the parlors of America and Britain. Otherwise little is known of him. Born and raised in New York, he worked in a butcher's shop until he became a

Figure 3.10. Engraving from a daguerreotype of Tom Briggs, early 1850s, reprinted in an unidentified newspaper May 22, 1880. From a clipping file in the Theatre Collection, Museum of the City of New York.

minstrel. He toured the United States, Britain (some of the time with Juba and Pell), and parts of Europe, and was sailing for San Francisco in 1854 when he caught the "Panama fever" and died. He was thirty years old. The narrative of a "good death" makes this just as much a moral tale as Brown's less savory story of Juba. What is most interesting here, and the reason I wanted to quote it at such length, is that two voices are at work.

The first is the voice of a representative of the writing classes, a reporter in California who acts as an apologist on behalf of polite society for Briggs, the minstrel man. He devotes most of his words in effect to writing against minstrelsy, arguing that Briggs was unusual by being so—to put it bluntly—civilized. He was well dressed to the point of foppishness ("linen ruffles and straw kids"), a trait, it was clearly explained, that might have but did not alienate him from his less refined colleagues; the clear statement here is that his attire could have caused a good deal of friction if he had been more aloof and self-important, or less masculine. He was not, like his "brethren," given to the vices of the working classes, instead devoting his time and energies to raising the value of his craft to the position of art. He was, to this writer, all that was good about the commodity capital of minstrelsy, the cleaned-up and more acceptable form that Dan Emmett, George Christy, and the early Ethiopian Serenaders with G. W. Pell were attempting to disseminate to the broader and better-paying audiences of the middle classes (see Cockrell and Lhamon in this volume). Of course this writer was not likely thinking of economics when he composed this encomium. He was more likely thinking of justifying the fact that he, a man of substance and influence (in potential, at least, as a writer and reporter in California), clearly loved the minstrel show. Audiences, I have suggested earlier in this essay and elsewhere, justified their enjoyment in part through pedagogy (it was an exhibition of culture); here the justification is through aesthetic sophistication.

The most unusual and salient point this writer makes concerns Tom Briggs's relationship with race. Put simply, he rises above blackface and the depiction of race in any way, making it irrelevant by means of beauty. Briggs is personally beautiful, so much so that this beauty, defined by whiteness, shines through the blackface; blackface makeup in this description becomes something that can obscure and corrupt. He is morally beautiful, never sullying his personal lifestyle with the vices of his colleague blackface minstrels. This statement suggests that by blacking up, the white minstrel men corrupt themselves, give themselves over somewhat to the wildness and dehumanizing forces of the "lesser race" they portray (see the discussion earlier of the "Gallery of All Nations"). The clothes—and makeup—make the man in this case, and though minstrel performers went to great lengths to emphasize that they were, after all, white men merely portraying race, this was an ongoing public relations struggle for them. Briggs is also, in this description, artistically beautiful, raising the level of sophistication of the banjo to a point at which it ceases to be a folk instrument, or properly of a piece with the minstrel performance of race. It is telling that this writer describes Briggs only as playing alone, both audience and fellow minstrels in thrall to his skills. In this description we can see, just barely, the descriptions of artistry that for a time were applied to Juba, thus justifying his positive presence onstage; but it also sounds a good deal like another kind of segregated performance, in this case not of a person of color on exhibition on a segregated stage but of a person of class giving a wholly other kind of concert, to be attended to quite differently from "mere" blackface minstrelsy. I read this part of the document as the work of someone who loves the minstrel show but does not like that he loves it. In his tribute to Briggs, he has found his own justifications.

Not so Eph Horn's toast to his friend and companion. Though this too is the work of the reporter, who would have paraphrased after the fact, it is sufficiently distinct in tone that I am persuaded it approximates Horn's own song of praise. Here there is no talk of fine clothing or polite demeanor; there is no sense that Briggs was a man apart, his companions watching him in awe. Indeed, Horn's first tear is shed at the realization that the partner with whom he has shared stage and road for several years is gone. The homosocial, close-knit subculture of minstrelsy is reinforced here, as is the working-class core of the tradition:

the post-funeral performance and tribute is held in a tavern, not a theater, and for fellow travelers and friends, not for the first citizens of San Francisco. This corroborates what we know about Briggs, despite the protestations of the writer of this piece; the team of Horn and Briggs were touring to primarily working-class venues, and they had a long-standing engagement in a tavern in New York prior to their ill-fated California trip.

What follows this call for a toast is an uncommon portrait of a man in love with performance. This Tom Briggs is obsessed with the banjo in a way that Horn admits moves past other performers. Briggs invests in expensive instruments, is always looking for ways to decorate and improve on them, innovates an early fingerpick, and shapes the nature of his music to the nature of the instrument (playing different kinds of music on the "heavy" and the "light" "Cremona"—a parodic reference to a city in Italy well known for its production of violins). He is clearly in love with playing and with performing for other people, and even more particularly other people "like him," from the working classes. He is, after all, on his way to the California goldfields, and Horn gives every indication that he is excited by the prospect of introducing his instrument, and what he can do with it, to all the other migrants there to mine a new life. Here, too, is a portrait of someone so obsessed with music that he speaks with his instrument, keeps it by his bed during extreme illness, and keeps playing it as he is dying. Even his last words, hardly profound, are only a lament that he can no longer play.

This is a romantic picture of an artist, to be sure, and we should not entirely trust it. But a part of the puzzle of minstrelsy that is often missed in the discussion of race, gender, and class does emerge in this rare description, however compromised by the reporter. The (mostly young) men who performed in blackface, and who created and disseminated the traditions we still experience, were in it for more than the money, or the opportunity to parody their "betters" and to portray heavy-handed racial caricatures. They were musicians, singers, and comedians who loved to perform. In this sense Horn's complete avoidance of the mention of race, or blackface, is significant. Although I do not in any respect wish to diminish the repercussions of racial impersonation here, it is no doubt true that some of these minstrels blacked up because the tradition stipulated it, if they wanted to play these instruments. For Briggs as for Juba—though perhaps not for Pell—their focus was on dance and music, and their legacy is the dissemination of innovation in those areas, emerging out from under the cloak of race prejudice. While it may seem too good to be true, there is another strain of blackface minstrelsy that is too often erased by the trickster-clown and the racial caricature—that of the skilled professional musician (and, in Juba's case, dancer) who was, in fact, collecting, creating, and disseminating an American folk idiom. (Figures 3.11, 3.12)

Figures 3.11, 3.12. Two images of the banjo from the late 1840s: on the left, a rough woodcut from a mid-1840s broadside advertisement, in the Sheffield Public Library; and on the right, an engraving from published sheet music showing W. R. Barlow (London: Lewis and Company, ca. 1854), in the British Library. The banjo had not acquired a standard shape at this point and was typically five-stringed and unfretted. No images of Tom Briggs playing his "Cremona" have been found.

Coda: The Strains of Minstrelsy

The microhistorical examination of individual documents does not lend itself very easily to concluding paragraphs. The deconstruction of documents tends to trouble, not to smooth, the narrative waters. At its core, in the midst of the individual eyewitness account of the singular event, anything might happen. A close reading of these documents in part reinforces some strains of the tradition that run throughout the history and legacy of minstrelsy and are prominent in recent studies, including the work in this volume. There is a strong inclination to control both the white and the black body by any means possible; the blacked-up white performer only pretends to lose control, but in fact is expressing just how controlled and controlling he is—in control of his own body while he imitates, on behalf of the society he serves, and controlling the black population he demeans through imitation. There is in these documents a sense of a number of clear and ever-present dangers, of poverty, of failure, of disease, of being "cast out" by those who must approve of us, whether that is the subculture of the minstrel profession or the patrons who have paid for and allowed performance. There is, of course, an overwhelming racism at the core of blackface minstrelsy, no less so for its complexity. It is really, however, a set of quite different, competing racisms, all of which might be performed and received at once, and all of which both repel and attract. On the stage of a theater in Sterling, Scotland, then, Pell, Juba, and "Poor Tom" Briggs sit side by side before a mixed-gender, mixed-class audience. Pell is a grotesque, out-of control, never-quite-reputable clown who teaches his audience that bad jokes and malapropisms are the norms of the southern black slave (though the audience will no doubt repeat them all), and who mocks the oppressive "powers that be" in ways that are quite attractive, if politically dangerous. Next to him is Juba, a powerful dancer of color who represents to this audience the exotic abandonment to feeling that is "natural" to his people, and unacceptable—though there is a good deal of enjoyment in the observance, and no doubt later the imitation, of his dance. And, finally, there is Briggs, who presents to this audience an instrument that has no credibility, that is a product of the lowest form of humanity (the audience knows this because they have seen the "Gallery of All Nations" at the local anatomical museum). And yet after his performance, young men (and, yes, women) in the audience want to learn how to play that instrument because he made it sing. In the moment—the microhistorical moment in which an individual member of the audience is confronted by "another other," but before that figure is put in its "proper" place, as stipulated by society's strictures—anything might happen. This is what is so dangerous about performance, and why so many have tried to suppress it. So what had by this point already become an antagonistically racist and segregationist form of entertainment may still be employed by young men to create and disseminate extraordinary dance, music, song, and humor, helping to create, in the long run, an environment for the creation—in and out of blackface—of blues, ragtime, jazz, and rock and roll, of tap, jazz, and many other variations of dance, and much of what we think of as American satire. It did not happen because of blackface minstrelsy, certainly; but we cannot simply say that it happened despite it (or to spite it).

It's complicated.

NOTES

1. Thomas Postlewait, "Writing History Today," *Theatre Survey* (November 2000): 104. The use of the term "exceptional normal" is from Edoardo Grendi, quoted by Giovanni Levi, "On Microhistory," in *New Perspectives on Historical Writing*, ed. Peter Burke (Cambridge: Polity, 1991), 109. See also Robert Darnton, *The Great Cat Massacre and Other Episodes in French Cultural History* (New York: Vintage Books, 1985), 5, where he also talks about looking for the joke we don't understand; and more generally Thomas Postlewait, *The Cambridge Introduction to Theatre Historiography* (Cambridge: Cambridge University Press, 2009).

2. Early narrative histories consulted include those listed in note 9 of the introduction to the volume. A range of periodical literature also exists in what has been a rich field of research in recent years. Providing the crucial "macrohistory" without which this kind of closer study cannot be done, see Eric Lott, *Love and Theft: Blackface Minstrelsy and the American Working Class* (New York: Oxford University Press, 1993); Dale Cockrell, *Demons of Disorder: Early Blackface Minstrels and Their World* (New York: Cambridge University Press, 1997); William Mahar, *Behind the Burnt Cork Mask: Early Blackface Minstrelsy and Antebellum American Popular Culture* (Urbana: University of Illinois Press, 1999); and W. T. Lhamon, *Raising Cain: Blackface Performance from Jim Crow to Hip Hop* (Cambridge: Harvard University Press, 1998). Cockrell and Lhamon are, of course, represented in this volume.

3. Col. T. Allston Brown, *New York Clipper*, 1876 (undated clippings, Museum of the City of New York).

4. For "genius of the heel" see *Theatre Journal*, n.d (fugitive clipping, British Library); for reference to whirling dervishes and the wilis, see *Era* (London), June 14, 1848; for "dances of his own simple people," see *Manchester Guardian*, October 18, 1848. As further examples, see *Era*, June 18, 1848: "It is the most wonderful conglomeration of every step that was ever thought of, and reminds the spectator more of one of the 'dancing dervishes,' or fabled willis, than anything else he can think of"; *Manchester Examiner*, October 17, 1848: "Surely he cannot be flesh and blood, but some more subtle substance, or how could he turn, and twine, and twist, and twirl, and hop, and jump, and kick, and throw his feet almost with a velocity that makes one think they are playing hide-and seek with a flash of lightning! Heels or toes, on feet or on knees, on the ground or off, it is all the same to Juba; his limbs move as if they were stuffed with electric wires. . . . His legs must be of India rubber; his feet of jointed iron: how else the former can have so much elasticity, and the latter can bear so much beating on the floor, we know not"; *Morning Post* (London), June 21, 1848: "His pedal execution is a thing to wonder at, if his flexibility of muscle did not confound us. He jumps, he capers, he crosses his legs, he stamps his heels, he dances on his knees, on his ankles, he ties his limbs into double knots, and untwists them as one might a skein of silk, and all these marvels are done in strict time and appropriate rhythm—each note has its corresponding step and action. Now he languishes, now burns, now love seems to sway his motions, and anon rage seems to impel his steps"; *Mirror and United Kingdom Magazine* (London), July 1848: "We fancied we had witnessed every kind of dance, from the wilds of Caffraria [*sic*] to the stage of the Academie at Paris; but all these choreographic manifestations were but poor shufflings compared to the pedal inspirations of Juba. Such mobility of muscles, such flexibility of joints, such boundings, such slidings, such gyrations, such toes and such heelings, such backwardings and forwardings, such posturings, such firmness of foot, such elasticity of tendon, such mutation of movement, such vigour, such variety, such natural grace, such

powers of endurance, such potency of pastern, were never combined in one nigger. Juba is to Vauxhall what the Lind is to the Opera House."

5. Most writers on early minstrelsy include a discussion about Juba; most of these are based on one article by Marian Hannah Winter discussed in this chapter. Many more documents related to Juba are now available at *The Juba Project,* www.utm.utoronto.ca/~w3minstr/, along with a bibliography of my own publications on this performer.

6. "[Juba's] first performance was 'Miss Lucy Long, in character.' With a most bewitching bonnet and veil, a *very* pink dress, beflounced to the waist, lace-fringed trousers of the most spotless purity, and red leather boots,—the ensemble completed by the green parasol and white cambric pocket handkerchief,—Master Juba certainly looked the black demoiselle of the first ton to the greatest advantage. The playing and singing by the Serenaders of a version of the well-known negro ditty, furnished the music to Juba's performance, which was after this fashion:—Promenading in a circle to the left for a few bars, till again facing the audience, he then commenced a series of steps, which altogether baffle description, from their number, oddity, and the rapidity with which they were executed." *Manchester Guardian,* October 18, 1848.

7. Marian Hannah Winter, "Juba and American Minstrelsy," *Dance Index* 6, no. 2 (February 1947): 28–47.

8. I have published on the subject of early minstrelsy and the anatomical museum in "'Surely he cannot be flesh and blood': The Early Victorian Anatomical Museum and the Blackface Minstrel," in *The Body in Medical Culture,* ed. Elizabeth Klaver (Albany: SUNY Press, 2009), 61–88. The discussion of Juba in this chapter revises and revisits that discussion.

9. For this and all further discussion in this essay, the crucial references on the nineteenth-century anatomical museum have been Michael Sappol, *A Traffic of Dead Bodies: Anatomy and Embodied Social Identity in Nineteenth-Century America* (Princeton: Princeton University Press, 2002), focusing on the United States; Maritha Rene Burmeister, "Popular Anatomical Museums in Nineteenth-Century England" (Ph.D. diss., State University of New Jersey, New Brunswick/Rutgers, 2000); and Ruth Richardson, *Death, Dissection and the Destitute* (London: Routledge and Kegan Paul, 1987). All three corroborate the complex class conflict surrounding the corpse and the museum during these years. See also Tony Bennett, *The Birth of the Museum: History, Theory, Politics* (London: Routledge, 1995); and Martin Kemp and Marina Wallace, *Spectacular Bodies: The Art and Science of the Human Body from Leonardo to Now* (London: Hayward Gallery; Berkeley, University of California Press, 2000). On race, science, and exhibition, see Bernth Lindfors, ed., *Africans on Stage: Studies in Ethnological Show Business* (Bloomington: Indiana University Press, 1999); Nancy Stepan, *The Idea of Race in Science: Great Britain, 1800–1960* (London: Archon Books, 1982); and especially Sander L. Gilman, *Difference and Pathology: Stereotypes of Sexuality, Race, and Madness* (Ithaca: Cornell University Press, 1985). Research included the examination of a range of playbills and catalogues for anatomical museums located in the John Johnson Collection, Bodleian Library, Oxford University; the Wellcome Library for the History of Medicine; and the British Library, in particular, *Catalogue of Dr. Kahn's Anatomical Museum* (London, 1851), which lists and describes 341 items; and *J. W. Reimers's Gallery of All Nations and Anatomical Museum* (Leeds, 1853), which lists 410 and claims more than 450 items on display.

10. See the *Sheffield and Rotherham Independent* and the *Sheffield Times,* July–October 1852. For a sense of the displays, see *Sheffield and Rotherham Independent,* August 28, 1852:

GREAT SUCCESS— . . . Exhibited with Great Success both in London, Manchester, and Glasgow. . . .

Programme

No. 1—The famous MODEL of the ENTIRE HUMAN BODY . . . .

No. 2—A beautiful Model, termed the ANATOMICAL VENUS . . . explained every hour by Dr. Cherry, who will also in his description, illustrate the Physiology of the Circulation of the Blood, Degestion, Nervous System, &c., with other highly interesting information relative to the construction of the Human Body.

No. 3—Highly Magnified Models of the FIVE SENSES. . .

No. 4—A vast number of Wax Models, taken from nature presenting faithful delineations of the frightful consequences of vicious indulgence.

No. 5—Models in Wax, showing Extraordinary Freaks of Nature.

No. 6—Nearly Two Hundred large coloured diagrams which strikingly portray the wonderful formation of the Human Body.

The Museum contains other objects not here enumerated.

P.S.—Mr. Woodhead solicits an early Visit, as his stay in Sheffield is rapidly drawing to a close. Of the Thousands who have crowded the Museum since its arrival, multitudes have repeated their visits several times, with increased interest and delight. For confirmation of these facts, see all the Sheffield Newpapers.

11. The first is a reference in Henry Mayhew, *London Labour and the London Poor*, vol. 3 (1861–62; repr., New York: Dover, 1968), 191, recording the words of an itinerant street minstrel, in a quotation also pertinent to the discussion of G. W. Pell in this chapter: "I used to wear a yellow waistcoat, in imitation of them at the St. James's Theatre. . . . The first came out at St. James's Theatre, and they made a deal of money. . . . Pell's gang was at the top of the tree. Juba was along with Pell. Juba was a first class—a regular A1—he was a regular black, and a splendid dancer in boots."

12. See Sappol, *Traffic in Dead Bodies;* and Burmeister, "Popular Anatomical Museums." I have found numerous exemplary documents, including a *Catalogue of Dr. Kahn's Celebrated Anatomical Museum . . . now exhibiting in the Music Hall, Nelson Street, Newcastle-on-Tyne* (n.d.) in the British Library. It includes a full description of the "Gallery of All Nations."

13. See, for example, Stephen Johnson, "Juba's Dance: An Assessment of Newly Acquired Documentation," *Proceedings of the 26th Annual Conference of the Society for Dance History Scholars* (2003): n.p.

14. As in, for example, this description from the *Manchester Guardian*, October 18, 1848: "He is apparently about eighteen years of age; about 5 feet 3 inches in height; of slender make, yet possessing great muscular activity. His head is very small, and his countenance, when at rest, has a rather mild, sedate, and far from unpleasing expression."

15. The exhibition of race and the exotic in this period was widespread. See Richard Altick, *The Shows of London* (London: Belknap Press, 1978), among a range of more recent writing. More specifically, the *London Morning Chronicle* of May 27, 1846, advertises the Ethiopian Serenaders in the same column as the exhibition of a Maori chieftain and Scottish dwarfs. The *London Observer* of May 2, 1847, advertises the exhibition of South African Aborigines, or Bushmen. Such displays were numerous, and included, at least as advertised, a group of African Americans. See also Douglas A. Lorimer, *Colour, Class and the Victorians* (Leicester: Leicester University Press; New York: Holmes and Meier, 1978).

16. Reporting on his appearances in Manchester, the *Era*, August 4, 1850, noted: "[Juba is] jumping very fast at the Colosseum, but too fast is worse than too slow, and we advise [Juba] to be wise in time. It is easier to jump down than to jump up"; *Era*, August 11 1850:

"Juba has jumped away—by the way of an earnest yet friendly caution, let us hope that he will not throw himself away. Be wise in time is a wholesome motto." See also the *Huddersfield Chronicle and West Yorkshire Advertiser,* November 30, 1850: "The performances of Boz's Juba have created quite a sensation in the gallery, who greeted his marvellous feats of dancing with thunders of applause and a standing *encore.* In all the rougher and less refined departments of his art, Juba is a perfect master." This review damns by faint praise, a far cry from the rapturous reviews of 1848–49.

17. Roland Barthes, *Camera Lucida: Reflections on Photography,* trans. Richard Howard (New York: Hill and Wang, 1981), 13, 15.

18. Merseyside Record Office M614 M I 1 1/5, entry no. 190, Liverpool Central Reference Library, Local History Collection.

19. In addition to the secondary sources already noted, the history of early minstrelsy has been written about with enthusiasm almost from its inception. T. Allston Brown published what amounts to a (surprisingly accurate) documentary history in the *New York Clipper* in an 1876 series, revised and expanded in 1912. An abundance of newspaper articles can be found in files and scrapbooks in the New York Public Library (particularly in the Townsend Walsh Collection) and the Harvard Theatre Collection, among other archives. By their existence and content it appears that minstrelsy had a strongly loyal and long-lived fan base, which was keenly interested in the origin of the genre and its changes over time. Information on Gilbert Pell for this brief chronology has been taken from Brown's "history," as well as a survey of a wide range of London newspapers. These documents can be explored on the database that is part of *The Juba Project.*

20. See Hans Nathan's study of Dan Emmett, one of the original Virginia Serenaders, *Dan Emmett and the Rise of Early Blackface Minstrelsy.* The information in this discussion exists as well in a range of fugitive clippings in the New York Public Library and the Harvard Theatre Collection. For an example of the reference to a "glut" of minstrels in 1840s Britain, see *John Bull,* October 24, 1846: "So many things of this kind have been brought forward lately, by Henry Russell, the Hutchinson Family, the Ethiopean Serenaders, and we do not know how many others, that they are getting quite stale; and any further attempt of the sort must have some wholly new features in order to become attractive." Studies of Rice are common, but see Cockrell, *Demons of Disorder;* and Lhamon, *Raising Cain,* in particular (as well as the work of these two authors in this volume).

21. The members of the first Ethiopian Serenaders were Frank Germon, Moody Stanwood, George Harrington, Gilbert Pell, and William White. James A. Dumbolton was the "agent," though his relationship with the troupe is unclear, since Pell was certainly the most prominent member, and Germon seems to have handled the press. See T. Allston Brown, "Early History of Negro Minstrelsy: Its Rise and Progress in the United States," *New York Clipper,* March 30, 1912, for reference. Brown reports that a group called "The Original Boston Serenaders," including some of the troupe later making their way to England as the Ethiopian Serenaders—George Harrington, Gilbert Ward Pell, Moody Stanwood, and Frank Germon—performed for the president of the United States (Tyler) early in 1844 as the "American Ethiopian Serenaders." For reference to the "cleaned-up" performance, see the *Court Gazette and Fashionable Times,* February 14, 1848: "In addition to their drolleries, they are vocalists of a very superior class, and their sentimental effusions are given with the most delicate accuracy of expression—and the most perfect finish and effect"; and *John Bull,* January 24, 1846: "We must confess, that we were by no means prepared for so rich and varied a musical treat; as we did not suppose the vocalists, or the instruments they

employed, could have discoursed such eloquent music." A full description of the talents of the original Ethiopian Serenaders exists in a fugitive clipping in the Harvard Theatre Collection, including the (odd and certainly untrue) statement that "Pelham, subsequently known as Pell, did not sing." For the range of venues and audiences, see, for example, the *Observer*, May 16, 1846, for reference to regular morning concerts, to private performances, and a more self-serving reference to the "vulgar imitations" of other blackface minstrels; the *New York Clipper*, October 7, 1876, for a reprinted program of a performance by the Serenaders for the duke of Devonshire at a party at Chiswick House (May 30, 1846; a playbill exists in the archives of the dukes of Devonshire); the *London Observer*, June 27, 1846, for a review of the performance for the royal children; and the same newspaper for June 7, 1846, for their appearance at "The Horns, Kennington," on a dark night at the St. James's. Their appearance at Arundel Castle for the royal family was in early December 1846.

22. When the original Ethiopian Serenaders returned to the United States, playbills trumpeted their performance for the queen and their other successes. From the scant evidence they were not financially successful, which must have been a great disappointment after their extraordinary popularity in Britain. There is no evidence as to why this happened, though there may have been a backlash from working-class audiences against their more "polite" entertainment. In any event, dissension seems to have entered the troupe, which quickly split into two, identically named. One, with Dumbolton and Stanwood, continued in America, returning to England in 1849. The itinerary of Pell's (and Juba's) version of the Ethiopian Serenaders, along with those of other troupes, and Pell's subsequent history can be traced through *The Juba Project*.

23. See the *Theatrical Journal* for November 13, 18, 20, and 27, 1847, in which reviews of Richard Pelham draw comparisons with his brother (then in America), followed by advertisements in answer: "Mr. R. W. Pelham (from America), the originator of the Ethiopian concerts, and the first person in England, Scotland, Ireland, or America, that ever introduced a band of minstrels before the public. . . . Mr. Pelham begs further to state that he was the first person who introduced his brother Mr. G. W. Pell, the celebrated bone player, of the St. James's Theatre, before the public. Some persons may ask why the names differ—The answer is this, when he arrived in this country with the Ethiopian Serenaders, Mr. P. had been here upwards of two years."

24. See English Census records for 1871 under "Richard Ward Pelham"; and "Among the Minstrels of the Past," *New York Clipper*, ca. December 1876, fugitive clipping, Harvard Theatre Collection. Pelham's death is noted here as occurring in October 1876, corroborated in the death registries for Lancashire in that quarter (October–December). This lengthy obituary and retrospective discusses his career; his place as an originator of minstrelsy; his survival in Liverpool thanks to Samuel Hague, another minstrel entrepreneur; as well as the Liverpool benefit for Pelham's wife and children, now "devoid of means." A system for sending contributions from America was organized by the *Clipper*.

25. Blackface as a theatrical convention has persisted in American popular culture to the present. See the introduction to this volume.

26. See note 15.

27. *New York Clipper*, March 30, 1912: "The retired bone player, died on Dec. 21, 1872, and was buried in the Cemetery St. Helen's, Lancashire, Eng." Though the source is from 1912, these histories are expanded revisions of less accessible publications from the mid-1870s, written for the same periodical. It is likely that Brown was a collector of minstrel ephemera.

28. Among many examples, William Whitlock died "at Long Branch, N.J.[,] March 29, 1878," and Frank Brower was "interred in the Woodlands Cemetery in Philadelphia" (*Clipper,* March 2, 1912); W. H. Granger "died in Toronto, Can., in April 1867" (*Clipper,* March 16, 1912); and see this statement concerning the death of E. P. Christy: "He died on May 21, and his remains were interred in Greenwood Cemetery. On the plate on the lid of the coffin were inscribed the words: 'Edwin P. Christy died May 21, 1862, aged 47 years 6 months and 23 days'" (*Clipper,* March 23, 1912).

29. The Minstrel Fund Association was registered in New York City in 1861. Charlie White noted at the time: "There are many individuals of other pursuits who occasionally resort to positions in the ranks of Minstrelsy, as circumstances allow; but I confess the profession would be greatly benefitted by closing the door against all such limited pretenders." From a fugitive clipping signed by White, in the Harvard Theatre Collection, probably from the *New York Clipper,* announcing the Association and listing its inaugural members.

30. See James Lees-Milne, *The Bachelor Duke: A Life of William Spencer Cavendish, 6th Duke of Devonshire, 1790–1858* (London: Murray, 1991). Reference to the duke's personal scrapbooks courtesy of correspondence with the archives at Chatsworth. There is a playbill in the Portsmouth Public Library for an amateur dance school from this period thanking the duke for his patronage. The information on the performance in Brighton comes from a local newspaper. The musician's letter exists in numerous newspaper advertisements: "I am directed by his Grace the Duke of Devonshire to inform you how much pleased himself and Friends were by the performance of yourself and Company at his House, and also at your public concert." I have written about the testimonial in early minstrelsy in "Testimonials in Silk: Juba and the Legitimization of American Blackface Minstrelsy in Britain," in *Testimonials in the American Marketplace: Emulation, Identity, Community,* ed. Marlis Schweitzer and Marina Moskowitz (Basingstoke: Palgrave Macmillan, 2009) 23–49.

31. The letter quoted rests in the archives of the dukes of Norfolk at Arundel Castle. My thanks to the archivists there for access, for the reference to Queen Victoria's personal diaries, and for the crash course they gave me on *Burke's Peerage.*

32. George Wilkes, "The Dying Minstrel," published in the *New York Spirit of the Times,* December 18, 1858 ("written some years ago in California" and "originally published in the *Pioneer,* a California monthly magazine").

33. Thomas F. Briggs, *Briggs' Banjo Instructor: containing the elementary principles of music. . .* (Boston: Oliver Ditson, 1855). A 1992 reprint (Bremo Bluff, Va.: Tuckahoe Music) was taken from an archival copy at Brown University. For early minstrel music, see Nathan, *Dan Emmett;* and Robert B. Winans, "Early Minstrel Show Music, 1843–1852," in *Inside the Minstrel Mask: Readings in Nineteenth-Century Blackface Minstrelsy,* ed. Annemarie Bean, James V. Hatch, and Brooks McNamara (Hanover, N.H.: Wesleyan University Press, 1996); also Karen Linn, *That Half-Barbaric Twang: The Banjo in American Popular Culture* (Urbana: University of Illinois Press, 1991).

4

The Uncanny History of Minstrels and Machines, 1835–1923

LOUIS CHUDE-SOKEI

On or about December 1835, sometime early in the month, though the details remain appropriately mythical and therefore necessarily fuzzy, American popular culture officially began. It may seem obvious that this is merely a restating of Virginia Woolf's famous declaration of the change in sensibilities that signals the formal birth of what we call literary or cultural modernism, but in truth it comes from Judith Wilt's paraphrasing of Woolf in a well-known essay that begins, "In or around December, 1897[,] . . . Victorian Gothic changed—into Victorian Science Fiction."[1] Wilt's exploration of the birth of science fiction "in the light of imperial anxieties" is largely rooted in questions of genre; the interest here, however, is in exploring how those racial anxieties were shaped in American popular culture within that space between the formal birth of science fiction—Victorian or otherwise—and modernism.[2] This is a modernism from which American popular culture emerges as a result of those anxieties associated with slavery, colonialism, and industrialism. Though characteristic of the Victorian era, they will in the twentieth century become the primary tensions of race and technology at the core of an American imperial epoch.

This periodization ends with 1923, the date of the introduction of the word "robot" into the English language, a term coined for use in Nobel laureate Karel Čapek's *R.U.R. (Rossum's Universal Robots)* but derived from the Czech word *robota,* meaning serf if not slave labor. Much more will be made of this remarkable play, particularly since its anthropomorphizing of late-nineteenth- and early-twentieth-century anxieties about technology become superimposed on extant anxieties about race and empire in that long fin de siècle. But the periodization begins in 1835, when the notorious P. T. Barnum "bought" or acquired the rights to display the slave woman Joice Heth, so-called mammy to George Washington, allegedly 161 years old, from an itinerant showman named R. W. Lindsay.[3] To say that American popular culture began at this moment may be an intentional overstatement, but it is a perception shared by those aware of the uncanny intersections at work in the relationship between Barnum and the woman he called "Aunt" Joice. As James W. Cook puts it, "If we were to pick a single moment to mark the birthdate of modern American popular culture, this just might be the one: on that fateful afternoon in July 1835, when an aspiring impresario from Bethel, Connecticut[,] took off his grocer's apron and began to think seriously about how to market Joice Heth as a popular curiosity in New York City."[4] (Figure 4.1)

It is generally accepted that Barnum built his entire career on the display of this woman, who was called everything from an "Egyptian mummy" to a "living skeleton," from "venerable nigger" to "The Greatest Natural and National Curiosity in the World.".[5] In his own words, the "accident" of Joice Heth "seemed almost to compel my agency," and it was she who "first brought me forward as a showman."[6] She was his introduction into an American public life that he irrevocably changed and a popular culture that some—including himself—argue he essentially invented. But whereas Cook identifies the meeting of Heth and Barnum in July 1835 as that originary moment (or perhaps the meeting of Barnum and Lindsay, Heth being mere property and whose complicity or participation remains enshrouded in fable and confusion), it should be pushed four months further to New Haven, where she was first displayed alongside perhaps the best-known machine of the age of both wonder and reason. It should be pushed to the December meeting between Joice Heth—a human reduced to object—and the infamous chess-playing machine "The Turk," an object raised to the tentative status of human, and which has such a long and complex history of display and literary and cultural reaction (ranging from Descartes to Edgar Allan Poe to Walter Benjamin) that the attempt to account for it here fully would be both unsatisfying and impossible (Figure 4.2).

Very briefly, "The Turk" was constructed by Wolfgang von Kempelen in 1769 for the entertainment of Empress Maria Theresa of Austria, but it would for years stun, terrify, and entertain much of Europe with its eerie mimicry of human beings, playing a game already established as a visible display of reason. This "thinking machine" was eventually acquired almost a century later by Johann Nepomuk Maelzel, purveyor of dioramas, court mechanic of the Hapsburgs, and close friend of Ludwig van Beethoven.[7] Although Barnum claimed that the pairing of Joice Heth and "The Turk" took place in Boston (Figure 4.3),

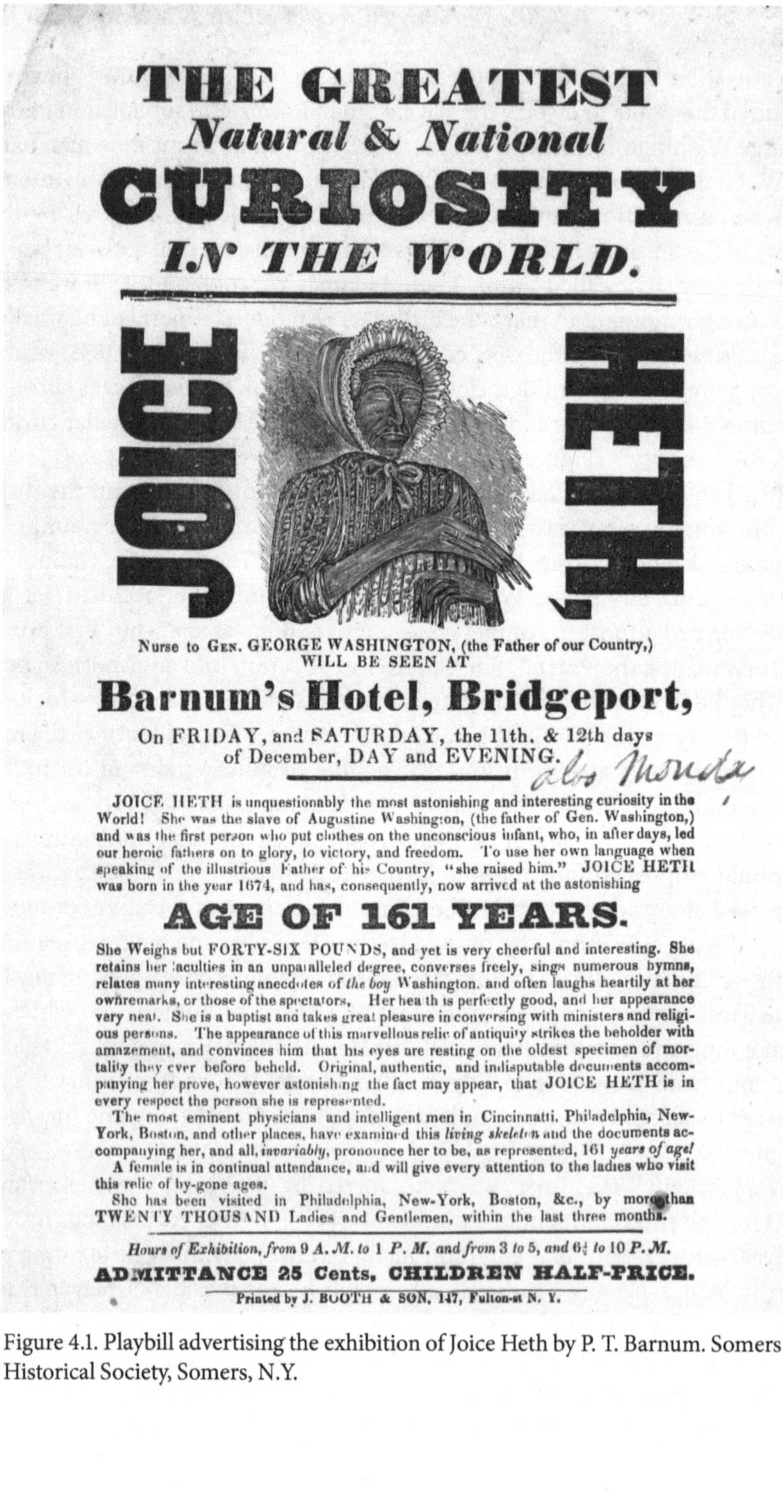

Figure 4.1. Playbill advertising the exhibition of Joice Heth by P. T. Barnum. Somers Historical Society, Somers, N.Y.

Figure 4.2. An engraving of the original chess-playing automaton "The Turk" from Karl Gottlieb von Windisch's book *Inanimate Reason* (London, 1784).

Figure 4.3. Patrons visiting Joice Heth in Boston. Illustration from *The Life of P. T. Barnum as Written by Himself* (New York, 1855).

Maelzel's

EXHIBITION,

MASONIC HALL.

PERFORMANCE EVERY EVENING.

ON SATURDAY, MAY 17 1834

There will be two Exhibitions, one commencing at [illegible] M. the
at the usual time—Doors open half an hour pr[illegible]

Doors open at half-past 7 o'clock. Performance to commence at 8 preci.

PART FIRST.

THE ORIGINAL AND CELEBRATED

AUTOMATON

CHESS PLAYER.

Invented by DE KEMPELIN, Improved by J. MAELZEL.

The Chess Player has withstood the first players of Europe and America, and excites universal admiration. He moves his head, eyes, lips, and hands, with the greatest facility, and distinctly pronounces the word "*Echec*," (the French word signifying "*Check*") when necessary. If a miss-move is made, he perceives and rectifies it.

THE

Automaton Trumpeter.

The Trumpeter is of a full size, and dressed in the uniform of the French Lancers. The pieces executed by this Automaton are performed with a distinctness and precision unattainable by the best living performers; the measurement of time being, from the nature of the mechanism, absolutely perfect. In double-tongueing, his superiority is particularly manifested, not only in the clearness of the tones, but also in the number of the notes which are sounded. All the sounds are actually produced in the Trumpet, there being no pipes whatever within the figure. The pieces he plays were written expressly for him by the first composers. He will perform on each evening, two favorite pieces. 1st. the French or Austrian Cavalry Manoeuvres. 2d, A March, with an accompaniment.

THE

MECHANICAL THEATRE,

Purposely introduced for the gratification of Juvenile Visiters.

IT CONSISTS OF THE FOLLOWING PIECES;

1 The *Amusing Little Bass Fiddler.*

2 The *French Oyster Woman*—who bows to the Company, and performs the duties of her station, by opening and presenting her Oysters to the audience.

3 The *Old French Gentleman*, of the ancient Regime, who drinks the health of the Company with great glee.

4 The *Chinese Dancer*, accompanying the Music with his Tamborine.

5 The *Little Troubadour*, playing on several instruments.

6 *Punchinello* will go through his comical attitudes in imitation of the celebrated Mazurier.

THE SPEAKING FIGURES

AND AUTOMATON

Slack Rope Dancers.

These are the only Figures known that produce distinct articulation by mechanical means. A small Automaton will, in the hands of any person, say "*Maman*" and "*Papa*," with the French accent, and the most perfect distinctness. One of the Rope Dancers uses the French exclamation, "*Oh! La! La!*" when on the rope as well as in the hand. The performance on the Slack Rope is unrivalled; the most surprising feats being executed with the greatest agility, and without any apparent mechanism.

PART SECOND.

THE GRAND

TOURNAMENT.

IN THREE ACTS,

Displaying with grace and accuracy various feats of Horsemanship and Dexterity, as performed at the ancient European Courts, together with many of the most difficult evolutions of the Circus. During the performance, a splendid Landscape and Fountain will be exhibited by Sun-set, when the surrounding atmosphere is illuminated by the descending orb.

To conclude with the

DIORAMA

OF THE INTERIOR OF THE

Cathedral of Rheims

This splendid Painting, by Ciceri, the most celebrated scenic artist in Paris, is a perfect representation of that ancient and magnificent edifice which was erected at the establishment of Christianity in France. Many historical incidents of importance occurred here, and within its walls the Kings of France have, for centuries, been anointed and crowned. From the rear of the Cathedral, a perspective view is had along the great length of its interior, (438 feet, by 93 in breadth) presenting two rows of stupendous columns, upwards of 100 feet high. The assembled congregation, the pews, the great central lamp suspended from the Dome, 116 feet high; the Grand Portal through which the view extends along one of the streets of the city to an almost illimitable perspective, and people are seen walking to and fro, and moving about in all directions; the variegated windows, and, particularly, the famous rosettes of beautiful stained glass, splendid relics of antiquity, which so peculiarly characterize this building, are all well calculated to impress the beholder with interest and admiration.

To complete the illusion bells will be heard, and the

MELODIUM,

Will perform on each evening, a select piece from the most celebrated compositions of Rossini, Mercandante, Auber, and other great masters.

ADMITTANCE, 50 CENTS—CHILDREN, HALF-PRICE.

The Two Front Benches are exclusively appropriated for Children.

Tickets may be had during the day at the Exhibition Hall, or at the Door in the Evening.

N. B. Mr. Maelzel offers for sale the Diorama of the Cathedral of Rheims.

Printed at the Athenian Buildings, Franklin Place, Philadelphia.

Figure 4.4. Playbill advertising Maelzel's exhibition of "The Turk" at the Masonic Hall, Philadelphia, May 17, 1834. From the Library Company of Philadelphia. P. T. Barnum and Maelzel met while touring their respective exhibitions.

it actually occurred in New Haven, where they were on display in contiguous rooms. It was in Boston, however, where Barnum first met Maelzel, who would inspire him and through whom he would be instrumental in reinvigorating a tradition of automata that had long fascinated and flummoxed Europe (Figure 4.4). Maelzel would will his collection of automata to Barnum, whom he very much thought of as his American protégé. But despite the showman's passion for automata and the fact that mechanical oddities would become as much a part of his repertoire as were racialized monstrosities, the display of "exotic" peoples and blackface minstrels—this was, after all, a mere three years after T. D. Rice's staggeringly successful performance of "Jim Crow" in New York—Gaby Wood is right to point out that Barnum ultimately "led the way for human oddities to replace mechanical curiosities in the public imagination."[8]

What makes the meeting of black slave woman and machine a necessary introduction to this essay was what happened next, something far more obscure than the now well-documented and richly theorized history of freakery, ethnographic display, and the complex birth of both the museum and the Western carnival-circus complex. Though he is notoriously unreliable, it is best to have Barnum himself tell the story despite the narrative sleight of hand at work in that relentless presentation of innocence characteristic of all of his autobiographies:

> When the audience began to decrease in numbers, a short communication appeared in one of the newspapers, signed "A Visitor," in which the writer claimed to have made an important discovery. He stated that Joice Heth, as at present exhibited, was a humbug, whereas, if the simple truth was told in regard to the exhibition, it was really vastly curious and interesting. "The fact is," said the communication, "Joice Heth is not a human being. What purports to be a remarkably old woman is simply a curiously-constructed automaton, made up of whalebone, India-rubber, and numberless springs ingeniously put together, and made to move at the slightest touch, according to the will of the operator. The exhibitor is a ventriloquist, and all the conversations apparently held with the ancient lady are purely imaginary, so far as she is concerned, for the answers and incidents purporting to be given and related by her are merely the ventriloquial voice of the exhibitor."[9]

There is little doubt that Barnum himself or his associate Levi Lyman was in fact "A Visitor"; there is also little doubt that the very idea of suggesting to the public that Joice Heth was a machine came from Maelzel himself, given his long history of passing off a machine for human, and particularly that personification of a machine as someone clothed in the skin and costume of Orientalist fantasy. Barnum continues: "Maelzel's ingenious mechanism somewhat prepared the way for this announcement, and hundreds who had not visited Joice Heth were now anxious to see the curious automaton; while many who had seen her were equally desirous of a second look, in order to determine whether or not they had been deceived. The consequence was, our audiences again largely increased."[10]

The presence of "The Turk" clearly had some impact on conditioning the public to imagine Joice Heth, too, as a construct of the age of industry, an American version of an automaton but masked in the dark flesh and withered femininity of a far more intimate, local, and familiar racial stereotype. But certainly that was not enough to guarantee the success of the hoax. Of course "The Turk" was revealed to have functioned by means of a steady sequence of diminutive chess prodigies hiding behind the machine mask; but though it played chess, it was clearly a manmade artifact, carved largely of wood. Most notably, *it did not speak*, and the phonograph and the spectacle of recorded speech were still decades away. So the question is this: Why were P. T. Barnum and the early market for freakery and human oddities so easily able to sustain this particular humbug? Why was it credible and indeed logical? And what would be the repercussions of this masquerade in which race, Africa, sexuality, and technology or artificial intelligence all came together in one performance? This essay is an attempt to answer these questions by situating them as the central concerns of American modernism and a popular culture for which they are its primary forces and tools of knowledge making.

Were we to trace Euro-American modernism back toward some elementary set of issues, influences, and obsessions, we could isolate two primary clusters of meaning among the intersecting many at work within the shock of America's relentless global expansion, which, as it was, was generated far more by cultural and technological influence than by techniques and axioms of territorial domination. The first cluster of concern here is the so-called machine aesthetic, produced by and through the West's difficult and ambivalent responses to industrialization, and which would ultimately find its political and social fulfillment in an America that announces its global presence via the language of inevitability, the language of the *new*. In America, technology would become celebrated as being central to its democracy, but also as a natural sign of it despite its initially disorienting and continually irruptive presence in a nineteenth century in which, as a defining issue, it was arguably second in importance and controversy only to slavery.

Yet despite the "triumph" of industrialization and the fetishizing of technology in the United States, the dominance over the landscape and the erasure of the frontier would only strengthen the nostalgia for nature that, as Leo Marx famously identified half a century ago, continues to define an American political and literary sensibility.[11] Utterly absent from Marx's otherwise magisterial work (despite being so central to his analyses and despite so many points of entry, even given the limitations of his time) is the issue of slavery, which is much more thoroughly implicated in both the pastoralizing and technologizing of the American literary and cultural landscape than he would allow. Largely because of the African slave's central function deep within those very notions of "nature" and nostalgia, race is a primary factor not only in nineteenth-century industrialization but also in the process of modernization and the cultural experience of modernism through its assumed special intimacy with nature. Therefore, the second cluster of interest in this essay is the cultural legacies of West Africa, which will be here called the "African aesthetic" despite being a category with such a gloriously troubled history that one can only use it as a sign of still troubling conflicts embedded behind and among its multiple masks and their plural meanings.

But it is precisely that tendency to read Africa as an omnivorous and endlessly capacious sign for a diaspora of interlinked black differences and a complex set of aesthetic positions vis-à-vis the West that undergirds this notion of an "African aesthetic." This aesthetic describes a tendency and a sensibility rooted not in any quantifiable or provable historical authenticity despite the dependence on anthropology and ethnography that characterized so many of the modern movements that would draw from it. Instead "the African aesthetic" functioned—functions—as the flexible rationale for the metonymic relationships between and among blacks and their varied cultural products during and after slavery; it functioned as a loose network of meanings between and among all that was taken to represent or speak for an African continuum. It has been well documented how modernist movements from cubism, surrealism, dada, and futurism to primitivism, negritude, Pan-Africanism, and Harlem's Renaissance depended on some invention of "Africa" or some construction of an "African aesthetic" either to highlight a contrast with or to enable a critique of a "Western culture" also of their devising. Because the Negro in all of these dialectical manipulations inexorably represented "nature," "the natural," the primitive, *and* the pre-technological—and because "Africa" was both the Negro's point of origin and irreducible essence—these constructs ultimately manifested a complex set of relationships with its dialectical other: technology, industry, or a civilization that had already been describing itself in such terms certainly since Thomas Carlyle.

So it suffices to say that from the sun setting of Rule Britannia to the pallid emergence of an American century, all of these patently modern tendencies, movements, and transformations in figuring the "Negro" and "Africa" in *some* relationship to "the new," to technology and new techniques, also established links between "race" and that other significant twentieth-century sign of otherness, "the machine." During the period marked by the dates 1835 and 1923, both of these categories would share the cultural spotlight in America; and the interbreeding and interdependence of their *uncanny* anxieties would require strategic moments when the two blend and pass for each other rather than function as the antinomies that they did and still do represent. In these moments of miscegenatory masquerade, all that was relatable to "Africa" would share and exchange space with all that was imaginable via the metaphor of "the machine" and the social and historical formations that quickly came to be described thus. In analyzing these two clusters and historicizing their fundamentally modern influence on each other, what we then find in the nineteenth century are two of the twentieth century's most distinct products facing and doubling each other: the blackface minstrel and the robot.

As is well known, in the years beyond this designated period the various figurations of the Negro and estimations of its cultural impact generally employed Africa in complex yet often contradictory ways. Africa could safely signify everything from an abyssal or timeless anteriority to the recolonization of the West by a suppressed primitiveness, or of the superego by the id. It could also be, on the one hand, the presence or return of a nonrational instinct in the midst of a materially powerful but internally decaying *cogito* or, on the other hand, the dangerous threat of atavism lurking beneath the slick processes of a democracy forced to contend with the new type of "humanity" represented by blacks after slavery. These uses of Africa were made affectively accessible via the presence of jazz, primitivist literature and art, banana-skirted dance spectacle, or the complex legacies of blackface, particularly after it became technologized in sound via "coon songs," in film, and in advertising. They would also be both strengthened and contested by the various claims on "Africa" and its legacy deployed by black modernist cultural and political movements operating both within and against the interests of Euro-American modernism. This complex and ambivalent fascination with colonial Africa, African America, and the Caribbean was most certainly the case during the interwar period, a moment characterized by a crisis of faith in technology inspired by the trauma of World War I. Indeed it was this crisis and the anxieties it generated that would enable the rise of a widespread cultural tendency that can be described by Sieglinde Lemke's seemingly oxymoronic but utterly accurate term "primitivist modernism."[12] In the words of Wilson Harris, "the gift of every advance in technology is fraught with ambiguity in its innermost content."[13] "Africa," the Negro, and the primitive became signs of that ambiguity and ambivalence as manifest in the realm of culture.

More important, the various movements and cultural tendencies of modernism would deploy the tensions generated by the juxtaposition of these two clusters of influence in order to explore and exploit the anxieties they depended on. For example, as a symbol of the natural and the pre-technological, the "African aesthetic" and the Negro who represented it were either untouched by or opposed to the industrial technology that had brashly come to define "newness" in America, a newness that made American modernity exceptional; or the Negro pioneered a quite novel set of sensibilities in which tradition and the modern, the organic and the technological, were made somehow to "jive" or "swing," particularly in the music and dance spectacles of 1920s American popular culture, which, though now remembered as organic and rooted in black vernacular culture, were initially seen and heard as machine age spectacles, as elaborate rituals of the submission of "art" to the logic of the machine, of whites to the depersonalized rhythms of industry—hence Adorno's notorious description of jazz as a form of fascism in blackface.[14] These observations about "primitivist modernism" can, however, be traced back two generations to the birth of plantation minstrelsy, particularly as the form found ways of dramatizing the demise of its own socioeconomic rationale and the inevitable transformation of slaves into humans and the movement from an agricultural economy to an industrial one. Though an admittedly simplistic binary, these clusters of influence and anxiety did bring together two specific ways of reading and experiencing the cultural influence of Africa and "the machine" in that long American fin de siècle. On the one hand, there was an old romantic fear of a dehumanizing, depersonalizing technology and its concurrent loss of "nature." Although this was an evenly distributed fear as significant to northern transcendentalism as it would be for, say, a southern plantation owner, it was felt most potently in the South because of its connection to a specific and increasingly threatened socioeconomic way of life. But on the other hand, there was a much more specific and explicitly American fear: that of an increasingly humanized—which is to say liberated—African American social, cultural, and political presence. It was an overwhelming fear of a black subjectivity that had previously been demarcated by law and by science as inhuman or subhuman, reasonless and most certainly soulless. In the South, this too was uniquely felt and uniquely feared.

It is worth noting that it was in the nineteenth century that our contemporary meanings of "technology" would begin to congeal, just as would the current meanings of "race" and "culture." In that century the very notion of "the machine" or even "industry" would evolve from merely material descriptions, tools, and objects into signs and metaphors of abstract social and historical processes. These metaphors would also begin to function as markers of specifically Western forms of power and descriptions of social and political systems and, as Locke would have it, of a deterministic social order. This would be the case just as the category of "race" would itself evolve beyond raw physical or biological data in order to provide abstract historical and cultural formulations confirming non-Western and specifically African inferiority, largely in the name of or under the aegis of science and ultimately in the rhetoric of development. These terms—"race," technology, culture, and "the machine"—would be given transformative impetus by the fresh legacies of Darwinian evolution amidst the industrial revolutions in colonial England and in an American slave economy that was buttressed by it. This latter economic and cultural system is of great significance because it was the source of what would become blackface minstrelsy and the complex and variegated world of American racial stereotypes and the popular culture that would be based on them. Far in advance of modernism, the Jazz Age, and a formalized primitivism, the plantation sealed the relationship between blacks and machines and expressed it in performance via blackface minstrelsy.

As a *system,* the plantation was a significant precursor to the regimentations and formal, time-driven depersonalizations known as Fordism and Taylorism. It is this insight that has motivated Caribbean thinkers such as the venerable C. L. R. James to stress the plantation as a "dominant industrial structure" and to have argued consistently that it was in the context of the plantation that slaves became disciplined into distinctly modern subjects in advance of formal freedom.[15] As he writes in his famed appendix to *The Black Jacobins,* "From Toussaint L'Ouverture to Fidel Castro": "Wherever the sugar plantation and slavery existed, they imposed a pattern. It is an original pattern, not European, not African, not a part of the American main, not native in any conceivable sense of that word, but West Indian, *sui generis,* with no parallel anywhere else."[16] For James, because the plantation was "a modern system," slaves "from the very start lived a life that was in its essence a modern life."[17] So it is largely through a Caribbean lens—one attuned to the ambivalent complexities of creolization—that this exploration of race and technology will largely be framed. This same technologization of the pastoral through the plantation system in America and the Caribbean is what also motivates Sylvia Wynter's description of the plantation not as a perverse pastoral environment but as a "social machine" in which "the Negro then becomes the *symbolic object of this lack which is designated as the lack of the human.*"[18] She refuses the logic of naturalization that in and after slavery worked so hard to render the plantation the organic and natural home of the *darky* while simultaneously denying that patrimony by way of its innate "African-ness." For her the plantation is instead a *machine* that "colonized, above all, Desire."[19] A complex social machine, it allowed desire to "work 'freely,'" a process which suggests that instead of erasing black subjectivity (that which was already being erased by slavery), a new kind of black *non-African* subjectivity was being produced on the plantation on the eve of slavery's demise. This essentially *modern* subjectivity may have been produced in the name of an industrial notion of "freedom," but it would limit the very meaning of the word in advance of its formal achievement.

Wynter's description of the Negro-in-the-machine importantly evokes Aimé Césaire's famed *Discourse on Colonialism,* in which he describes the machinery of colonialism's process of "thingification," whereby the "indigenous" becomes transformed into "an instrument of production."[20] But the Sambo stereotype/archetype simultaneously drew its charge and value from the suggestion that the Negro was actually the antithesis of production and the lacuna of an industrial temporality. In this guise, he was not only lazy but also immune to the work ethic, a position dialectically necessary in the construction of a certain kind of technological whiteness: "Central to the bourgeois ideology is the idea of the atomistic individual as a responsible agent. By constructing Sambo as the negation of responsibility, the slave master legitimated his own role as the responsible agent acting on behalf of the irresponsible minstrel."[21] It is important to point out that Wynter does acknowledge that Sambo is merely the double in a pair of stereotypes including "Nat," the rebellious figure drawn from Nat Turner. Nevertheless, despite the obsession with racial "resistance" that delimits much scholarly conversation and inquiry, Wynter finds in Sambo a far more liberating set of possibilities; in other words, she sees in the comic something far more complex than the melodrama of formal refusal. In the relationship between master and childlike mimic, the primary terms may have been racial, but indeed the overwhelming context was one of a struggle with a capricious "nature," the wilderness of both the unconscious and an American landscape that was seen as yearning for domestication. Yet for whites during the early years of industrialization in America, that comic figure offered the spectacle of escape from what was beginning to seem an all-encompassing deindividuating system, one that not only erased "nature" but also robbed whites of their own "organic" sense of agency and power in an increasingly regimented socioeconomic order. It is no exaggeration to suggest that it is the fear of this order that has fueled generations of science-fiction narratives in which whites fear their own mechanization and dehumanization in a context in which what Aristotle called "animated tools" gain consciousness and either seek revenge or claim their evolutionary due.

It is this rapidly changing agrarian landscape, a dramatically shifting industrial economy, and the threatened transformation of slaves into citizens—animals into humans—that will fuel the "theft" side of the dialectic in Eric Lott's foundational work on blackface minstrelsy, *Love and Theft.* To play or enjoy blackface masquerade was also to resist the new industrial regime with its responsibilities and its clockwork temporality. In Wynter's words, blackface offered southern whites "the barest minimum of an affective and emotional life . . . to be sustained in the wilderness of technological rationalization."[22]

The Sambo mask was an escape from mechanization through the pleasures of an always flexible and always performative "African aesthetic" that was the chthonic doorway into a raw, primitive, and hypersexual nature as distinct from whiteness and "the West" as possible despite the fact that this mask was an indigenous product of modernity. This use of minstrelsy to construct a debased yet popular culture that enables and maintains a white sense of humanity in that wilderness of industrial modernity goes much further than spectacle and its economies of pleasure and play. It is through the minstrel stereotype and blackface mask that the white colonial/racist "self, to constitute itself as human in the normative conception, must then conceptualize the possibility of lack, the lack of the intellectual faculties, of being the non-human, of being Sambo."[23] Wynter's long-standing critique of the onto-historical category of the "human" preempts and predates Donna Haraway's "cyborg feminist" conceptual apparatus by some years; and it reminds us that during slavery, blacks were poised not merely between the categories of "human" and animal. The Negro was poised also between rational agent and soulless machine, between mindless brute and what George Lamming once described as "man-shaped ploughs."[24]

In light of Wynter's description of the experience of blackface performance as an experience of the "possibility of lack," it must be emphasized that the Negro was in fact neither human nor animal but something or somewhere either in between or incommensurably beyond. Or, as Wilson Harris would no doubt suggest, the carnivalesque blackface Negro occupied some other dimension entirely that refracts rather than reflects the foundational biases of slavery as it reimagined "unfathomable kinships" in the act of an organic masquerade.[25] Harris, after all, is a thinker much more attuned to the productive and cross-cultural value of the uncanny than any of those whose analyses are rooted in the binary logic of American racial differences. To return to Wynter, the "possibility of lack" was experienced through Sambo not as a complete being but not as an inanimate object either. Instead "he" was a figure of pure, unadulterated liminality, of the relentless possibility for "unfathomable kinships." Indeed, as she argues, Sambo is less a sign of racial binaries than "the scapegoat-carrier of all alternative potentialities that are repressed in the system. Sambo becomes the representation of all desire that flows outside the dominant order."[26] Because Sambo was necessarily kinetic with the mask relentlessly in motion, because the Negro was *not* inert and recognized as central to labor and the economy, this liminality could incorporate the *idea* of machinic production. Machines, after all, were in fact also others that bore some uncanny relationship to the very slaves they would eventually replace.

Before the twentieth century and in the period under consideration, the idea of machinic production had already been anthropomorphized, embodied. It had been visualized and culturally registered by automata, those figures of artificial life that were also popular spectacles in sideshows and carnivals alongside the display of African or other natives and which featured all manner of blackface coonery. Though dating back centuries, these machines—many of which were clearly fraudulent, featuring bodies buried behind or below the machine mask, like "The Turk"—were resurgent in nineteenth-century America in no small part because of the efforts of "America's greatest showman," P. T. Barnum. As Benjamin Reiss puts it in his comprehensive study of Barnum and Joice Heth, the relationship between blacks and machines was so established in the antebellum period that there were a great many "automaton 'Negroes'" produced in America which were on display in the same spaces where oddities, curios, freaks, Negroes, and minstrels were often featured: "Black people and apes were fitting forms for automata since they both posed—in different degrees—questions for white audiences about bodies that resembled dominant conceptions of 'the human' but that may or may not have lacked fully human powers of intentionality or rational agency. Black automata, additionally, repeated at the level of amusement slavery's system of bodily domination."[27] In the spirit of providing a non-binary, creolized view of this history, it is worth mentioning here also the work of the African American entrepreneur John W. Cooper, who slightly reversed or supplemented this conventional power dynamic with his own fabrication and display of black machines sometime around 1909. His black minstrel automata shows lasted at least ten years and were good enough to earn him the title "The Black Napoleon of Ventriloquism."[28]

In a rare and important attempt to take seriously just how the "discourse of technology was and still is imbricated within discourses of race, civil rights, and slavery," the literary critic Michael Chaney points out how "proslavery ideology conceptualizes so-called inferior races as functional commodities dehumanized to the status of mere tools."[29] As Reiss would put it, "In their natural state [blacks] were like beasts; but in a perfect state of slavery, they could become, if guided by a master's rational will, something like machines or prosthetic devices."[30] But although he is three or four generations late in locating this intersection of race and technology "alongside the Civil Rights and feminist movements" and the concurrent discourses of cybernation when it is in fact a Victorian conceit, Chaney is right to argue that "slavocratic society may also reflect a commonplace recourse in prescience literature, which assuaged patriarchal anxieties regarding a technological revolution that was then unfolding," one that presaged "the new age in technology in terms of a return to the age of slavery."[31] This passage should be clarified since the "return" in question here is more accurately a fear among whites of their own transformation into slaves by machines, *not* a return to the age defined by America's peculiar institution in which blacks were slaves. What Chaney describes is instead a fear of *reversal,* of a sudden loss of power rather than a return to an antebellum status quo. This fear of reversal will attend each technological change and ultimately racialize it since it is almost always (and has always been) articulated in the language of racial slavery—from automata to cybernetics.[32] So because Donna Haraway's still influential "ironic political myth" of the cyborg emerges from and depends on the primary transgression between the categories of human and animal, Chaney is on point to make the claim that *that* myth is perhaps doubly political or triply ironic in that it is ultimately rooted in "the category disputations over the black body in America, between what constituted human and animal"; and so Haraway has provided, in essence "a theoretical abstraction of African-American slave subjectivity" through the lens of gender and technology.[33] But in truth, P. T. Barnum got there first.

It is precisely this promiscuous liminality, with its relentless slippages between the categories of Negro and animal and machine, inhuman, nonhuman, and subhuman, that makes the Freudian uncanny necessary in making sense of those forces that maintain and depend on the historical relationship between Africa and "the machine." As discussed earlier, Wynter's critique of the "human" frames these "unfathomable relationships" within a Caribbean discourse of creolization in which Sambo is its most colorful product or manifestation; and it is from that discourse that Sambo and "the comic" can be deployed without the excessive trauma that the icon/image is made to evoke in a North American context in which minstrelsy's possibilities still remain stigmatized. Her use of Sambo thus broadens Chaney's valuable insights beyond the borders of the American plantation, especially since these category disputations around the Negro's "nature" were enacted throughout the African Diaspora and were routed through a generalized understanding of Africa as the source of that "nature." Wynter's thinking also precedes and completes Haraway's by questioning the "human" in order to detail its limits and to explore the very possibility of entry into it by those subjects previously named antithetical to the category; and as demonstrated in her discussion of Sambo, Wynter's thinking too is dependent on the uncanny. The uncanny, after all, entails that which is dreadful, fearful, and terrifying, but also that which is simultaneously familiar, long known, and intimate. It produces intellectual uncertainty and epistemic ambivalence precisely because it pollutes self with other, binding the former to the latter despite repressing the latter as an irreconcilable otherness.

The uncanny, however, is also a source of humor. As Eric Lott puts it: "Clowning is an uncanny kind of activity, scariest when it is most cheerful, unsettling to an audience even as it unmasks the pretentious ringmaster.

Blackface performers, often inspiring a certain terror as well as great affection, relied precisely on this doubleness."[34] In Freud the uncanny signifies the presence of a double, albeit one "concealed and kept out of sight."[35] It includes "the impression made by wax-work figures, artificial dolls, and automatons," and that "intellectual uncertainty whether an object is alive or not, and when an inanimate object becomes too much like an animate one."[36] For Henri Bergson, working in the considerable wake of Freud's essay, these figures of artificial, synthetic life would be examples of a comic sensibility precisely because of their being uncanny semblances of humanity via automation: "This is no longer life, it is automatism established in life and imitating it. It belongs to the comic."[37] Bergson's *Laughter: An Essay on the Meaning of the Comic* demonstrates just how imbricated the discourse of uncanny doubles and machines was with the anxieties of race. It updates and completes the Freudian uncanny by way of its own uneasy relationship to minstrels and machines: "We begin, then, to become imitable only when we cease to be ourselves. I mean our gestures can only be imitated in their mechanical uniformity, and therefore exactly in what is alien to our living personality. To imitate any one is to bring out the element of automatism he has allowed to creep into his person. And as this is the very essence of the ludicrous, it is no wonder that imitation gives rise to laughter."[38] This is what Wynter argues is the psycho-affective disequilibrium healed by Sambo, by his kinetic mask and racial masquerade. It is also classic performance theory, classic parody, and of course classic minstrelsy and carnival. As we will see shortly, Bergson's analysis is also a product of a long and familiar history of romantic racism in which the other is prized for its ability to heal the imbalances of the white or Western self—particularly in the context of alienating new technologies and their attendant ideologies of subject formation, social organization, and of course commodification. These insights will ultimately express how from analog to digital, the black other is almost always implicated in or conscripted by a white need to make sense of new relationships to new technologies as they "creep into his person." And these technologies accomplish this fearsome invasion of the self initially by way of imitation—by "nature" mimicking and therefore drawing attention to the "element of automatism" that is already there but masked as "nature."

Given what will prove to be his racialization of the comic through mimicry and the uncanny, Bergson in effect describes the therapeutic value of blackface minstrelsy: as a cure for the modern white disease of "automatism." This is evident when he asks, in a much more problematic way than with Freud's talk of androids:

> And why does one laugh at a negro? The question would appear to be an embarrassing one, for it has been asked by successive psychologists . . . and all have given

> different replies. And yet I rather fancy the correct answer was suggested to me one day in the street by an ordinary cabby, who applied the expression "unwashed" to the negro fare he was driving. Unwashed! Does not this mean that a black face, in our imagination, is one daubed over with ink or soot? . . . [A]nd so we see that the notion of disguise has passed on something of its comic quality to instances in which there is actually no disguise, though there might be.[39]

The most obvious aspect of this passage is of course its not so subtle dependence on blackface minstrelsy in a description of a "real" Negro, a black person so overdetermined in "*our* imagination" that she or he irrevocably partakes of that comic tradition even without the mask. Bergson goes so far as to leave us with the dangling possibility that even when there is no "ink or soot" (or burnt cork), the mask's traces exist in perpetuity, epistemologically "unwashed." The memory of the mask contaminates the experience of flesh, and the presence of organic flesh merely articulates a previous strategy of masquerade. Less obvious is the fact that by this 1911 essay, the very notion of "automatism" had already become so racialized that the Negro was merely one in the list of doubles for white subjectivity and the "human" as enumerated by both Freud and Bergson. Here, far in advance of the cyborgs of Haraway and Chaney, the linkage of Negro, dolls, and automata, blackface and machine, already operated with an unquestioned logic, each as a mask of the other.

To clarify the previous point, Bergson's various references to "our living personality" or "our imagination" clearly do not include the Negro as a subject. In the essay, the Negro is much more closely related to androids than to even "an ordinary cabby." The Negro is a mere doppelganger for "our living personality," being a sign not of life nor of the category of "human" but a double for it—innately comic and irrevocably in disguise. After all, it is not the Negro who is prone to or victim of "automatism," nor does the Negro benefit from the experience of uncanny doubling; he merely comments on it all, brings "our" attention to it, and thereby allows "us" to laugh at and transcend it. In this reading the Negro does not share in the full experience of "the uncanny" or "the comic" quite simply because he—or "it"—is so deeply linked to its primary cause or source. But it is Bergson's conclusion that seals the link between blackface and automata, contextualizing that most fully realized historical expression of a racialized uncanny, which was the epochal meeting of America's greatest showman and a female African slave in 1835. Bergson writes: "Let us then return, for the last time, to our central image: something mechanical encrusted on something living. Here, the living being under discussion was a human being, a person. A mechanical arrangement, on the other hand, is a thing. What, therefore, incited laughter was the momentary transformation of a person into a thing. . . . WE LAUGH EVERY TIME A PERSON GIVES US THE IMPRESSION OF BEING A THING."[40]

Of course, the opposite corollary is also true and even more significant in the context of American slavery *and* in terms of blackface minstrelsy: "we" fear and dread the moment whenever a *thing* gives us the impression of being a person. In a "slavocratic" racial economy, this slippage occurs just when a designated thing dares assert itself as a person via mimicry of "human" codes, thereby suggesting the capacity for reason, for literacy, and thereby making a claim on kinship. This moment of slippage, of what Judith Butler has dubbed a "category crisis," though evident and traceable in performance, must be located in much stronger materialist circumstances as Chaney suggests. The uncanny as it characterizes the relationship between white and black, human and inhuman other, must be rooted in something more historically concrete than the mere dis-ease in sensibility described by both Freud and Bergson. Bill Brown is therefore to be commended for identifying it as a product of the "contradictory legal status of the American slave—both human and thing."[41] Given the history of American law and its ambivalence as to the category status and substantive quality of the black slave, Brown is absolutely correct to attribute a specifically "American uncanny" to U.S. law through which "the slave becomes the source of uncanny anxiety."[42]

This "uncanny anxiety," however—and the "intellectual uncertainty" whether the Negro was human or not despite being too much like both an ape and a "human" (read "white" person)—must be read beyond the bounds of the United States. This is not simply because Joice Heth was consistently advertised as an African but because she was brought over from the continent as a child. Wynter's deployment of Sambo should then also be read against the exceptionalism that claims minstrelsy as exclusive to a North American historical or cultural climate since the form depended on and in turn influenced so many discourses in and beyond the plantation of an American context. The racial or "American" uncanny must be read thus for two primary reasons: first, because the ramifications of U.S. law were globally inscribed, and the influence of its attendant racial and social assumptions were of no small influence in other parts of the world, most certainly in the Caribbean. Second, in the United States and in the Caribbean, the American Negro functioned as the necessary mediating link between America, the African Diaspora, and the "dark continent" itself. Sambo contained in his mask simultaneous and mediating relationships between the West and the non-West, America and the Caribbean, America and Africa. "He" was also a cultural presence in those sites because of the eventual migration of minstrel theater and music but also because he was a circulating product of local performances of race and colonialism in various plantation or imperial economies in which minstrelsy would be indigenized, from the Caribbean back to the African continent.

But it is the complex ambivalence in both U.S. law and colonial racism itself—this kinship-alienation dialectic, this animal-human-machine problematic—that is of greater consequence in the partial definition of a racial uncanny (since the uncanny can be only partially defined, being a fragmentary sense of completion in relation to a plenitude that is relentlessly suggested but always refused on the basis of race). It is this philosophically partial yet legally institutionalized definition that enables Wynter to posit a diasporic, creolized "Sambo" as the ultimate product and sign of "category crisis"; again, "it is in the sense that we should view the Sambo stereotype as the scapegoat-carrier of all alternative potentialities that are repressed in the system. Sambo becomes the representation of all desire that flows outside the dominant. Which is to say that through the Sambo figure and its logic and legacy of primitivism, through its doubling for and mimicking of the white rational subject, all forms of otherness—like machines—also have an echo and, eventually, a (black) voice and face. Recall that what links the uncanny other to the fragile self is not just the vague anthropomorphism of the former but its penchant for mimicry, for daring to seem like you, in fact to perform you as well as you perform it. Recall also that from automata to a "mimetically capacious machine" like the phonograph, machines were widely feared for possibly possessing reason or thought and as terrible replacements or substitutes for humans.[43] It is through those machines—particularly the phonograph—that the sound of black voices, for example, will make such a cultural impact that they will begin a history in which race or its aural signifiers come to function as a mask for the socioeconomic regime that the machine itself actually stands for, much in the way that Sambo will speak racism and white anxieties through a black mouth. It is worth adding here that many would first encounter the phonograph in those very sideshows and spaces of curiosity and freakery where both automata and Negroes were displayed or performed. The uncanny is therefore the space of epistemological uncertainty and cultural anxiety where the minstrel meets the machine. As a generalized sensibility, it contains them both and makes necessary the two best-known responses to severe anxiety and cultural uncertainty: laughter and terror. It is to his credit that so early in the history of American mass media and popular culture, P. T. Barnum would so astutely realize the power and possibility that lay in simultaneously commodifying them both (Figure 4.5).

Sambo, then, is a product of a changing American pastoral landscape which entailed a severe transformation in both technological development and race relations and which helped lay the foundation for an American popular culture. "He" must be read against an emergent global empire that depended as much on technological advancement *and* popular culture as it did on biological racial categories: "For a deep chord has been struck here by early twentieth-

Figure 4.5. Minstrel automaton, nineteenth century, in the Czech Museum of Music, National Museum, Prague. For an alternative image of the minstrel automaton, see Figures 7.1 and 7.2.

Figure 4.6. A scene from *R.U.R. (Rossum's Universal Robots)*, by Josef and Karel Čapek, performed in New York City (1922), showing a new image of the "automaton," now renamed "robot." From the Billy Rose Theatre Collection, Library and Museum of Performing Arts, New York Public Library.

century advertising and popular culture, substantiating the primitivism that Darwin connected to miming prowess."[44] As the missing link between animal and human, Sambo was the link to that other threat to white male centrality which was also the figure of a complex desire for cultural power and which also operated via mimicry: the machine. Though it would wait until 1922 to be provided with a permanent name, this economic and cultural "other" would be explicitly racialized in 1872 by Samuel Butler in his legendary *Erewhon,* which notably feared the inevitable coming to dominance of machines as they evolved into a distinct race of sentient beings. This anthropomorphization of this *other* uncanny other would once have been named an automaton by Freud and Bergson and most certainly by Samuel Butler and P. T. Barnum. But from the 1922 New York premiere of the Czech writer Karel Čapek's *R.U.R. (Rossum's Universal Robots),* it would quite rapidly begin to be called a *robot* in a play that told the story of a slave race of inhuman machines who not only evolve "souls" but then also emerge victorious over the (white) humans who had enslaved them (Figure 4.6). Perhaps the uncanny relationship between these narratives and

American racial and cultural anxieties is why, by the 1923 English publication of *R.U.R.*, the word "robot" so rapidly supplanted the much more common term "automaton," or even the ancient term "android" when used to describe this hypermodern figure of Wynter's "alternative potentialities" or Harris's "unfathomable kinships." Even more uncanny is the fact that the year when *R.U.R.* premiered in the United States, the African American modernist Jean Toomer would give the strange title "Rhobert" to a short story appearing in his famed collection *Cane.* In his criticism of a soulless northern black bourgeoisie adrift from its organic cultural roots, Toomer would echo Čapek by describing the titular character in the following way: "Rhobert wears a house, like a monstrous diver's helmet, on his head. . . . Rods of the house like antennae of a dead thing, stuffed, prop up in the air."[45]

But for a white status quo, the figure of the robot doubled and threatened a white rational subjectivity precisely while former slaves were increasingly asserting the rights of "the human" against the legacy of "slavocracy" and during the rise of industrialism. Nevertheless, the very question of the Negro's modernity—well, the Negro's modern*ism*—had already been rendered an open question in American minstrelsy back on the plantation. Temporal questions of the "African-ness" of the Negro vis-à-vis its American modernity were fully embedded in its fundamental narrative tensions, which depended on a rural-urban split; and in a context so defined by technology, one in which technological sophistication became increasingly the barometer for racial differences and cultural rankings, this question of temporality was dependent on a relationship to "the machine," or again, a civilization that increasingly defined itself in such terms and through such concepts. For example, most minstrel shows featured two distinct types of Negro, suggesting how blackface performance was divided as to whether or not "the Negro" was the rural or African past or the urban modern. In this temporal and historical dialectic, Sambo was simply the rustic plantation dweller inseparable from the symbolic economy of slavery; his bookend, Zip Coon, was linked directly to (and often known as) Jim Crow. Whereas the former represented nostalgia for the plantation and a ludic rejection of or a biological failure at the work ethic, the latter was its double, the slick urban dandy introduced into minstrelsy by George Washington Dixon in the 1820s. Zip Coon was notoriously "uppity," mocked for his aspirations, and did not know his place despite the fact that he was probably the earliest representation of a black hyper-consumer in American history (not to mention being the forerunner of all forms of contemporary post–hip hop pimpish masquerade). Zip Coon in fact *dared* or threatened to be placeless, divorcing himself from the economy of the plantation machine while claiming both the North and the freedom of migration. In shifting places as the itinerant and often flashy bluesmen and women soon would, he suggested that space should be or could be shared with urban, modern whites while reminding them that the plantation, "Africa," and even Sambo were irrevocably in the past. Zip Coon was thus a self-conscious and self-fashioned product of the coming machine age and of a changed, migratory sense of a black "nature." Of course, in performance, the gravity of his threat made him much more vulnerable to jokes about lynching and much more threatening to those blacks uneasy with the threats to the status quo represented by his masquerade. Zip Coon achieved all of this while the much more organic Sambo basked in the safety of a pre-technological and nondemocratic stupor, a stupor that was understood as being due to his fundamentally "*African* nature."

For Eric Lott the two types of Negroes in classic minstrel theater represented a geographical "sectional break" attendant on all the political, social, and ideological distinctions that would build up to the Civil War; but insofar as the South was linked to the past and the North the utopian site of post-emancipatory dreaming, the split was an equally temporal affair.[46] As is evident in the terms used to describe and refer to antebellum blacks and then to minstrelsy, the question of the Negro's temporality, of which century he belonged in, was framed also in global terms, rendering Lott's "sectional break" transnational. These terms of geographical, cultural, and historical otherness maintained the absent presence of racial origins that was the African continent. Given the assumptions of the time, in which race, culture, and origins were seen as innately bound, this African "nature" was rendered as a loose, self-governing network of discourses (an "aesthetic") alongside the belief that minstrelsy was indeed an autochthonous cultural form. Blacks, for example, would be simultaneously contained by the relentless descriptions of minstrelsy as "African," "Ethiopian," "Egyptian," "Dahomean," or similar designations, as seen in the very way Joice Heth would be advertised, even in advance of the blackface era. These were not random or throwaway terms, despite the fact that so many scholars of minstrelsy seem to treat them as such out of a desire to will blackface into being an exclusively and exceptionally American form and a particularly American experience of trauma. Even when deployed in descriptions of whites in blackface, the terms detailed a relationship to or a governing body of ideas *about* the African continent, emphasizing its pre-technological history-lessness and its people who—unlike, say, those in India and China—had not proven themselves worthy by the civilizational indices of literacy and technological sophistication.

Particularly relevant in the lexicon of a then nascent advertising and racialized media spectacle, minstrels and minstrelsy were continuously advertised by terms of inflated patrimony such as "Congo," "Senegambian," or even "Abyssinian." As Lott points out, this "national cultural form" was presented as and considered "the Æthiopian drama" while simultaneously acknowledged as "the lowest description of American farce . . . not without originality, considerable invention, and a rich vein of burlesque humor."[47] Certainly the terms were deployed mock-heroically. But that such a potent and patently American folk form should consistently draw attention to itself by way of signifiers of the African continent is curiously deflective and most certainly a technique of managing a racial uncanny rooted in a space external to the United States. It was most obviously meant to remind audiences and performers that the Negro was not truly a native, not indigenous despite being bound to the spatial and social economies of the plantation. The terms made it clear also that the Negro *and* the continental African were unfit for modernity and for the responsibilities of full citizenship because of that biocultural link to a place of unquestioned savagery and darkness. And they were deployed aggressively, relentlessly *Africanizing* the African American's primitive and premodern "nature" precisely when debates about its humanity and modernity were gaining ground in political discourse. Arguably this racist use of Africa was at the root of the still much-ignored *anti-Africanism* and black vanguardism in a good deal of late-nineteenth- and early-twentieth-century African American culture and politics. This black hostility and disdain toward the African continent would only be transformed—though never fully reversed—by the various movements of black modernism, from Ethiopianism to Pan-Africanism to New Negro-ism.

Now, despite the omnipresence of "Africa" in the discourses of minstrel masquerade, it is the case that Wynter strays a bit too far out of the realm of historical accuracy in her imaginative theorizing when she argues that "the American Minstrel show is a direct development out of the popular folk cultures of Africa, with possibly, as the Jonkunnu plays show, contributions from the parallel folk cultures of precapitalist Europe."[48] That it is "direct" is of course debatable, or respectfully *dismissible.* But in light of her reference to "Jonkunnu," a Caribbean folk festival of subversive masking and ludic play also rooted in slave culture, it is clear that in her view, blackface functions much more broadly within ritual forms of the carnivalesque in and beyond the African Diaspora than simply within the binary racial dramas of nineteenth- and twentieth-century America. Her strategy is ultimately to dislodge blackface from functioning as the almost exclusive sign of American racial trauma that so many desire for it to be and to see in it a longer continuum of "African" expressive play, one anterior to an ever-privileged American "blackness"—though it is also true, as some historians and scholars such as Alexander Saxton point out, that "early minstrels . . . had understood slave music not as African but as close to nature. Correspondingly, they perceived slaves as part of nature—part of the nature of the

South."[49] But the attempt in minstrelsy to render the plantation as the "home" of the darky and the organic site of his "nature" was in no way an attempt to *de-Africanize* black slaves, since that would be ultimately either to claim them as belonging to the same historical continuum as their white masters or to suggest that they had a prior, more authentic claim on the United States. Since "Africa" and the "nature" of African Americans were ultimately homologous in a time when race and culture were synonymous, these mock-heroic descriptions drew from a debased Africa to mock-authorize an emergent American form. This was a form that wore the mask of its Negro presence while speaking white anxieties about a changing landscape in a vernacular appropriated from slaves and former slaves. Such an intricate dance of belonging and disavowal, America and Africa was surely what allowed the form to be claimed by whites without attributing credit to blacks as its creators or its inspiration.

Despite the reluctance of so many to accept or admit the crossover from comic travesty to self-righteous militancy, the influence of minstrelsy was not present simply in a racist modernist American popular culture. It was equally notable in the cultural and political spectacles of black modernism. They inspire everything from Garveyism and its often willy-nilly appropriation of terms, icons, and signifiers from a wildly generalized African continent to the equally willy-nilly appropriation and deployment of those very terms in the poetry, music, and art of the New Negro movement.[50] These black moderns were arguably as ambivalent about Africa as they were about Sambo; or in some cases they would use the former to erase the latter. Being more Zip Coon than Sambo, the "African aesthetic" of black moderns was a myth that helped them claim a unique place within a modern urban civilization and allowed them to compete with white moderns in that aesthetic scramble for Africa at the root of primitivist modernism. For writers such as Langston Hughes, Claude McKay, and even Alain Locke and W. E. B. Du Bois, Africa was a point of orientation in the face of what the arch-primitivist Claude McKay would describe as "the ever tightening mechanical organization of modern life" in which blacks were now "milling through the civilized machine."[51] This was, after all, a civilization that still bore strong doubts about their humanity and still depended on Sambo despite the fact that many whites were turning to a symbolic Africa out of a fear of losing theirs. Ironically, what whites feared in this transition was the loss of a humanity that they had long denied to actual slaves and blacks themselves.

This now almost clichéd modernist malaise and its fetish for Africa mirrored the earlier movement from a slave economy into an industrial one—a movement that was dramatized by blackface minstrelsy. As Wynter points out, Sambo was the denial of that humanity rendered as masked spectacle; but as she also argues, he was the sign of affective life, too, for those threatened by the spiritual and emotional death of industrialism and modernization which would so feed modernist literary and cultural expression. For that generation after slavery, in the midst of what Claude McKay described as "a world-conquering and leveling machine civilization," Sambo would participate in the various movements, tendencies, and cultural explosions called cultural modernism as the link between "the African aesthetic" and "the machine," between a slave past, an industrial present, and a technological future.[52] Owing to the persistence of a racialized and technologized uncanny, blackface would become as much a sign of the modern as of the antebellum, as much a symbol of the pre-technological as a harbinger of the machine age. It is in the latter context that the influence of minstrelsy on modernism can be seen, not simply in the effect that blackface would have on black moderns, but most notably in the very translation of nineteenth-century American plantation racial economies into cultural forms that would disperse throughout the cabarets, sound recordings, literary texts, and images that fed cultural modernism. We should add to this cross-cultural mix the growing fetish for African masks that conditioned much of the modernist impulse alongside the brewing explosion of jazz, which was as much a product and signifier of technological artifice and machinic incorporation as it was an organic black musical form. As the noted 1920s-era anti-jazz crusader Daniel Gregory Mason put it in distinctly Adorno-esque terms, jazz was "so perfectly adapted to robots that the one could be deduced from the other. Jazz is thus the exact musical reflection of modern capitalistic industrialism."[53] The Sambo and the Zip Coon masks are ineluctably linked to West African masks, each a visual cue for—or perhaps an echo of—the other.

So even though parodic, imprecise, and dense with racist, romantic, and/or fuzzy nationalist intent, the presence and legacy of blackface minstrelsy did help popularize and domesticate a flexibly defined "African aesthetic" in the wider climate of early-twentieth-century American modernism in the wake of the fateful meeting of "America's greatest showman" and the African female slave. As is well known, the success of displaying Joice Heth both as decaying African animal and then as the epitome of mechanical engineering set Barnum on a career that profited greatly by the display of automata, black freaks, *and* minstrels. In this commercial and spectacular relationship, the blending of the "African aesthetic" and the "machine aesthetic" was already on the way to being naturalized in the American imagination with the discursive logic of one being buttressed by the historical and cultural associations of the other. This uncanny relationship and history are constitutive of cultural modernism and at the core of the discursive and economic effects that are American mass media and popular culture. This is, after all, a popular culture that functions largely by way of naturalizing artifice in the language of the inevitable, the language of "nature," and all too often the language of "race." Because of this history, the suggestion of the one *as* the other was not just credible but necessary to a form of commodification rooted in slavery and in racial travesty, one in which race would be necessary in domesticating a new system of technology and its attendant sociocultural and economic relationships. This miscegenatory birthing of American popular culture found its annunciation in the strange case of a wizened black slave woman and her passing for or being passed as a machine. Because she was a slave, however—a mere thirty years before a full legal emancipation into the "human"—she was actually being passed as a machinic simulacrum of something other than a human being, something that was already passing for something else and could therefore be used to pass for anything as long as it existed on the far edges of the "human." To put it in deliberately mythic terms, "Aunt" Joice Heth was the black Madonna of the coming machine age. In her infinite masks, an old social and economic system passed as a new one and a new technological system of culture and power masqueraded as an organic one. In this sequence of transubstantiations, dumbstruck audiences partook of the glory of a new commodity masquerading as an old one and witnessed an old performance of "nature" naturalizing and therefore legitimizing one that had already changed.

NOTES

1. Judith Wilt, "The Imperial Mouth: Imperialism, the Gothic and Science Fiction," *Journal of Popular Culture* 14, no. 4 (Spring 1981): 618.

2. Ibid. I'm particularly taken by Wilt's preliminary attempt at adumbrating "a theory of imperialism as a major contributing pressure for the mutation of gothic into science fiction"; this attempt modifies and specifies the work of Patrick Brantlinger in his well-regarded *Rule of Darkness: British Literature and Imperialism, 1830–1914* (Ithaca: Cornell University Press, 1988), a text that operates with a periodization not accidentally quite similar to my own. Another quite useful text is John Rieder, *Colonialism and the Emergence of Science Fiction* (Middletown, Conn.: Wesleyan University Press, 2008).

3. I emphasize the ambiguity in whether Barnum acquired/bought "the rights" for display or bought her outright; there is some confusion there as a result of his continual reinvention of his own history and autobiography to distance himself from slavery and his participation in it, particularly as he moved his racialized spectacles from slave states to free ones.

4. James W. Cook, *The Arts of Deception: Playing with Fraud in the Age of Barnum* (Cambridge: Harvard University Press, 2001), 3.

5. Ibid., 5–6; Benjamin Reiss, *The Showman and the Slave: Race, Death, and Memory in Barnum's America* (Cambridge: Harvard University Press, 2001), 1, 106.

6. P. T. Barnum, *Struggles and Triumphs; Or Forty Years' Recollections of P. T. Barnum. Written by Himself* (Buffalo: Warren, Johnson & Co., 1873), 73.

7. Gaby Wood, *Edison's Eve: A Magical History of the Quest for Mechanical Life* (New York: Knopf, 2002), 60.

8. Ibid., 217.

9. P. T. Barnum, *The Life of P. T. Barnum, Written by Himself* (New York: Redfield, 1854), 157.

10. Ibid.

11. Leo Marx, *The Machine in the Garden: Technology and the Pastoral Ideal in America* (New York: Oxford University Press, 1964).

12. Sieglinde Lemke, *Primitivist Modernism: Black Culture and the Origins of Transatlantic Modernism* (New York: Oxford University Press, 1998). For more on this familiar and much-remarked-on tendency, see Marianna Torgovnick, *Gone Primitive: Savage Intellects, Modern Lives* (Chicago: University of Chicago Press, 1991); Petrine Archer Straw, *Negrophilia: Avant-Garde Paris and Black Culture in the 1920s* (London: Thames and Hudson, 2000).

13. Wilson Harris, "Creoleness: The Crossroads of a Civilization?" in *Selected Essays of Wilson Harris: The Unfinished Genesis of the Imagination* (London: Routledge, 1999), 244.

14. For an effective yet incomplete exploration of this argument, see Joel Dinerstein, *Swinging the Machine: Modernity, Technology, and African American Culture between the World Wars* (Amherst: University of Massachusetts Press, 2003). See also Felicia McCarren, *Dancing Machines: Choreographies of Mechanical Reproduction* (Stanford: Stanford University Press, 2003). I have described Dinerstein's argument as incomplete simply because of its somewhat triumphalist assertions concerning the process by which race "tames" technology and domesticates it; though I do agree it is also true that it is by this very process that race becomes a sign of technology and of American imperial processes precisely because of its all too easy association with discourses of "resistance," which have become merely a new language of American exceptionalism.

15. *The C. L. R. James Reader*, ed. Anna Grimshaw (Cambridge: Blackwell, 1992), 306.

16. C. L. R. James, *The Black Jacobins* (New York: Vintage Books, 1963), 391–92.

17. Ibid., 392.

18. Sylvia Wynter, "Sambos and Minstrels," *Social Text*, no. 1 (Winter 1979): 152.

19. Ibid.

20. Aimé Césaire, *Discourse on Colonialism* (New York: Monthly Review Press, 1972), 21.

21. Wynter, "Sambos and Minstrels," 151.

22. Ibid., 149.

23. Ibid., 152.

24. George Lamming, *The Pleasures of Exile* (Ann Arbor: University of Michigan Press, 1992), 121.

25. Harris, "Creoleness," 44.

26. Wynter, "Sambos and Minstrels," 154–55.

27. Reiss, *The Showman and the Slave*, 121.

28. Steven Connor, *Dumbstruck: A Cultural History of Ventriloquism* (New York: Oxford University Press, 2000), 336–37.

29. Michael Chaney, "Slave Cyborgs and the Black Infovirus: Ishmael Reed's Cybernetic Aesthetics," *MFS: Modern Fiction Studies* 49, no. 2 (Summer 2003): 265–66.

30. Reiss, *The Showman and the Slave*, 121.

31. Chaney, "Slave Cyborgs," 265.

32. Donna Haraway, *Simians, Cyborgs, and Women: The Reinvention of Nature* (New York: Routledge, 1991), 149. The tension around this transgression is certainly present in

the work of Norbert Weiner, founder of the science of cybernetics, whose classic text *The Human Use of Human Beings* (New York: Houghton Mifflin, 1950) was once described by the so-called Afro-futurist Kodwo Eshun as W. E. B. Du Bois's *Souls of Black Folk* "updated for the Analog age." Though I find this a characteristically imprecise formulation, I think Eshun means that Du Bois's text and its metaphors of doubling are as dependent on analog technologies of duplication as they are on new modes of apprehending the mind. Weiner's now classic text is itself suffused with an anxiety about race, particularly in the inescapable conversation about slavery that emerges as he attempts to distinguish cybernetics and machine labor from "real" slavery. Kodwo Eshun, *More Brilliant Than the Sun* (London: Quartet Books, 1998).

33. Chaney, "Slave Cyborgs," 267–68.

34. Eric Lott, *Love and Theft: Blackface Minstrelsy and the American Working Class* (New York: Oxford University Press, 1993), 25.

35. Sigmund Freud, *Collected Papers,* trans. Joan Riviere and James Strachey, vol. 4 (London: Basic Books, 1959), 375.

36. Ibid., 378, 385.

37. Henri Bergson, *Laughter: An Essay on the Meaning of the Comic,* Project Gutenberg E-Book no. 4352 (2009).

38. Ibid.

39. Ibid.

40. Ibid.

41. Bill Brown, "Reification, Reanimation, and the American Uncanny," *Critical Inquiry* 32 (Winter 2006): 179.

42. Ibid., 199.

43. Michael Taussig, *Mimesis and Alterity: A Particular History of the Senses* (New York: Routledge, 1992).

44. Ibid., 211.

45. Jean Toomer, "Rhobert," in *Cane* (New York: Boni and Liveright, 1923), 40.

46. Lott, *Love and Theft,* 207.

47. Ibid., 89.

48. Wynter, "Sambos and Minstrels," 155.

49. Alexander Saxton, "Blackface Minstrelsy," in *Inside the Minstrel Mask: Readings in Nineteenth-Century Blackface Minstrelsy,* ed. Annemarie Bean, James V. Hatch, and Brooks McNamara (Hanover: University Press of New England for Wesleyan University Press, 1996), 75.

50. See Louis Chude-Sokei, *The Last "Darky": Bert Williams, Black-on-Black Minstrelsy, and the African Diaspora* (Durham: Duke University Press, 2005).

51. Claude McKay, *Banjo* (New York: Harper & Brothers, 1929), 324.

52. Ibid., 66.

53. Lawrence W. Levine, "Jazz and American Culture," in *The Jazz Cadence of American Culture,* ed. Robert G. O'Meally (New York: Columbia University Press, 1998), 437.

5

Surprised by Blackface

D. W. Griffith and *One Exciting Night*

LINDA WILLIAMS

According to current critical wisdom, D. W. Griffith's 1922 film *One Exciting Night* fails to deliver the excitement of its title. Indeed, many critics consider it the legendary filmmaker's very worst film, playing to all his weaknesses, both racial and aesthetic.[1] Not equipped for the tight plotting of mystery or for the light comedy required by the kind of clever modern stage play he was attempting to imitate, Griffith is deemed to have fallen flat. In a note on the film for the 2007 *Giornate del Cinema Muto* program, Steven Higgins concludes that the proof that Griffith lacked the ability to direct with a "light touch" resides in the fact that he "fell back upon the broadest and most offensive kind of racial stereotyping, portraying the character of Romeo Washington as a lazy good-for-nothing whose quaking in terror at the slightest provocation was clearly meant to incite riotous laughter in the audience. The fact that the part of Romeo was acted by Porter Strong, a white man in blackface, makes the effect all the more painful for modern audiences."[2] Higgins is surprised and offended by blackface, and especially by the evidence that audiences of the time found two of the primary performers, Porter Strong and Irma Harrison, to be not only "skilled burnt cork performers" but also "highly entertaining."[3]

Reacting much like the entire field of film studies in his surprise and offense at the survival of blackface performance traditions in this twentieth-century medium, Higgins naturally wants to distance himself, and this field, from the unenlightened souls who may have found blackface entertaining. Of course this is what we all might want to do. Audiences who laughed at the demeaning minstrel stereotypes of blackface or who thrilled at the spectacle of the Ku Klux Klan riding to the rescue of white women threatened by black brutes seem unfathomable to us today. And yet critics would sometimes rather express offense at racism than come to grips with the appeal and rationale of the many facets of blackface "lore" as it has operated throughout American culture.[4]

In this essay I aim to get beyond these initial registrations of surprise and offense to understand the basis of the appeal of burnt cork to Griffith himself and to the audiences of this 1922 film. I especially want to avoid the temptation, rife in Griffith criticism, to identify moments in his later films when the director "falls back" on seemingly archaic traditions—whether blackface humor, with its roots in minstrelsy, or black-white racial melodrama.[5] I hope to show that far from falling back on old-fashioned stereotypes, Griffith was not simply repeating his racist past; he was modernizing—which is not to say correcting—in racially new, but still white supremacist and offensive, ways.

D. W. Griffith had deployed burnt cork for both comic and melodramatic purposes long before the epoch-making *Birth of a Nation* (1915). In that film, however, he seemed to solidify a practice of Jim Crow segregation that depended on blackface delineation in all principal black characters.[6] The racist rule of thumb was essentially that if black characters were to enact major scenes with whites, and especially if black *male* characters were to enact major scenes with white *female* characters, then these black characters must be played by whites in blackface.[7] In other words, there were legal and practical reasons for blackface anytime the story of a film was about relations between black and whites. Laws against integration were strictly in force in the South. Conventions against it were also in effect in the North. And most movie theater audiences were segregated. Blackface, by the time it became a convention in fiction films of the 1910s and 1920s, was not only a residue of minstrel masks but also a way of reassuring audiences, and especially southern audiences, that the races were not mixing in fact, especially when they were mixing, necessarily, at the level of the fictions portrayed.

Thus the movie screen, like the theatrical stage of this period, was rigorously segregated. The one great exception to the rule against actual racial mixing occurred in the extraordinary career of the blackface comedian Bert Williams. This light-complexioned West Indian made his early reputation in the team of Williams and Walker as a slow-witted "darky" in many groundbreaking all-black musicals in the early years of the century. In 1910, however, after the death of George Walker, Williams was the first black performer to integrate the cast of the Ziegfeld Follies. This integration, which took place against considerable opposition by other Follies headliners, occurred only while Williams continued to wear his trademark sad-sack "darky" face, and it did not extend to the audience of the Follies, which remained strictly segregated, thus depriving Williams of his most avid fans.[8] The Follies paid the price of giving up touring southern towns where integration was legally forbidden.[9] Moreover, a stipulation in Williams's contract (put there himself for his own protection) forbade him to appear on the same stage with white women performers, thus limiting the actual integration of the cast to males alone. For an entire decade at the Follies, Williams would remain behind his minstrel mask. Just what could be done within the limits of this mask has been the subject of much intriguing analysis.[10] It is against the background of such analysis, a history that is now willing to probe black blackface, and one important step in the slow assimilation of blacks into American popular culture that I would like to examine a flip side to this innovation: D. W. Griffith's use of blackface as one awkward step in the painfully slow integration of American films. This is not an argument about progress—the incremental recognition of the humanity behind the mask—but it is an argument about change in a film director whose deployment of racial masks had enormous consequences in American history in that film we most love to hate: *The Birth of a Nation.* Nevertheless, the analysis of blackface in Griffith's films has not received the attention it is due precisely because we seem never to get beyond our surprise and offense. What follows, then, is an argument about how the conventions of burnt cork changed in the early twenties and how those conventions portrayed the white supremacists' imagination of the place of African Americans in the American homeland, indeed, in Griffith's iconic "old Kentucky home."

Griffith's Comic and Melodramatic Conventions of Burnt Cork

In Griffith's films of the teens, the counterfeit blackness of white performers functioned primarily to reassure white audiences that segregation was as much in effect within the film as it was in life in so many parts of the country. This meant, however, that Griffith had a dramatic problem in his particular brand of racial melodrama. He needed his black or mixed-race villains to lust visibly after whites, especially the white girl, and thus he needed to portray the racial mixing he abhorred even though this sexual-racial threat could be represented only by white actors in blackface.

The fictional representation of the threat of miscegenation so crucial to Griffith's racial melodrama would not be officially prohibited in Hollywood films until the "Don'ts and Be Carefuls" of the earliest version of the Production Code in 1927 and later codified in the 1930 Hollywood Production Code proper. In the latter document, miscegenation would be defined as "sex relationships between the white and black races,"[11] which was precisely the kind of relation Griffith had multiplied in his landmark film under cover of blackface. In *The Birth of a Nation* these relations proliferated: first, between the white

Reconstruction senator Austin Stoneman and his mulatta "housekeeper," Lydia Brown; second, in the intended forced "marriage" to Elsie Stoneman plotted by the mulatto politician Silas Lynch; and third in the intended rape of the Cameron family's "little sister" by the renegade black man, Gus, who pursues her to the edge of a cliff, over which she throws herself.

Since D. W. Griffith was never going to use an actual black actor (male or female) in any of these villainous roles of sexual predators mixing with whites, these racialized villains—Lydia Brown, Silas Lynch, and Gus—could be played only by whites in (various degrees of) blackface, thus undercutting the "realism" of the sexual-racial threat they supposedly depicted.[12] And precisely because they were villains of melodrama, these blackface characters could not perform according to either the comic or pathetic conventions of blackface minstrelsy. Not for them the faux awkwardness, ironic grace, sentimental pathos, or tongue-in-cheek irony so prevalent in minstrel representation. What, then, was their repertoire of movement under their different black masks? Consistently in Griffith, they are depicted as "naturally" servile creatures who first bow and scrape and then, only when encouraged by whites, aspire to higher things. A tension between a "natural" inclination to stoop is put in conflict with "unnatural" urges to stand tall. For example, when the proud and upright mulatta housekeeper Lydia Brown finds herself slighted by the refusal of a proud white man (Senator Charles Sumner) to treat her like a lady rather than a servant, she whips herself into a frenzy, falling to the floor and tearing her clothes in fury (Figure 5.1); her rage is viewed as hysterical, his reluctance to treat her as a lady as natural, justified by her regression to bestiality. In another example, the "renegade" Gus (Figure 5.2) is famously played by the white actor Walter Long with a slack jaw and animalistic crouch, reminiscent of the position of the first Africans brought to America (see Figure 5.9). But when he is soon promoted to captain, Lynch walks proudly down the street and seeks to "marry" the Cameron family little sister, thus alternately veering, like Lydia, between crouch and proud upright stance. Silas Lynch, who is similarly crouched and servile originally, is encouraged by his mentor Austin Stoneman to stand tall and take no orders from whites (Figure 5.3).[13]

In contrast to these originally crouching, sexually threatening blackface villains, the actors playing former house slaves, while literally servile to their masters, do not alternate between upright postures and a crouch. They are portrayed as taking proper pride in the status of their owners. Loyalty marks them as deserving to stand upright and to scold those other "niggers" who do not know their place. Mammy, the Cameron family's former house slave turned loyal servant after the Civil War, is comic in her obesity and even uses this weight at one point to foil two renegade black soldiers who squirm under her bulk to enable the escape of her former master (Figure 5.4). One might thus expect her to behave in the comic or sentimental tradition of minstrelsy. But she is not caricatured by the exaggerated, large bright lips of minstrel makeup or by the contrasting whites of flashing eyes. Though she will at one point throw herself comically into the arms of a white man who rescues the Cameron family, thus shocking the older Cameron sister (Figure 5.5), she does not imitate the broad facial caricature of the minstrel mask; and her misdeed, unlike white female–black male contact, is indulged. Indeed, she reacts as scandalized only when she observes such minstrel stereotypes as are displayed early in the film, when the northern Stonemans visit the southern Camerons, by the "free-nigger from de n'of" who scandalizes Mammy by wiggling his eyebrows (Figure 5.6). Thus Mammy criticizes the "free nigger" who does not know, as she does, his proper place.[14] As is the case in so many subsequent representations, Mammy is the black character with the most extensive, and least threatening, relation to whites.

By 1915, then, with *The Birth of a Nation,* we observe four basic types of blackface in Griffith. The first is the lustful black villain, like Gus; the second the lustful male or female villain, whose threat to the violation of the color line is, in the case of Lydia Brown and Silas Lynch, already visible in his or her mixed-black skin. The mulatto or mulatta, who is already the product of miscegenation, is the one who dares aspire the most boldly to sexual relations with whites, and who extends himself or herself upright, but only to revert to character in lustful crouches. In these cases the mask of blackface darkens but does not otherwise caricature the features. A third type of mask consists in the desexualized (usually by overweight or age) black servant. Here too the blackface mask does not exaggerate the mouth or bodily movements in minstrel fashion. If this servant character still does not know his or her place, a fourth type of mask is in order. This is the only instance, as in the case of the "nigger from de n'of," derived directly from minstrelsy. For Griffith, the Zip Coon who has experienced the liberties of the North is only momentarily, and only in a fiction depicting the antebellum period, a laughing matter.

There is also a fifth type of mask, though one that is not literally blackface. These are the faces of the African American "supernumeraries" or "extras" who are never named in the credits and who only rarely come into contact with whites. In *The Birth of a Nation* they include the soldiers who carry out the orders of Silas Lynch (Figure 5.7), the easily manipulated new black voters (Figure 5.8), and other groups of blacks who are not individuated. Perhaps the most striking examples of black masses are the bodies that Griffith seems to hold responsible for causing the sufferings of black-white racial melodrama itself.

Figure 5.1. Lydia Brown tears her clothes. From *Birth of a Nation.*

Figure 5.2. Gus, the renegade. From *Birth of a Nation.*

Figure 5.3. Silas Lynch is urged to stand tall. From *Birth of a Nation.*

Figure 5.4. Mammy throws her weight on two black(face) soldiers. From *Birth of a Nation.*

Figure 5.5. Mammy hugs her white rescuer. From *Birth of a Nation.*

Figure 5.6. Mammy and the "free-nigger from de n'of." From *Birth of a Nation.*

Figure 5.7. Supernumeraries: soldiers in the service of Silas Lynch. From *Birth of a Nation.*

Figure 5.8. Easily manipulated new black citizens. From *Birth of a Nation.*

Figure 5.9. "The bringing of the African." From *Birth of a Nation.*

In an opening tableau we see two shirtless Africans crouched and cowering before a white man who raises his hand over them as if in benediction. The film's first intertitle explains, "The bringing of the African planted the first seeds of disruption" (Figure 5.9). All America's problems stem from this first mistake of "planting" black bodies in a white land, Griffith seems to argue (in a prologue that is his own invention and cannot be blamed on Thomas Dixon Jr., on whose novel *The Clansman* the film was based). Although the first mistake is slavery itself—the bringing of the naturally servile African to America—it is compounded by the second mistake, the disaster of freedom that *The Birth of a Nation* recounts, the freedom that would alter the original crouch and urge these slaves to become upright, and thus "uppity." These bodies do not inhabit minstrel caricatures. Griffith wants them to inspire fear. They embody none of the affection, comic or sentimental, of the minstrel tradition.

Such are the basic conventions of black (and blackface) masks as enshrined in *The Birth of a Nation.* The racial mixing that blackface aimed to melodramatize may have required blackface, but it is probably a mistake to call this minstrelsy. It is racial melodrama of the most egregious sort, outrageously reversing the historical facts to make white women the victims of a bestial miscegenous desire when precisely the reverse had been the norm. Only the independent black producer-director Oscar Micheaux would set the record straight, at least for the very few who saw his film *Within Our Gates* (1919). In this film, which Jane Gaines has aptly described as a racial melodrama that directly answers Griffith, Micheaux dares to enact the drama of miscegenous desire between black and white bodies—and, boldly, with no blackface.[15] He shows a black woman in much the same position as Elsie Stoneman: racially and sexually beset.[16] The white-haired Arnold Girdlestone (played by a white actor) pursues the disheveled and frightened Sylvia Landry (played by the black actress Evelyn Preer) until he traps her and places his hands on her breast, ripping her bodice and revealing a scar on her chest by which he recognizes her as his own daughter—the product of his own previous mixed-race union.

Both Griffith and Micheaux depict the horror of miscegenation and its threat to the helpless, racialized woman. Both incur censorship, but the one who presents the story in blackface makes the most popular and galvanizing film in the history of the nation; the one who doesn't incurs community censorship and, with no avenue of distribution, reaches almost no viewers. Not only did Micheaux's film show miscegenation as it mostly was—a white male violation of black women—but also he dangerously enacted racial mixing in his very staging. By the time of the institution of the "Don'ts and Be Carefuls" promulgated in 1927 and in the Hays Code of 1930, American movies had decided to avoid either kind of racial mixing. Indeed, the Code's ban on depictions of miscegenation, though it eliminated the kind of vilification of black lust at which Griffith excelled, also eliminated the kind of vilification of white lust through which Micheaux could answer Griffith. Hereafter black men and white women, and white men and black women—in or out of blackface—would be kept even further apart. Indeed, once relations of miscegenation were strictly forbidden, depictions of all relations between the races became even more hierarchical and conventionally ordered, at which point, coinciding with the arrival of sound, minstrel stereotypes would enjoy a major resurgence.

During this period, as Thomas Cripps summarizes, "no studio depicted black despair, poverty, neglect, outrage, caste, or discrimination."[17] Even the eventual ban on any "willful offense to any nation, race or creed" had only the effect of eliminating the depiction of nonwhite races.[18] This is not to say that without the Code, African American experience would have been more positively depicted. It is only to say that portions of this experience might have been depicted more in relation to whites, though always within the bounds of white supremacy.

One Exciting Night (1922) thus catches Griffith and American film history in an interregnum that permitted a depiction of the threat of (or the desire for) black bodies that would be tempered or eliminated once the Code was in full force. This film neither proffers the incendiary, soon-to-be-outlawed "miscegenation" and racial offenses of the previous decade nor yet seeks the safety of omitting black representations and "serious" relations with whites altogether. While it is most often to *Intolerance* (1916) that critics turn when seeking a Griffith wishing to repair the "willful offense" to race of *The Birth of a Nation*, it is actually this later, overlooked film that shows us what racial apologia might look like in this director.[19] It is not a pretty sight, but it is a fascinating one.

One Exciting Night: A Modern Movie

The Bat: A Mystery Drama in Three Acts, by Mary Roberts Rinehart and Avery Hopwood, had opened on Broadway in 1920 and played a phenomenal 828 performances. Alexander Woollcott, writing about the play in the *New York Times,* derided the convoluted and nonsensical plot which invited the abandonment of rationality and the embrace of chaos. Yet he went on to admit that the play could be "no end of fun if you let yourself go."[20] Sudden blackouts and dramatic spotlights were part of the stage thrill of the original play, which Griffith hoped to outdo with cinematic thrills.[21] In a second discussion of the play, Woollcott diagnosed the work's popularity in a way that Walter Benjamin might have later appreciated: "The sharpened appetite for mystery plays [is] less a superficial matter of vogue than an actual relation to the frayed nerves of the post-war world."[22]

Unable to purchase the play itself for film adaptation, Griffith blithely wrote his own knockoff using the pseudonym "Irene Sinclair," a Kentucky "authoress." "She" gave him permission to imagine the original drama, which takes place in a nonspecific rural setting, in his own home state of Kentucky, and thus to introduce many putative "southern" conventions of black(face) melodrama and minstrelsy that were not in the original.[23]

The basic plot of the film is structurally quite similar to that of the play: an isolated country house is the hiding place for a large amount of money—funds stolen from a bank in the original play, ill-gotten bootlegger booty in Griffith's film. A murder is committed under the nose of various inhabitants of the house as a detective attempts to solve the crime and find the missing money.

The Bat had not been without its own racial component. A Japanese "houseboy" named Billy, most likely played in yellowface, is one of the play's first suspects.[24] Similarly, Griffith's southern locale affords him the opportunity to cast suspicion initially on a black man named Sam. But whereas *The Bat* quickly dispenses with our suspicion of the "inscrutable" Billy, Griffith enhances our suspicion of Sam and even creates a second Sam, Samuel Jones, who may be impersonating the first.[25] The first Sam belongs to an otherwise white gang of bootleggers. An intertitle announces, "It is well-known that Black Sam is the dark terror of the bootlegger organization." We see him slinking about outside the country estate that once belonged to the head bootlegger just before the murder of another member of the gang takes place. Our suspicion naturally falls on the ominous Sam, who is referred to by a partner in crime as a "nigger."[26] But this Sam soon disappears. When another black character named Samuel Jones (Frank Wunderlee) later turns up seeking work in the same house, we immediately suspect that he is the same man, now disguised as a servant to gain access to the house where the money is hidden. This Sam, whom we finally

Figure 5.10. Samuel Jones with shifty eyes. From *One Exciting Night.*

see clearly, has straight upright hair that contrasts sharply with his black(face) skin and shifty eyes (Figure 5.10). We assume that he is one of Griffith's typical black(faced) villains of racial melodrama. That he will not prove to be so is one of the ways in which we will be "surprised" by blackface.

In the mystery surrounding the identity of Sam, Griffith plays with our own racial responses, recasting the "chaos" mentioned in Alexander Woollcott's review of the original play in racial terms. We do not know from one moment to the next who is the racial victim and who is the racial villain of this work. The very proliferation of Sams suggests the quandary Griffith faces. If black men do not actually lust after white women but still do so in the white imagination, then how should such characters' relations with whites be presented? The vacillation over how to think of the black man would seem to be part of the film's very modernity—a modernity with roots, as in much modern art, in ideas about a primitive Africa. And indeed, in a convoluted backstory we learn that the mystery of Sam's identity lies in deepest Africa. Like Bert Williams and George Walker in the musical play *In Dahomey* (1902), but with solemnity rather than satirical fun, Griffith traces some of his characters back to Africa. To set up this backstory the film offers a seemingly endless set of introductory intertitles. He first instructs his audience to "watch closely the early scenes as they become important later on." Then he implores them, in anticipation of Hitchcock, not to "divulge the solution of the plot." Finally, the last intertitle reads, "In sombre Africa, stern source of the world's greatest fortunes, our story opens." As in *The Birth of a Nation,* the first image reveals a crouching African, this one seen in long shot (Figure 5.11). All that subsequently transpires in *Birth*—the Civil War, the violence of Reconstruction—is implicitly "explained" by the supernumerary Africans whose "bringing" to America "planted the first seeds of disruption." The question for Griffith in *One Exciting Night* is now whether this African too plants "seeds of disruption."

Figure 5.11. Opening shot of *One Exciting Night:* the African.

The African spied in the first shot of *One Exciting Night* is dressed in a turban and rags, and as closer views later suggest, he is also in blackface, a device that opens the way to his "relation" with white characters. The intertitles introduce this man as "The Kaffir," the South African equivalent of "nigger," a catchall term for native Africans who might otherwise be distinguished by the names of specific tribes.[27] We are informed that he is "deeply devoted to the husband of the young mother," the white woman we now see lying on a makeshift bed with her newborn child.

A white man and his female companion in safari costumes also attend the young mother. They are impatient to continue their quest for gold, which has been discovered by the young mother's husband. We soon learn that the husband, brother of the man who attends the young mother, has died. Upon hearing this news the mother dies too, leaving only the baby to inherit the gold. The brother, the white villain, disposes of the baby by giving it to his female companion. This baby will become Agnes (Carol Dempster), the film's heroine. The fortune she will eventually inherit is the gold her dead father's brother here steals.

In this convoluted backstory Griffith revises his earlier propensity to blame black Africans for the "seeds of disunion." In this case it is not the actually black African body that is blamed but "the mystery of GREED," as another early intertitle puts it. The African is linked to the source of the mystery, but he is not its motive. Indeed, the film will even go out of its way to link greed with racism in the next scene.

In this bedside scene the female companion of the gold hunter twirls a chain to which is affixed a locket. She does not notice when the locket, containing paired photos of herself, falls to the floor. The servile African retrieves it but does not notice that half of it remains on the straw-covered floor (Figure 5.12). He approaches the woman in his characteristic crouch to return the locket to her. Griffith's camera moves in closer for the details of this approach, and part of the action is repeated, the better for us to notice the white woman's revulsion to this dark-skinned, striped-turbaned creature. She puts her hand before her nose as if to brush away his smell and turns away from him (Figure 5.13). But he persists until she finally notices and takes the locket. In pointing to where he found it, however, he inadvertently touches the back of his bare arm to her white sleeve and hand. Repulsed at his touch, she slaps him across the face. He slinks backward, still crouching. His knees tremble, though not in the comic caricature of the superstitious and fearful "darky" but in an intriguing tension between fear and rage. In separate shots we see the woman wipe the contamination of his touch from her sleeve and hands as the "Kaffir" clenches his fist but then, thinking better, shrinks back in fear. Head down, he discovers the other half of the locket with its photo of this white woman in her safari hat. This time he does not try to return it. The reason Griffith imputes to him is a native belief in magic. In the words of an intertitle, "Pictures—white man's magic to be treasured."

Figure 5.12. The African retrieves the locket. From *One Exciting Night.*

Figure 5.13. The white woman repulsed by the black African. From *One Exciting Night.*

Figure 5.14. The African overhears the plot. From *One Exciting Night.*

Later, the black(faced) African listens in as the brother and his companion plot to have her raise the child herself so it will be ignorant of this inheritance. As he listens, we see several views of his face (Figure 5.14). The film seems to ask what we should make of these black(face) features now that they have been deemed so revolting by a woman capable of robbing a child of its inheritance and beating a subservient black man. Is this African a Tom-like victim persecuted by Simon Legree–like villains, a man we should pity and love, or is he a primitive whose rage must be feared? The question hangs suspended over the entire film and will be answered only in the denouement. What is "new" and "modern" in the film is thus partly this suspense involving racial feeling toward the black(faced) man, which becomes part of the larger mystery. Although this African sequence has been criticized as unnecessary padding, it is what this convoluted film is most deeply about.

Almost as elaborate, and as seemingly unnecessary to the main plot about money hidden in a Kentucky country estate, is the blackface minstrel comedy that takes place in the present story sixteen years later. Augmenting the conventional romance between the now grown Agnes and the dashing young millionaire who loves her despite her betrothal to an older villain is the comic romance between one Romeo Washington (Porter Strong) and an unnamed mulatta maid (Irma Harrison). This racialized doubling of the white couple has, as with the African backstory of the "Kaffir," no parallel in the play Griffith was adapting. Indeed, it has no parallel in mainstream American entertainment of the time, which, although no code would specify it, observed a tacit ban on the portrayal of black-on-black romance in both theater and film.[28]

In the film's main plot the young hero, Fairfax (Henry Hull, who had recently starred in yet another Broadway haunted house play, *The Cat and the Canary*), and the young heroine, Agnes (Carol Dempster, still in the early stages of her work with Griffith), find themselves comically mirrored by the black(faced) servants in the manner of romantic Roman Plautine comedy, which is often about masters and cunning slaves. These blackfaced characters' vigorous wooing contrasts with the rather languorous sighs of the white couple. The film's introduction of Romeo Washington is as elaborate and leisurely as its introduction of the "Kaffir's" story. An intertitle sets up his entrance: "Fired with ambition, young Romeo Washington hustles out to get a job." Cut to a rural whistle-stop whose population is devoid of all ambition and hustle. Romeo, suitcase in hand, arrives as all the local "darkies" doze.[29] If Romeo steps into this scene with initial energy, he almost immediately loses it through the infectious somnolence. He blinks and yawns at the tableau formed by a Mammy type who neglects her potato peeling, men asleep in chairs, and banjo strummers who snooze in the background (Figure 5.15). Romeo, in checkered cap and matching collar and a light-colored suit and vest, makes his entrance as the modern incarnation of the northern Zip Coon on a sleepy Kentucky afternoon. Unlike the authentic black supernumeraries, none of whom will come into contact with the white principals except those disguised by blackface, he is in full minstrel guise.

Griffith clearly intends the very idea of Negro ambition to be comical in contrast to the general, and supposedly more natural, somnolence of his supernumerary black community. It will be the work of the film to put the hustling, amorous Romeo right back here where he started into a more "proper"—that is, less ambitious—place. Until that moment, however, it will be his business—unlike that of the rooted supernumeraries—to *move*. Looking for work, Romeo finds his way to the hero's mansion. When a disapproving white majordomo asks him with a sigh if the reference he presents is all he has, he replies in an intertitle: "Yeah Sah. He sid my face would do the rest." In a close-up that gives us further opportunity to glimpse white features under the mask, Romeo clamps his white lips together and widens his eyes (Figure 5.16). Most of the facial action is located in the eyes, typified by two quick blinks followed by a long stare—an action repeated when he flirts with his paramour.

Hired to clean out the room in which the bootlegger had been murdered, Romeo repeats the blinks and the stare, but this time the big smile disappears. He puts his checkered cap back on, beats a hasty retreat to the kitchen door, and picks up his suitcase to leave. Only then does he notice the comely maid swaying in a dance as she prepares food. A comic push-pull follows, acted out in Romeo's body, between his desire to join the maid in her infectious dance and the fear that pushes him to leave.

Poised at the door, suitcase in hand, Romeo stares at the maid, blinks, looks back toward the scary murder room, then back again at the maid's lascivious movements. Dropping the suitcase, still watching the dance (she has now

Figure 5.15. Romeo encounters the sleepy black community. From *One Exciting Night.*

Figure 5.16. Romeo's black mask. From *One Exciting Night.*

Figure 5.17. Romeo scoots toward the maid. From *One Exciting Night.*

Figure 5.18. Romeo rolls his eyes in figure eights. From *One Exciting Night.*

noticed him noticing), he involuntarily taps his foot to her rhythm. In a long shot we see his body bend at the knees. While his head and upper body are held stiff (representing the part of him that is still afraid), his lower body (representing the part that is seduced) scoots sideways, with legs splayed, toward her (Figure 5.17). She hikes up her skirt and smiles as she continues her dance. Soon they are moving together. The maid rolls her eyes flirtatiously. He outdoes her, rolling his own eyes in figure eights, first in one direction, then in another (Figure 5.18). His courtship includes showing off his war medal for, he tells her, "catching myself 15 Germans in one day." An intertitle undercuts the boast: "He forgets to mention he found it." Though Griffith does what he can to undermine the notion of any real bravery on Romeo's part, its very possibility, in this period following the Great War, changes the film's attitude toward him. Although the film will work overtime to frighten him in the haunted house, and to undercut his would-be heroic status, Romeo's attraction to the maid helps him overcome his fear. He informs the butler: "Mister my mind wiggles. I takes de job."

The place of the black man in American white supremacist society is thus very much an animating question in Griffith's film. The same could be said of *Birth of a Nation,* which ends with scenes showing mounted and robed Ku Klux Klan members preventing black extras from voting, thus directly stating that their only proper place is as nonvoting less-than-citizens. In *One Exciting Night,* however, the mobile Romeo suggests a character who, like the "New Negro" soon to be described in a collection of essays by Alain Locke (1925), has been abroad, perhaps fought for his country, and clearly does not initially fit into the somnolent community that fails to welcome him. "Fired with ambition" like the uppity "free-nigger from de n'of" in *Birth,* Romeo is seduced by the charms of the black(faced) mulatta maid. Though his romance with her is obviously caricatured, it is important to realize that Griffith may have thought he was being extremely modern and "realistic" in depicting it, for black-on-black romance was a major taboo not only in the films of this era but also on the stage, even where one might have expected to see it—in those all-black-performed and black-produced works that had forged the path of black representations in the Harlem Renaissance.[30] Thus romance between blacks, whether played by actors of color or white actors in blackface, was relatively new both on stage and in film. Although Romeo will be amply punished for wiggling more than his mind at the maid, perhaps the striking fact is that his desire for the maid and her desire for him gets so much initial, almost joyous play.

The maid is afraid to spend the night in the house alone and so contrives to have Romeo—the decorated war hero—sneak inside later that night to "protect" her. Romeo primps for his date, puts on a different hat, and walks to the "big house." Along the way, the wind is taken out of his sails as he is haunted by one of the scary creatures that lurk about the mansion. For no apparent reason—beyond Griffith's desire to get the puffed-up black man back into the characteristic crouch of the servile African—he ends up arriving at the house crawling on all fours. During the course of the long night of haunting, both he and the maid will have no time for the romance that is their purpose. This romance will be interrupted by the terrors of a haunted house which will repeatedly transform Romeo's proud, medal-displaying erect posture into an almost permanent crouch and quake and that will eventually reduce the couple to praying in the kitchen on their hands and knees. They climb up stairs only to fall back down them more than once. Such, it would seem, is the price they must pay for their romance. Yet when all the suspects are eventually rounded up in one room, the detective in charge will ask why Romeo, who had earlier been sent away, came back. "I loves her!" is his proud answer, in what may be one of the first black-on-black(face) declarations of love in the history of American film.

Reviewers were divided between those who found Porter Strong's depiction of a "scared darky" merely conventional, such as the one who notes that he "does his stint in the usual burnt cork fashion,"[31] and those who offered higher praise. An anonymous reviewer writing for the *New York Times* singles out Strong's comedy as "of the broad and busy kind, but he's funny, so he qualifies."[32] Another review describes the subplot as that of "a negro and his mulata [*sic*] love, scared out of their instincts, and thereby creating oceans of laughter."[33]

It would have been helpful if the reviewers had bothered to specify what produced such "oceans" of merriment. In contrast to the large amount of ink spilled in specifying what exact type of "New Woman" Carol Dempster's Agnes was meant to represent, it is clear that burnt cork comedy, which so surprises us today, was taken for granted in 1922. It is proof of the stubborn endurance of what W. T. Lhamon Jr. has called the "lore" of blackface.

To Lhamon, an evolving lore of gestures—originating in a kind of overtly performed insouciance, athletic jumping, wheeling, and turning—began with indigent blacks dancing for eels at Catherine Market in New York City, and continued in the appropriations of white performers in blackface as early as 1815. Variations of these gestures further solidified into a genre and a whole evening's entertainment with the performances of the Virginia Minstrels in New York in 1843. And they continue today as a circulating set of expressive behaviors for the depiction of blackness, performed by all races and ethnicities. Lhamon writes, "Lore does in culture what stereotypes do in discourse . . . hold current beliefs together in highly charged shorthand," but because "its axis wobbles when it turns, lore never returns to the same place. Every group's members must adjust their lore cycle."[34] The question is: How was D. W. Griffith adjusting his? What wobble keeps him from simply recapitulating blackface minstrelsy and blackface villainy?

The Storm

One indirect answer to our question might be viewed in the trademark last-minute rescue that Griffith added to the end of the film. Before he conceived of the idea of adding a hurricane and rescue to the already chaotic and inflated proceedings, Griffith's denouement had revealed that the murders in the supposedly haunted house belonging to the young and handsome Fairfax had been committed by the white villain, Rockmaigne, who had obtained his betrothal to Agnes by blackmailing her mother. Eager to earn the love of her cold mother, Agnes had agreed to the engagement despite her budding love for Fairfax. When Rockmaigne is (literally) unmasked as the true agent of the many murders in the mansion, the way is clear for Agnes and Fairfax to wed, but not before Griffith has given us every opportunity to suspect the more conventional racial villain, Sam. At one point late in the proceedings, this black(faced) shifty-eyed servant sneaks into the bedroom of the Fairfax mansion where Agnes and her mother sleep. He first approaches the bed of the daughter in a crouch, hovers over her, hands extended, then mysteriously moves to the bed of the mother, where he reaches out to the breast of the sleeping woman (Figure 5.19). Just as he is about to grasp her breast, the film fades to black, holds it a moment, and then fades back in. Sam is still poised in the same position, but now instead of moving toward the white woman, he withdraws.

What heinous deed has this fadeout concealed? Readers of *The Clansman,* as Griffith certainly was, might remember that in Dixon's novel, not only does Gus the renegade seek to rape the young virgin who would rather throw herself

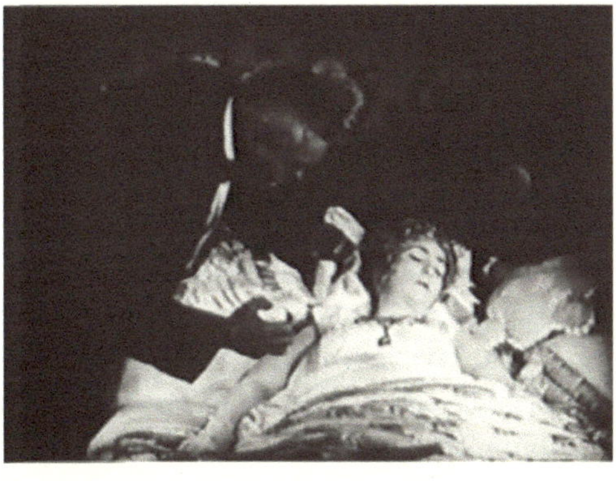

Figure 5.19. Sam reaches out to the white woman's breast. From *One Exciting Night.*

off a cliff than endure "the fate worse than death" of miscegenous rape, but also Dixon marks with an ellipsis at the end of one chapter and the beginning of another the unwritten rape of both mother and daughter, who then both throw themselves off a cliff rather than confess their shame.[35]

Sam is thus pictured at this point as a likely suspect for harboring miscegenous desire toward both white mother and daughter as well as the most likely suspect in the murders at the mansion. When the innocent Fairfax is accused by the detective of murdering one of the guests, it is Sam we see lurking in the background and to whom circumstances point. Yet at the same time, we are aware that Griffith is overtly playing with both his own and his audience's racist expectations even while sometimes comically defusing them. For example, soon after Sam withdraws from hovering over the sleeping older woman, he bumps into a chair, precipitating a series of terrified reactions that end in Agnes hiding herself comically under the covers of her bed. A tone mixing sinister sexual threat with physical comedy marks a major adjustment in Griffith's schema of racial representation and is a fair approximation of the abandonment of rationality and embrace of chaos that Alexander Woollcott had diagnosed as apt for the "frayed nerves of the post-war world" in the original Broadway play.

Griffith's self-congratulatory modernity thus translates the chaotic comic thrills of the original play into racialized terms. He does so by first causing us to suspect the worst of the black(faced) villain and then pulling that rug out from under us by revealing that Sam is actually the film's formal hero. Samuel Jones, whom we suspect of being the same person as "Black Sam" the bootlegger, is in the end revealed as none other than the loyal "Kaffir" of the film's African prologue. Out of loyalty to Agnes's father, he has devoted his life to tracking Agnes down in order to restore her inheritance of the African gold. We are thus belatedly asked to reinterpret Sam's invasion of the mother's and daughter's bedroom. It was not an act of miscegenous desire but rather an attempt to retrieve the other half of the locket that the false "mother" had lost back in Africa in order to identify her. We are furthermore asked to believe that the "primitive" and crouching Kaffir who once believed that the photo in the locket was "White man's magic to be treasured" has been transformed into the erect, dignified, ratiocinating Samuel Jones. Finally, we are asked to believe that he has joined forces with a Scotland Yard investigator to identify Agnes as the rightful heir.

Thus the real hero of *One Exciting Night* proves to be not the rather useless Fairfax, who actually does little to get the girl, but the extremely useful, brave, and persistent "Kaffir—Sam," who has spent a lifetime and traveled across continents to save her. If anyone deserves to "get the girl" it is Sam. This might be the deeper reason why Griffith suddenly decided to add a hurricane and a last-minute rescue from his oldest bag of tricks: it would finally give the dashing young Fairfax something to do other than express dismay at the accumulation of corpses in his mansion.

Griffith argued that his audiences had come to expect these big epic flourishes from his films. But Carol Dempster gets the blame for turning a modest picture that might have earned his studio some profit into a money drain by complaining to him that *One Exciting Night* "lacked a 'Big Griffith finish.'" Richard Schickel writes that the film was already cut, previewed, and ready for release within budget when Dempster put the idea of the storm into Griffith's head. Her real cause for complaint, according to Schickel, was that the film had no compelling climax comparable to those lavished on her rival Lillian Gish. Griffith immediately devised a hurricane that would strike just as a masked and still unrecognized Rockmaigne is fleeing the house with the money. Agnes races out into the storm in hot pursuit. Unlike Gish, who passively awaited rescue in Griffith's previous epics and even suicidally throws herself into the storm toward the end of *Way Down East,* Dempster's Agnes exhibits a "New Woman" conquer-or-die gumption in pursuing the villain under perilous circumstances. Fairfax, hampered by the handcuffs the detective has put on him, simply follows. When a tree falls and traps Agnes, with yet another tree about to fall on it and kill her, in an act of much-delayed heroism Fairfax extracts her in the nick of time, thus earning some right to "get the girl."

It is readily apparent, however, that the real rescue of the heroine has already consisted in the exposure of the cold mother as a false parent and the consequent restoration of Agnes's fortune. The storm is unnecessary window dressing which only gives the illusion that Fairfax is an action hero. When it is over, the detective from Scotland Yard explains that ever since Sam found the other half of the locket back in Africa, "in his primitive way he [had] searched for this conclusive proof" of Agnes's identity. A flashback to his presumably nefarious acts in the bedroom of the mother and daughter fills in the ellipsis that had previously concealed the entirety of his actions. What we have been led to mistake for racialized lust was instead a ratiocinative search for the clue of the locket. We see the burnt cork hands finding and removing the photo from the locket around the false mother's neck, fitting it into the other half, and then taking it away (Figure 5.20). Of course, we might wonder, if Sam has managed to play the observant detective, in what way is he still primitive? This is the question Griffith cannot answer. His reworking of blackface convention can only vacillate between melodramatic victim and villain. There is no middle ground in his melodrama of black and white.

After the detective explains Sam's pure motives, Sam and Agnes are coupled in the same shot. An intertitle interrupts this framing to offer Sam's one and only verbal explanation for his kindness: "In Africa, Miss, your father was

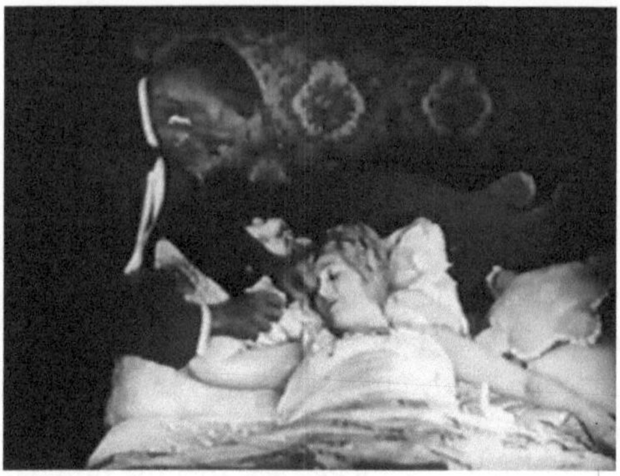

Figure 5.20. What was missing in the ellipsis. From *One Exciting Night.*

about the only person who ever was kind to me." In a close-up he completes these lines of affectionate reminiscence with a benevolent look, then his features grow sad and he stoically looks away from her, steeling his body and moving back (Figure 5.21). Their brief moment of interracial intimacy is over, and all subsequent shots contrive to distance them—as when the Scotland Yard detective is located at the apex of a triangle formed with Agnes and Sam, as if he were policing any further closeness between them (Figure 5.22). The next shot is taken from a greater distance and now includes the false mother, whom the detective signals to leave (Figure 5.23). When Agnes reaches out to prevent her from leaving, the camera moves in to isolate just the detective and Agnes, with the effect of excluding both the "mother" and Sam from the former family unit, as if they were now both exposed as false kin (Figure 5.24). It is thus the detective, not Sam, who bids Agnes a kindly farewell and leaves. An even more distant shot shows that the "mother" follows him and, after a pause, so does Sam, as if he, like her, were being marched off to prison. Agnes says no words of farewell to Sam. Left with young Fairfax and his aunt, she momentarily feels alone until Fairfax exuberantly offers to furnish her with "MOTHER, FATHER, HUSBAND, SWEETHEART—EVERYTHING!"

This, Griffith seems to think, is all we need to know about the fate of Samuel Jones. His at least dignified exit might be viewed as an improvement over the inelegant tiptoeing away of blacks at the end of *The Birth of a Nation.* Yet where does he go? Back to Africa, where he will find other white masters to whom he can devote his life? To England with the Scotland Yard detective? It is obvious that Griffith has imagined no place for this black(faced) African in his happy ending union of the white couple. The result is that Sam's fate is ingloriously linked to that of the guilty false kin. I have written elsewhere about the difficulty that black-white racial melodrama has in forging an American home for its African (American) protagonists. This was no less true for Harriet Beecher Stowe, whose African characters dream at the end of *Uncle Tom's Cabin* of a return to Africa, than it is for Dixon and Griffith, whose "solutions" tend

Figure 5.21. Sam stoically looks away from Agnes. From *One Exciting Night.*

Figure 5.22. Sam and Agnes "policed" by the detective. From *One Exciting Night.*

Figure 5.23. The detective signals to the mother to leave. From *One Exciting Night.*

Figure 5.24. Agnes and the detective, with Sam and the "mother" excluded. From *One Exciting Night.*

toward the outright disappearance of black bodies, certainly from any potential roles as citizens.[36]

The storm of *One Exciting Night*, however unwise an addition to an already bloated film, thus works to erase our sense that Agnes should be indebted to Sam, not to Fairfax. Having spent so much money on this storm to lend his white hero much-needed virtue, it would seem that Griffith could not resist also using it for more "comic" business with his other black(faced) romantic hero, Romeo Washington. Unlike the African who quietly exits the scene, Romeo, as the quintessentially stereotyped and blacked-up American "Zip Coon," will be welcomed at film's end with a place in the sleepy Kentucky community he was initially too "fired by ambition" to join. He will even, like Fairfax, get the girl he loves, but not before he once more has the wind taken out of his sails. After Agnes has been rescued and Rockmaigne captured, Griffith indulges in adding another five minutes to a film that has already run well over two hours to show "Romeo home at last." Just what kind of "home" he might have acquired is a mystery, since in the course of his day it has been pretty clear that Romeo is a transient, as signaled by his prominent suitcase. In any event, it becomes quite apparent in what follows that Griffith relishes the physical dismantling of such

Figure 5.25. Romeo's disintegrating house. From *One Exciting Night.*

Figure 5.26. Romeo and house lifted into the air. From *One Exciting Night.*

a hypothetical home.[37] Wandering into the frame, Romeo sees the windows and doors fly off his flimsy shack (Figure 5.25). Taking shelter in the doorway, Romeo is terrified to find himself being lifted into the air (Figure 5.26). Both he and the shack turn cartwheels, finally landing on their side. Both he and his "home" are thrown about, buffeted, and turned rootless by the storm.

If Sam, the African racial villain revised into hero, quietly exits the frame, finding no home in America, least of all in the household of the woman he has saved, then Romeo, the minstrelized African (American), will finally be rewarded with his "proper place" in a modern America of athletic New Women, nefarious bootleggers both black and white, evil cads, and charming young millionaires. Yet Romeo's place will not be among these modern go-getters but rather right back where he started, with the black supernumeraries in a kind of unspecified, liminal "old Kentucky home." In a circular trajectory that corrects the linear, upwardly mobile ambition that originally "fired" him, we find Romeo in the very location from which he first set out: the sleepy whistle-stop where a mammy still peels potatoes, other black folk laze about, and somnolence rules.

The only difference, albeit a considerable one, is that the "colored maid," as the film's cast of characters calls her, is seated beside him and his arm is proprietarily placed around her. As in the beginning, the black community that occupies this liminal space, presumably near the train station where Romeo first arrived, is played by real black supernumeraries (Figure 5.27). We find Romeo telling a tall tale about his exploits in the haunted house. Just as in his war stories, he casts himself as the hero: "Two murderers running loose and I reaches out and captures both of them" (Figure 5.28). While the seemingly credulous maid approvingly plants a sleepy kiss on him as he tells his story, a black youth is the first to break the straight-faced reaction with a smile (Figure 5.29). Romeo feigns outrage, but when the maid also cracks a smile and the rest of the community does too, he soon relents and qualifies—"Well, I seen him anyway." Amid the general hilarity (Figure 5.30), with Romeo now laughing at himself, he contentedly kisses the maid (Figure 5.31). Fade out on Romeo in "his place." Fade in on Agnes and Fairfax in theirs: a big church wedding.

Such, it would seem, is the twofold nature of Griffith's modern racial "tolerance" as played in blackface, both caricatured and "straight." In one move, the film first indulges in, then corrects, any suspicions of black male miscegenous desire. We are chastened for any racist assumptions the film first urges us to make about the black(faced) man's desires. But the narrative pauses only one small beat for *Uncle Tom*-style pity and then gets rid of Sam, lest we begin to see him as a real hero with some right of entitlement to the girl he saves or her property. In a second move, the minstrel tradition of Kentucky homes and kind masters seems to invite Griffith to "generously" include Romeo Washington and his "colored maid" in a larger, homey community of the ambitionless,

Figure 5.27. Romeo, settled into the black community of supernumeraries. From *One Exciting Night.*

Figure 5.28. Romeo tells his tall tale. From *One Exciting Night.*

Figure 5.29. A black youth smiles at Romeo's tale. From *One Exciting Night.*

Figure 5.30. The community laughs at Romeo. From *One Exciting Night.*

Figure 5.31. Romeo kisses the maid. From *One Exciting Night.*

though only after he has been buffeted by ghosts and a storm and taught that his place is very circumscribed. Thus, whereas Sam renounces desire, Romeo, as his name suggests, is its comic blackface embodiment. Though his story ends on a kiss, we have seen what it takes for the black(faced) man to "get the girl."

I have not tried to argue that *One Exciting Night* deserves a place among D. W. Griffith's great films. There is no question that the film was hastily knocked off between the much more carefully crafted previous big film, *Orphans of the Storm* (1922), and the subsequent, and more modest, *The White Rose* (1923). Among the film's numerous flaws, the allegory-mongering intertitles are some of the worst the director ever wrote or illustrated;[38] the plotting is ponderous and alternates between unnecessary confusion and an overelaborate connecting of dots; and the storm that forms its climax is, as both Higgins and Schickel note, narratively unmotivated and, compared to the ice storm of *Way Down East,* decidedly fake.[39]

Nevertheless, the film's elaborate blackface subplots pose with a new acuteness the persistent question of the proper home for the African (American) in the post–Great War era. Offering both the Tom and the anti-Tom solutions to this question—exiling one blackfaced man and incorporating the other into a quasi-antebellum somnolence—Griffith's answer is as conflicted as the white America of this period. His early 1920s use of blackface lore should thus not surprise even if it does offend.

D. W. Griffith probably believed he was being modern and tolerant when he accepted Romeo's chastened Zip Coon into the community of the "Kentucky home," even as he delighted in destroying Romeo's home. He also probably believed he was being modern and tolerant by inventing the thriller for the screen, faking us out about victims and villains in a newly racialized way. Burnt cork performance has always told much more about the white fascination with or dread of blackness than it does about black people. It is, as Eric Lott writes, a counterfeit "necessary to construct and preserve a fundamentally 'hegemonic' 'misrecognition' of black people."[40] It will not do, then, to classify what Griffith does here as a simple return to minstrel stereotypes. If some minstrel lore was put to use by Griffith this late in his career, at a moment when he was quite strenuously attempting to display his credentials as a modern filmmaker, then we can recognize what is new and different, while still white supremacist and ugly, in this work.

NOTES

Many thanks to Jonathan Lee for research and editorial acumen. Thanks to Paolo Cherchi Usai for the Griffith Project, which devoted itself to *all* of Griffith's films, even the bad ones. This essay is a revised version of "Surprised by Blackface: D.W. Griffith, Blackface and *One Exciting Night*," in *The Griffith Project*, vol. 12, ed. Paolo Cherchi Usai (London: BFI, 2008), 122–39.

1. Richard Schickel, *D. W. Griffith: An American Life* (New York: Simon and Schuster, 1984), 474.

2. Steven Higgins, "*One Exciting Night*," in *The Griffith Project*, vol. 10, ed. Paolo Cherchi Usai (London: BFI, 2006), 139–42.

3. Ibid., 99. Indeed, reviews of the film tended to be quite generous. Also see Schickel, *D. W. Griffith*, 474, and critics cited later in this chapter.

4. The term "lore" is from W. T. Lhamon Jr., *Raising Cain: Blackface Performance from Jim Crow to Hip Hop* (Cambridge: Harvard University Press, 1998), 70. See further discussion later in this chapter.

5. I argue in *Playing the Race Card* that the poet Vachel Lindsay's *Art of the Moving Picture* (New York: Macmillan, 1915) set the trend. Lindsay claims that whenever Griffith follows *The Clansman*, his film is bad, but whenever "it is unadulterated Griffith, which is half the time, it is good" (*Art*, 75–76). Lewis Jacobs, James Agee, and the contemporary Griffith biographer Richard Schickel have followed suit. I have argued that this persistent tendency to attribute what is great and wonderful in Griffith to his position as godlike, autonomous originator positioned outside of time and history and to attribute what is embarrassing and racist in him to his local, time-bound influences as a southerner is deeply flawed. It is as if Griffith were a genius and a visionary artist when he transcends history and a victim of his own melodramatic tendencies conceived as atavistic throwbacks when he is bad. See Linda Williams, *Playing the Race Card: Melodramas of Black and White from Uncle Tom to O. J. Simpson* (Princeton: Princeton University Press, 2001). See also Susan Courtney. *Hollywood Fantasies of Miscegenation: Spectacular Narratives of Gender and Race, 1903–1967* (Princeton: Princeton University Press, 2005).

6. See Jacqueline Stewart, *Migrating to the Movies: Cinema and Black Urban Modernity* (Berkeley: University of California Press, 2005), 57, which notes that burnt cork had not always been the norm in the earlier pre-Hollywood cinema. Stewart writes, for example, that during this period, which she calls "preclassical," blackface "did not entirely supplant Black actors, who continued to appear in nonfiction films and occasionally in minor background roles in fiction films during the transition period." Thus blackfaced mammies could appear with "real Black babies and children" in the 1908 *Mixed Babies*.

7. This practice was not universal, which is why I see Griffith here solidifying a practice

that could have gone either way. In 1914, for example, Robert Daly produced a film version of *Uncle Tom's Cabin* that featured Sam Lucas, a black actor who had long played Uncle Tom onstage. Though Lucas's age (he was then seventy-two) rendered his intimacies with Little Eva innocuous, the very fact that one black character played outside of blackface had serious dealings with a white female character shows that in certain contexts—especially the context of a desexualized and doddering Uncle Tom—it had been possible, before the vast popularity and institution of "anti-Tom" sentiment made nationally acceptable by *The Birth of a Nation,* to mix white characters with black characters in serious drama. See Williams, *Playing the Race Card.* See also Michael Rogin's groundbreaking discussion of the racial politics of *Birth of a Nation* in "His Sword Became a Flashing Vision," in *Ronald Reagan, the Movie: And Other Episodes in Political Demonology* (Berkeley: University of California Press, 1987). Rogin sees the result of Griffith's decision to "have no black blood among the principals" as ending in the absurdity of whites "in white sheets" defeating "whites in blackface" (223). See also Rogin's *Blackface, White Noise: Jewish Immigrants in the Hollywood Melting Pot* (Los Angeles: University of California Press, 1996).

8. See Camille R. Forbes, *Introducing Bert Williams: Burnt Cork, Broadway, and the Story of America's First Black Star* (New York: Basic Civitas Books, 2008), 199. See also Daphne Brooks, *Bodies in Dissent: Spectacular Performances of Race and Freedom, 1850–1910* (Durham: Duke University Press, 2006).

9. See Louis Chude-Sokei, *The Last "Darky": Bert Williams, Black on Black Minstrelsy, and the African Diaspora* (Durham: Duke University Press, 2006), 20.

10. See Eric Ledell Smith, *Bert Williams: A Biography of the Pioneer Black Comedian* (Jefferson, N.C.: McFarland and Company, 1992), 132; also Forbes, *Introducing Bert Williams;* and Chude-Sokei, *The Last "Darky."*

11. Jon Lewis, *Hollywood v. Hard Core: How the Struggle over Censorship Saved the Modern Film Industry* (New York: New York University Press, 2000), 301.

12. See Ann Douglas, *The Feminization of American Culture* (New York: Avon, 1977), and *Terrible Honesty: Mongrel Manhattan in the 1920s* (New York: Noonday Press, 1995).

13. Except for Stoneman, that is. When Silas asks for the hand of Stoneman's daughter in marriage, he is rudely rebuffed, an indication of Stoneman's "true" and virtuous rejection of miscegenation.

14. The irony of Mammy's disapproval of the "free-nigger from de n'of" is that he is played, in blackface, by the same muscular actor who later plays her white rescuer.

15. Jane Gaines, *Fire and Desire: Mixed-Raced Movies in the Silent Era* (Chicago: University of Chicago Press, 2001), 176–90. See also her essay "Fire and Desire: Race, Melodrama, and Oscar Micheaux," in *Black American Cinema,* ed. Manthia Diawara (New York: AFI/Routledge, 1992), 49–70.

16. Note that Jane Gaines draws the parallel with Gus and the Cameron little sister, but the sexual pursuit in the enclosed space of a room and the maturity of both Elsie and Sylvia Landry make a comparison between them apt as well.

17. Thomas Cripps, *Slow Fade to Black: The Negro in American Film, 1900–1942* (1977; reprint, New York: Oxford University Press, 1993), 119.

18. This language is from the 1927 "Don'ts and Be Carefuls." The 1930 Code would more specifically eliminate the use of the word "nigger." See Lewis, *Hollywood v. Hard Core,* 301, 306.

19. *Intolerance* combined a modern story of reformist meddling with the ancient story of Babylon, the France of the St. Bartholomew Massacre, and the story of Christ to deliver

a message on the problem of intolerance over the ages. Yet the film did not actually treat any relevant American racial themes and did not (re)address racial tolerance at all. Richard Schickel writes that "the film was in no way an apologia for the ideas expressed in *Birth*" but was rather an assault on the earlier film's critics and their intolerance of Griffith's "right to say what he wanted to say" (*D. W. Griffith,* 303). Nevertheless the film has often been presented as the more politically correct counterbalance to the overt racial prejudices of *Birth.* Certainly the NAACP and many individual African Americans read it as, in the words of the Hays Code, a "willful offense" to the black race.

20. Alexander Woollcott, "The Play: A Reinhart Mystery Staged," *New York Times,* August 24, 1920. For the play, see Mary Roberts Rinehart and Avery Hopwood, *The Bat: A Mystery Drama in Three Acts* (New York: Samuel French, 1920).

21. Griffith seems to have maintained the spotlight-manipulating manner of the original in several scenes that have an unmotivated spotlight.

22. Alexander Woollcott, "Second Thoughts on First Nights," *New York Times,* April 30, 1922.

23. Griffith also used this pseudonym for the screenplay of *Dream Street* (1921) and *The White Rose* (1923).

24. The role was played by Harry Morvil; one of several photos from the original production shows him as Billy with darkened face and slicked-down hair.

25. Griffith uses the name Sam or variations of it frequently for black men. Samuel Jones, for instance, is a name he had already used for a black character, played by Porter Strong, in *Dream Street* (1921). Besides being a common name, Sam is obviously a name that connoted blackness to Griffith.

26. This is before the "Don'ts and Be Carefuls" of the early Hays Code began to prohibit ethnic name-calling with a clause stipulating that "willful offense to any nation, race or creed" would not be tolerated. See Lewis, *Hollywood v. Hard Core,* 301.

27. The *American Heritage Dictionary* notes that "Kaffir" was originally an Islamic term, translated as infidel, "used especially in southern Africa as a disparaging term for a Black person."

28. This ban operated in all black productions as well as blackface ones. Camille Forbes notes that the all-black off-Broadway production of *Darktown Follies* in 1914 had been the first to portray black-on-black romance. When Florenz Ziegfeld borrowed the first-act finale from that show, he included a romantic duet called "Rock Me in the Cradle of Love," which depicted a romance between a black(faced) woman and man (*Introducing Bert Williams,* 257–58). See also James Weldon Johnson, *Black Manhattan* (New York: Knopf, 1930), 174.

29. This mix of main character in blackface supporting characters played by blacks is typical of both Griffith, as noted earlier, and the one Bert Williams film I have seen, *A Born Gambler* (1916).

30. For example, the groundbreaking Williams and Walker musicals *In Dahomey* (1903) and *Abyssinia* (1906) avoided any hint of intraracial romance. See Forbes, *Introducing Bert Williams,* 138, 258. In the earlier blackface minstrel tradition, romance had always been portrayed between white men in blackface and white men in blackface dressed as women. It would seem that the tradition of the "tragic mulatta" derives its tragedy from the fact that there was no one, black *or* white, with whom she could have a "legitimate" romance.

31. Frederick James Smith, review, *Los Angeles Times,* October 28, 1922.

32. Review, *New York Times,* October 24, 1922.

33. Ralph T. Jones, review, *Atlanta Constitution*, April 17, 1923.

34. Lhamon, *Raising Cain*, 70. See the introduction to this volume for a rehearsal of these early years of minstrelsy, and the revisiting of the subject in the essays by W. T. Lhamon and Dale Cockrell.

35. Thomas Dixon Jr., *The Clansman: An Historical Romance of the Ku Klux Klan* (1905; reprint, Lexington: University Press of Kentucky, 1970).

36. See Williams, *Playing the Race Card*.

37. See my discussion of the significance of the humble cabin home throughout the long tradition of American racial melodrama, from Uncle Tom's cabin, to the cabin that is the locus of the reunion of "former enemies of North and South" who fight in defense of their "Aryan birthright" in *The Birth of a Nation*, and on to America's fascination with Tara in *Gone with the Wind*. Williams, *Playing the Race Card*.

38. For example, "The sacrifice of youth on the Altar of Greed and Passion" is followed by an image of a white woman literally on a sacrificial altar while an evil, dark-skinned, biblically robed man looks on; such forced allegory does not sit well with the more modern manipulation of thrills and laughter.

39. Despite claims that Griffith's crew simply took advantage of a storm that passed their way while filming. See Higgins, "One Exciting Night"; Schickel, *D. W. Griffith*.

40. See Eric Lott, *Love and Theft: Blackface Minstrelsy and the American Working Class* (New York: Oxford University Press, 1993), 123.

6

"Gentlemen, Please Be Seated"

Racial Masquerade and Sadomasochism in 1930s Animation

NICHOLAS SAMMOND

In 1932 Walt Disney Productions released *Trader Mickey*, a new cartoon short featuring its rapidly rising star, Mickey Mouse. This cartoon followed a fairly standard format for the early sound era: a minimal plot and a centerpiece musical production number highlighted the wonders of the still relatively new technology of sync sound, and its use of popular melodies and dance numbers played on the trends of the day. The story, in this case, is that Mickey and his dog, Pluto, become shipwrecked on a distant shore, are captured by cannibals, and dance their way to freedom by playing on the natives' inherent susceptibility to jazz rhythms.

The film is significant not only for its inflection of the popular swing-era trope of jazz as "jungle music," but also because Mickey's capture at the hands of these animated cannibals is an instance of cultural contact between a blackface minstrel (Mickey) and the less oblique racist stereotypes that historically had charged that figure with its libidinous, animalistic, and uncivilized appeal. Reading what seemed at the time an innocuous cartoon short, then, offers a shorthand look at the complex of race, violence, and desire that charged fantasies of blackness in the late-nineteenth- and early-twentieth-century United States. It also provides an avenue toward understanding how the figure of the minstrel became so embedded in animation during its silent era that by the time of Mickey's arrival, an easy and direct association between trademark cartoon characters—Mickey, Felix, Bimbo, Bosko—and blackface minstrelsy was settling into an array of conventions that maintained a less direct relationship to (an imagined) blackness. That is, by the 1930s, trademark cartoon characters such as Mickey were becoming *vestigial minstrels,* carrying all (or many) of the markers of minstrelsy yet rarely referring directly to the tradition itself.[1] By 1932, the live performance of blackface minstrelsy was waning along with vaudeville, and its place in live cinema (initially so important to early sound offerings) was increasingly limited to serving as a marker of bygone performance styles and simpler times, yet the minstrelsy of animation was at this point deeply embedded in the visual, auditory, and performative traditions of the genre.[2]

Reinscribing Mickey and his fellow cartoon tricksters as minstrels isn't merely an act of (empty and symbolic) reparation; it is an effort to place the often marginalized but always extremely popular form of the animated cartoon short more firmly within a racial matrix that included the vaudeville stage, the minstrel show, the midway native village, and the black-and-tan review—all of which, within a complex, varied, and sometimes contradictory fabric of racial discourses, produced, contested, and regulated real relations on the ground.[3] Yet beyond simply revealing the racial (and racist) undertones of beloved animated characters, the point of understanding those characters as minstrels is, first, to witness how stereotypical ideas considered increasingly unacceptable in one forum may pass relatively unnoticed in another. But seeing Mickey or Bugs or Bimbo as a minstrel also admits a nuanced and detailed view of animation as a fantastic, violent, and excessive popular art form, one whose very mundanity contributed to the trivialization of the violence of racial formations of the time.

The issue here isn't about misunderstanding the operation of race in animation as an unfortunate turn in an otherwise benign and childlike medium—although that misunderstanding does continue to operate. Rather, the problem of understanding the role and place of race in cartoons is of the same sort as and of a piece with the discussion of violence in them. Generally, criticisms of cartoon violence attempt to imagine bracketing it from the form itself, as if cartoons could simply be made less violent and still be vital and interesting. This attitude ignores that the form itself, with its stretching, squashing, and metamorphosis of bodies, relies on a certain abstract violence as an essential demonstration of its distinct formal properties, of what it does best and differently from live cinema. Likewise, the idea that cartoons could easily be evacuated of their racial overtones fails to attend to how fundamental those overtones were to the social and cultural circumstances within which the form appeared. And finally, combining the racial and racist fantasies within which animation emerged with its propensity for physically violent interaction with the human (or anthropomorphic) form itself isn't merely additive; racial stereotyping is itself a form of social violence that was often made literal in the visual iconography of animation. In short, the vibrancy and magic associated with the cartoons of this period depend on a sadomasochistic racial fantasy of encounter and resistance that is played out again and again.

Trader Mickey encapsulates this strange intersection of the traditions of blackface minstrelsy that undergird American animation and the violent and excessive racist caricatures that permeated the jazz-inflected cartoons of early sound cinema. Thus, tracing the difference between the minstrel and the racist caricature may better serve to alienate a few of the practices that we have come to see as natural in animation—particularly its tendency toward excessive yet seemingly inconsequential violence. For although by no means the most vicious of the cartoons of the early sound era, even *Trader Mickey* is rife with violence threatened and enacted, and Mickey—who has become so intimately associated with sweetness and light that Disney recently had to mount a PR campaign to introduce his new "edge" for a video game that requires him to be aggressive—is no exception.[4] *Trader Mickey* is useful for describing the difference between an animate minstrel and a racist caricature because the cartoon illustrates how the minstrel's intimate associations with voice, silence, and violence made it an appropriate avatar for the artisan animator increasingly constrained within an industrializing art form.

Heart of Darkness

The very term "Mickey Mouse," with all of its various connotations, speaks to the character's semiotic weight. To describe something as "Mickey Mouse" is to call it trivial. Why? Not yet at the height of his fame in 1932, Mickey was already widely and enthusiastically praised by critics and Disney's public, was becoming a merchandizing juggernaut available in myriad forms, and was on his way to being a ubiquitous household object.[5] Yet it is that very ubiquity which has contributed to the rodent's triviality. Mickey Mouse was simultaneously a beloved cartoon character and a trademark icon on every bit of gimcrackery one could imagine, from watches and water glasses, to toothbrushes and notebooks, to frocks and flatware. So one sense of "Mickey Mouse" is to become cheapened through excessive commodification (Figure 6.1).[6] Mickey Mouse was the exemplar of the paradoxical figure of the animate commodity, the apparently living thing that signified itself—yet seemingly producing its own value, held none of it. The figure of Mickey was (and is) contradictory: important in its triviality; handmade yet seemingly alive; capricious and willful yet ultimately good-natured and obedient; and simultaneously racially coded as both black and white. It is within this dense and self-refractory matrix of meaning that Mickey appears in *Trader Mickey,* and through which one may approach the

Figure 6.1. An issue of *Mickey Mouse Magazine* from 1933, which was included in deliveries of milk in Maryland, gives a sense of the ubiquity of the character. The magazine featured stories about Mickey's life and work, as well as contests offering prizes of other Mickey merchandise, such as watches.

sadomasochistic complex that informs both the trademark animated character and the traditions of blackface minstrelsy upon which it is based.

Trader Mickey opens on Mickey and Pluto cruising upriver in a makeshift paddlewheel steamer loaded with cargo, past hippos and crocodiles (Figure 6.2). Mickey is perched atop his cargo, merrily plucking away at a banjo. Within a few shots, this seemingly harmless cartoon confection has presented us with a wealth of information. Making his way into the heart of darkness several years before the tropical kitsch of Trader Vic appeared in the United States, Mickey plays a trader in Africa like a vaudevillian donning a loosely fitting costume. A trader of what? His makeshift boat is loaded with goods of some sort, but we aren't sure for what (or whom) he expects to trade those goods before he heads home on his return voyage. The paddle wheel on his boat could just as easily signal the Old South as it does a colonial adventure in an African rain forest. To be blunt, at best Mickey plays a dry-goods merchant working the byways of some colonial zone; at worst he is slave-trader Mickey, and his trade is in the savage bodies he is soon to encounter. Neither fully white nor fully black—the minstrel a figure whose ideal blackness is painted on, and which rests uneasily above its ostensibly material body—he is a liminal figure in a liminal zone.

Here Africa, the originary locus of the slave body, threatens to collapse into the site of that body's eventual forced labor, the South. This is not so much an act of pentimento as the generation of a continuous alternative space of subjugation. One of a number of representations that imagined the Old South as symbolically contiguous with Africa (and, in the Jazz Age, with Harlem), the film posits (or accepts) a geography based on race. Blackness simultaneously signifies the plantation and the jungle. This repeats one of the foundational conceits of minstrelsy, in which early minstrel performers framed their shows as anthropological reports: having visited the plantation, they had witnessed the primitive dances of enslaved Africans (themselves barely removed from the jungle), and were pleased and privileged to reproduce them for an audience distanced by geographical location and/or cosmopolitanism from their meanings.[7] Black or white, but always in blackface, minstrel performers were sometimes called "delineators," as if what they performed were less a representation than a re-presentation. The woolly wigs, burnt cork, and greasepaint that literally delineated the head, the eyes, and the mouth of the minstrel were only the beginning, as were the gloves that increasingly became a trademark of the

Figure 6.2. The beginning of *Trader Mickey* (1932) finds Mickey Mouse and Pluto on a paddlewheel steamer surrounded by hippos. The setting combines in the banjo-playing Mickey the popular trope of the trader or white hunter and the minstrel returning to his origins.

Figure 6.3. Mickey Mouse strumming the banjo in *Trader Mickey* and playing "Turkey in the Straw" ("Old Zip Coon") in *Steamboat Willie* (1928). The combination of Mickey's gloved hands, his wide, almost painted-on mouth and eyes, and the use of minstrel standards reinforces his link to the minstrel stage.

form as the nineteenth century progressed. What were delineated as well were the dances, the songs, the speech patterns, the jumbled and confused thoughts of the primitive savage attempting to communicate in the tongue of his master—the mangling of which revealed both the limited intellect of the minstrel and the social and political contradictions of the common sense of the day.[8]

But more than location connects this short to minstrelsy. Mickey is happily strumming a raggedy tune on a banjo (Figure 6.3), and this isn't the first time he has played music specifically associated with the minstrel stage. In his first outing in synch sound, *Steamboat Willie* (1928), Mickey played the minstrel standard "Turkey in the Straw" (also known as "Zip Coon") on the bodies of various farm animals as that steamboat made its way upriver.[9] Although *Steamboat Willie* is often erroneously celebrated as the first sound cartoon, rarely do those accolades mention its indebtedness to the minstrel stage for its sonic performance. And as has often been noted, the film was not the first sound cartoon, merely the first cartoon to demonstrate effectively the potential of synchronized sound (and to link that performance to an effective public relations campaign). Of particular note were successful experiments by the Fleischer brothers in sound animation, which predated Disney's work by several years. Yet in efforts such as their Song Car-Tunes, the Fleischers also sometimes relied on standards of the minstrel stage, encouraging audiences to sing along by following the bouncing ball to songs such as "Dixie," "My Old Kentucky Home," or "Old Black Joe" (Figure 6.4). The images that accompanied these cartoons matched the songs. In other words, though not commonly discussed today, the literal trope of the minstrel and the minstrel show, alongside the ubiquity of the

Figure 6.4. In the Fleischer Song Car-Tune *My Old Kentucky Home* (1924), a crudely drawn pickaninny serves as the bouncing ball for an audience sing-along to the Stephen Foster minstrel classic originally titled "Poor Uncle Tom, Good Night!"

vestigial minstrel, was quite common in the cartoons of the late 1920s and early 1930s. So in *Trader Mickey*, the mouse is, quite simply and quite reasonably, a minstrel traveling steadily toward the headwaters of the tradition that helped spawn him.

It isn't just the happy strumming that signals him as such, though: Mickey sports the uniform of white gloves, black face, exaggerated mouth, and wide eyes that marked both the popular animated characters of the day and their progenitor, the blackface minstrel (Figure 6.5). But beyond those obvious physical markers, he also performs the minstrel's traditional role of the trickster, the imp who operates on the margins of social and material convention, and who embodies significant destructive and productive powers. He is a force of disruption—albeit one somewhat tamed by an emerging "Disney" aesthetic.[10] And as that force he exists in a world of hurt, an animated cosmos in which incredible violence circulates through seemingly indestructible bodies, visiting itself upon hero and villain alike.

Here and elsewhere, Mickey is more than just a trickster, a lord of misrule. As a vestigial minstrel, he is an indexical marker, an oblique gesture toward the Old South, the plantation, and slavery. Epitomized by minstrelsy's end men Tambo and Bones, the minstrel did more than signify a generic African American body; it even signified more than an enslaved African American. The body that the minstrel performance invoked, and which informed the trickster figure of the trademark cartoon character—Mickey, Felix, Ko-Ko, Oswald—was one that imagined the recalcitrant (ex)slave who, through an artful combination of stereotyped laziness, cunning, and the performance of a studied ignorance, avoided the forced labor and regimes of punishment that were the condition of chattel slavery. For the central tropes of minstrelsy—the singing and dancing, the stump speech, the good-natured misdirection of the interlocutor by the end men—all derived from the necessary fantasy of the slave as a creature closer in the natural chain of being to the (equally stubborn) mule or the cunning Br'er Rabbit. This figure felt less pain than its white counterpart, and was more naturally inclined to hard physical labor in the open air. As Dennis Childs has described it in relation to the chain gangs that were contemporary with the cartoon minstrel: "The physical branding that slaves received upon their kidnapping onto the coffle and slave ship [was] coupled with their epistemic branding as animalistic, infantile, and lazy; as such the forebears of the plantation 'darky' [were] incapable of feeling the pain of internment, of recognizing the enormity of their dispossession, or of performing industrious labor without the spur of punishment. For those humans branded as savage 'monkeys,' terror and collec-

Figure 6.5. Mickey Mouse hanging from a cannibal's spear in *Trader Mickey* offers a clear view of his defining minstrel characteristics: white gloves, painted-on mouth and eyes, and outsized clothes. Blackface minstrelsy was common to the popular continuing characters of early animation, such as Felix the Cat, Oswald the Lucky Rabbit, and Bosko.

tive disappearance are an occasion for joviality, merriment, and song."[11] By the time of the emergence of those chain gangs in the late nineteenth century, and of the beginnings of the American cartoon thereafter, that rhetoric was very much operative. For example, Alex Lichtenstein reports that in 1912, the assistant director of the U.S. Office of Public Roads, arguing in favor of chain gang labor, declared that the "negro is accustomed to outdoor occupations . . . [and is] experienced in manual labor . . . [and] does not possess the same aversion to working in public . . . as is characteristic of the white race."[12]

For Saidiya Hartman, this sort of fantasy marked slave and minstrel bodies alike as provisional subjects, lacking full autonomy and available for appropriation by others: "The bound black body, permanently affixed in its place, engenders pleasure not only ensuant to the buffoonery and grotesqueries of Cuff, Sambo, and Zip Coon but above all deriving from the very mechanisms of this coercive placement; it is a pleasure obtained from the security of place and order and predicated upon chattel slavery."[13] It wasn't just the capering of Tambo, Bones, or Mickey that afforded audiences pleasure, then, but the very association of those characters with the enslaved body, and the system of chattel slavery which it embodied. The pleasure could be described as sadistic, deriving from the forced subjection of others. At the same time, though, according to Hartman, it was witnessing this systematic yet distanced performance of the effects of slavery that made sense of that institution, as fixed in a natural order through which one's humanity could be affirmed—if one had the luxury to identify as white. Blackface minstrelsy celebrated the black body as outside of and resistant to (white) civilization, a body that through its very necessary subjugation and its defiance thereof demonstrated the very humorous foibles and failings of that civilization.

That in minstrelsy this performance was most often offered by a white man in blackface only added to its frisson. One could, at a distance, participate in the subjugation and exchange of another person, visiting that economic and social control on a body simultaneously white and black. As in the sadomasochistic act, this pleasure combines the fantasy of subjection with the fantasy that its objects willingly entered into it, that the subjection is pleasurable in its own right to the masochist.

In those not infrequent cases of black performers required to black up in order to gain access to the stage (and a livelihood), the pleasure of subjugation and engagement in that system of domination was asserted even over the ostensibly free black body. The black performer seemed to yield willingly to a significatory system that made reference to his or her own (potential) enslavement, in order to perform that enslavement as the positive condition of the happy darky. "In this regard," Hartman argues, "the donning of blackface restaged the seizure and possession of the black body for the other's use and enjoyment. The culture of cross-racial identification facilitated in minstrelsy cannot be extricated from the relations of chattel slavery."[14]

As far as the animated minstrel was (and to some extent still is) concerned, this was no less true. The animated continuing character carried the physical markers of the minstrel—the white gloves, the black face (or, in the case of the Fleischers' popular trickster Ko-Ko, white but still painted on), and exaggerated eyes and mouth—as well as the bodily elasticity, the propensity to dance (and, with the coming of sound, to sing), and a willfully disobedient disposition.[15] But it was particularly in the interplay between the character and its animator in cartoons of the early silent era that this subjugation made itself most evident. Characters such as Felix and Ko-Ko frequently tested the bounds of the screen itself, and (especially in Ko-Ko's case) were often punished for asserting themselves (Figure 6.6). As with the minstrel character created by whites to be subjugated by whites, the early animated character was created and disciplined by the same animator.[16] (With the exception of Winsor McCay's early struggles with Gertie, Max Fleischer's epic ongoing struggle with Ko-Ko, and Walter

Figure 6.6. In *Ko-Ko the Barber* (1925), Ko-Ko the Clown take scissors from his (drawn) barbershop to cut through the paper on which he is drawn, in order to escape his animator and nemesis, Max Fleischer.

Lantz's shenanigans with Pete the Pup, that discipline was usually meted out by nothing more than a photograph of the animator's hand, which was easier to photograph frame by frame than a live hand.) By the time of *Trader Mickey*, though, even the trope of the intruding hand of the animator had largely disappeared. Yet the animated minstrel was nonetheless still regularly subjected to violence, constraint, and punishment, if not by hostile figures such as the cannibal king before whom Trader Mickey is brought, then by the environment itself. Animated characters by their nature were the victims of torture—for the sake of amusement.[17]

Instrumental Interlude

Yet this only begins to tell the tale of why early animators would make the minstrel a key figure in the emerging cosmos of animation, and why the violence sublimated in the song and dance of the minstrel stage might reemerge with a vengeance in the cartoon world. The "security of place" about which Hartman speaks points back to the plantation, but it also organizes the North (where almost all early animation was made) and the South into contrasting fantastic realms of free and unfree labor. Minstrelsy is not simply a bodily regime; it is also spatial. The ritual torment of the animated minstrel character externalized fantasies of freedom and unfreedom in which that character acted up and was punished, thus establishing the real world of the animator as less free (and ultimately less able to support rebellion) than the cartoon character's world, but more secure in its demonstration of mastery because of that act of creation and discipline.

To return to the cartoon, when Trader Mickey sets foot on the river bank, slaps his feet on the mud of the Mississippi/Congo, he is met by a tribe of ravening cannibals. Led by a buffoonish king who can't stop laughing, mouse and dog are seized and Mickey is thrown into a pot and prepped for cooking, while the king and his tribesmen sort through the items he has brought for trading. Strangely, they find that much of Mickey's stock consists of trumpets, trombones, tubas, and the like—the instruments for a jazz band. Mystified, the grotesquely caricatured Ubangis try to play them but only end up injuring the instruments, themselves, and one another. Beginning in this moment, the cartoon reveals a continuum of animate being. Although the instruments are inanimate, they still strike back at the cannibals when abused (Figures 6.7, 6.8). Likewise, in later scenes the cannibals play not only the instruments but also one another. In other words, both cannibals and trombones are relatively animate instruments, plastic beyond the usual bounds of their being. Their interaction reveals their mutual instrumentality, their common primitive bond. More tool than human, sharing a certain happy deformability while one is instrument for another, they are both finally instruments for those above them.

But this gets ahead of the story. Just when it seems that all is lost, the chef who is preparing Mickey tries to use an alto saxophone as a ladle. Mickey gets hold of it and begins playing, and of course the natives can't help but dance. That dance will bond the trader and cannibals under the sign of rhythm, which the black body, true to stereotype, cannot possibly resist. The tune that Mickey belts out sets off a medley of standards, including "St. James Infirmary Blues" and "Darktown Strutters' Ball," which signify both the Harlem demimonde and the Old South. Suddenly, even though the cannibals continue to play their instruments incorrectly, the tune is clear, and the audience witnesses a full-blown production number with Mickey and the king of the cannibals as its co-stars.

This production number, which is the centerpiece of the cartoon, literalizes the fantasy of jazz as "jungle music," replete with the thrills of cannibalism, upriver crossed with uptown. As any number of critics have noted, this implicit message, carried forward from the minstrel stage, was literalized in 1930, when Paul Whiteman, in *The King of Jazz,* announced that "jazz was born in the African jungle to the beating of voodoo drums."[18] Discussing the Fleischers' use of otherworldly motifs in their live-animated jazz series, which featured Cab Calloway several times, Daniel Goldmark suggests that early American animation repeatedly invoked the jungle and the plantation to signal the primal roots of African American culture: "The dark jungles represent jazz's supposed primeval origins, while the caves that appear in all three Calloway cartoons work as metaphors for the urban source of jazz, Harlem nightclubs. The portrayal of these exotic locales in cartoons provided white audiences with a safe outing to a strange and unusual world, much like a visit to the Harlem clubs."[19] But Africa, Harlem, and the South aren't the only realms invoked in the production number. Mickey and his captors blithely make use of the copious human bones that litter the village. They play them like percussion instruments, they use them to adorn ad hoc costumes, and they dance atop piles of skulls; mass death is everywhere in the frame, even as they all happily rollick their way through the Black Bottom and the Charleston (Figure 6.9). As in the Fleischer Brothers' contemporaneous Betty Boop shorts, which featured jazz greats such as Calloway and Louis Armstrong live and then imagined as animated creatures (Figure 6.10), this visual iconography also placed African American social and cultural life in an underworld teeming with death and violence, fusing the seemingly innate joyousness of the natives to an ever-present mortal threat.

Figures 6.7, 6.8. The cannibals in *Trader Mickey* struggle—and demonstrate their mutually plasmatic instrumentality–with the trumpets, trombones, tubas, and other instruments that Mickey has brought to the jungle to trade for some unspecified commodity. As the cannibals deform the instruments, the instruments resist them.

Figure 6.9. Two cannibals in *Trader Mickey* play the bass on a pile of human bones, further linking blackness to an underworldly and inhuman realm of being.

Figure 6.10. In *I'll Be Glad When You're Dead, You Rascal You* (1932), Louis Armstrong morphs into and out of the head of a ravenous cannibal, chasing Ko-Ko and Bimbo. Here, jazz animates and embodies the jungle, chasing down its descendant, the minstrel.

Chains of Being

Trader Mickey takes things a little further, though. As the natives dance and play, small details flit across the screen. Many of the cannibals wear bracelets and anklets, some of which have an odd extra ring attached to them, as if they were once shackles (Figure 6.11). It is a fleeting and random image, suggestive perhaps of an escape from bondage—or of being ready for chains. The chronology matters little; the gesture is toward the association—the linking—of the ostensibly black body with a condition of slavery, of being both subject and chattel. As if this offhand gesture weren't enough, chains or no, some of the natives dance and play their instruments upright, while others play on all fours as if they were prehuman missing links. Here the much noted anthropomorphism of the classic cartoon takes on a more subtle gradation: while somehow Mickey, an oversized mouse, is the most civilized creature present, the apparently African natives, who are meant to read as human, gambol apelike, playing their jazz instruments with either hands or feet with equal ease (Figure 6.12).

Figure 6.11. In several sequences in *Trader Mickey* the cannibals wear shackles on their legs, suggesting that they have been or will be slaves. This sequence, in which they dance with Mickey to popular jazz tunes, suggests a genealogical connection between the minstrel and the slave.

Figure 6.12. Some of the cannibals in *Trader Mickey* play equally well with their hands and feet, or use their mouths to play their instruments.

But even within the social order of the cannibals, there are necessary gradations of humanity. At the other end of the spectrum, like Mickey, both the king and the chef wear the white gloves of a minstrel (Figure 6.13). A chain of being presents itself in the number, which, like a minstrel show, is performed face-forward, and in many of the shots the characters clearly acknowledge their audience. This performance describes a developmental timeline that begins at the proto-human (those cannibals not yet upright), continues to cannibals on two legs, then on to those who have donned the minstrel gloves but are still essentially savage, and ends at Mickey, an anthropomorphic minstrel mouse who dances for his life—and toward a civilization he will never fully occupy.

It would be enough to point out that this libidinous dance of life, death, and dirty blues produces a sadomasochistic fantasy in which ostensibly black bodies are so steeped in their own physicality, their own animal nature, that they revel in a world in which pain is an unremarkable part of an innate celebration of a sensual yet inherently incoherent life. It would be enough to point out that this particular cartoon hints at that primal fantasy about which Hartman speaks—one that traces the minstrel body back to the quasi-animal realm of the (imagined) African native, and that it further implicates that minstrel figure

Figure 6.13. Like the cannibal king in *Trader Mickey,* the chef—here confusing a saxophone for a ladle—wears the gloves of the minstrel, suggesting a continuum from the savage subjects of the tribe, to its elites, on to Mickey as the returning minstrel.

in the slave trade. (For again, what do these natives have that Mickey would want?) It isn't hard to read the cartoon as another in a long line of cinematic and performative fantasies in which the very nature of blackness masochistically invites its own torment.

But pointing out one more node in that hierarchy and its location in attendant fantasies about the African or African American body as a missing link between a white modern humanity and its roots among the apes does not tell the whole tale, nor does it fully account for the anxious violence that attends the cartoon minstrel. In addition to recapitulating a fantastic primate taxonomy, *Trader Mickey* also illustrates the minstrel's relationship to the slave as chattel, as object, and as tool. What the landscape of the cannibal village reveals (and this is also true of animation in general) is that no body, no thing, is completely human nor completely an autonomous subject. Both because they are animated, and because they are located on a taxonomic continuum from the ape to the minstrel, every thing and every person in the cartoon, up to and including Mickey, is to some degree a useful object for someone else in the cartoon. Of course Mickey, being more civilized, is more likely to use than to be used, but this becomes assured only after he has employed jazz to channel the brute force of the cannibals into song and dance.

Fetishism

The animated minstrel, then, stands as a fetish for a set of relations that are present but not fully nameable. He is a Marxist fetish in the sense that he is a commodity, a crystallization of the social and material relations that obtain around his creation, and he occludes those relations through his status as a social object. He is a Freudian fetish in that his apparent condition as a living being is a disavowal of the violent hand of the maker behind him, and of the violent appropriation of the labor that went into his making. He is at one and the same time a subject and an object—or better, an object masquerading as a subject.[20] In this instance the animated cannibals who threaten Mickey serve to underscore that disavowal; they too are alive, yet they seem unable to demonstrate their humanity completely. They make Mickey seem more human. Yet at the risk of stating the obvious, no matter how much Mickey behaves like a human, he is a mouse. Mickey is anthropomorphic; the cannibals are zoomorphic; together they offer a visual treatise on the racial underpinnings of subject-object relations circa 1932.

This is the fetishistic magic of animation: any object in the animated world has the potential to come to life, and any living thing may be reduced to an object. Subjectivity is ephemeral and uncertain, granted by external circumstances and revocable. Thus, while *Trader Mickey* allows for the neat turn of providing a primer on the fantastic relationship between the savage and the minstrel, a compressed history of minstrelsy's anthropological conceit, Mickey would be a minstrel, and his subject status contingent, regardless of whether he were threatened by cannibals. He was a minstrel before and after this particular cartoon. What this scenario permits is a study in contrasts: the cannibals are classic racist caricatures, but they are not minstrels. They do not obtain the status of pretenders to civilization because they have not yet bought into (or more accurately been sold into) relations of exchange. Mickey, by contrast, as a trader in goods, has. As a minstrel, Mickey stands as the embodiment of the animator's alienated labor. Like the blackface minstrel who enacts the imperfect resistance of the recalcitrant slave, he may take pleasure in his rebellion, but he will never fully realize its fruits. As a commodity that apparently lives and works, Mickey enacts the fantasy of seeming to have free will yet without ever being fully the owner of his self or his own labor power. Minstrelsy is instrumentalism illustrated. For example, the end men Tambo and Bones are both characters put on by their performers and the personification of the instruments they play, the tambourine and the bones; they are essentially instruments playing instruments.

Likewise the free laborer maintains the real fiction of self-possession, of being able to divorce one's own body from its products in the act of exchange. This requires, of course, a notion of surplus labor: the free laborer is understood as entering into negotiation with an employer to actualize the value of her or his labor, the tacit understanding being that the employer will realize a profit from whatever excess value the laborer is forced to give up in order to complete the contract. (This, as Marx points out, is how the commodity relation operates. The employer imagines profit as deriving from the commodity itself when it is sold; the worker understands profit as deriving from her or his inability to realize the total value of her or his labor when *that* is sold.) It is a necessarily unequal operation, an unfriendly transaction masquerading as a friendly one, a hiving off and selling of a portion of one's self in order to maintain the rest. Animators who went to work for studios in the formative years of the American animation industry did so freely, and in doing so agreed to perform extremely creative work under onerous working conditions. Animation production at that time was not unlike other piecework industries, with journeyman animators churning out hundreds of drawings a day. As John Randolph Bray, one of the men most responsible for the rationalization of animation, put it in 1917: "In each foot of moving picture film there are about sixteen pictures, or sixteen thousand separate pictures to the thousand-foot reel. A one-reel cartoon contains, therefore, sixteen thousand sketches. . . . In my studio we turn out not less than one [cartoon] a week. Allowing that there are twenty of us at work, it makes nearly six months' work each to be done in one week."[21] Animator Shamus Culhane, remembering those early days of animation, referred to this as like working in a "sausage mill."[22]

Which part of the worker is alienated from which? An exception necessary for the rule, the slave in its vocal and physical abjection seems to give a perverse voice to the mute cries of the supposedly free worker's body as it has its labor wrested from it during a seemingly voluntary participation in the labor market. The performance of this abject black body, engaged in what Corin Willis describes as overdetermined signification—for the minstrel, expressed in everything from the verbal excess of the stump speech, to the sartorial excess of gigantic cuffs and collars and white gloves, to the bodily excess of an oversized mouth and eyes, or of jumping Jim Crow—articulates and delineates the mute cry of the alienated worker parted from itself.[23] Even beyond the particulars of work in the animation industry, the cartoon minstrel as resistant trickster speaks to and of a culture moving from nineteenth-century craft modes of production to rationalized twentieth-century mass production. Read in this light, Mickey and his ilk would be examples of what Fredric Jameson has called "a kind of homeopathic strategy whereby the scandalous and intolerable external irritant is drawn into the aesthetic process itself and thereby systematically worked over, 'acted out,' and symbolically neutralized."[24] Jameson was reading the impulse toward repetition and the use of mass-cultural icons in modernist avant-garde production; extending that model to cultural workers of the same period suggests only that the shock of the modern was felt by more than simply those of delicate and refined sensibilities.[25]

The animate minstrel, who progressed from the silent and self-manipulating Felix to Bugs and Daffy with their logorrheic hijinks, became the yet more fantastic embodiment of that shock, the displacement of the violence of the separation of one's labor from one's self (if not one's self from one's self).[26] A figure representing the descendant of the recalcitrant slave, this character was created as willful and resistant by animators, made to be punished for resisting its own subjection, its own abjection. Hence, perhaps, the extreme mayhem in cartoons, and the increasing violence of those cartoons when they were given voice in the 1920s and 1930s. The continuing characters of the silent era, such as Felix, Ko-Ko, or even Alice, lacking the power of speech, visually marked and remarked on their made environment, of which they were an uneasy part, using it against itself, sometimes even attempting to escape the bounds of the world into which they had been forcibly placed (Figure 6.14). Truly formed as an objection, apparently autonomous yet without free will, these continuing cartoon characters were forced to appear to resist the conditions of their mak-

Figure 6.14. In *Ko-Ko Needles the Boss* (1924), Ko-Ko the Clown steals a sewing needle that Max Fleischer has been using to stitch the background against which the clown appears, using it to duel with the pen-wielding animator.

ing, then to submit to their master for punishment for that very act of refusal. When they were given voice, they seemed to turn their attention inward, as did Mickey, who, for example, accepted the bounds of the frame but struggled happily against his cannibal captors.[27]

The animated minstrel, then, embodied a protest at the conditions of its own making, and begged punishment for that very protest. This performance of condensation and displacement was the mechanism by which the minstrel was so easily integrated into the animated cartoon. Roughly a mere fifteen years passed between the industrialization of animation in the United States and its transition to sound. In that time a robust but relatively insular cartoon business arose, based on a journeyman-apprentice system that trained up artists to be industrial workers, and within which workers regularly shifted from one company to another in search of better wages, working conditions, and recognition.[28] This system engaged entry-level workers in repetitive tasks such as washing cels, erasing pencil lines, and (at best) "tweening"—drawing the motion of characters between one gesture and another, over and over. Even lead animators, who were charged with character and story development, had that pleasure tempered with repetitive task work and long hours. Within this milieu, conventions not only cohered quickly but also spread from company to company through migrating workers. Popular characters were imitated, with only enough marginal differentiation to avoid litigation. Likewise, as in vaudeville and the silent live comedies of the period, gags that worked were lifted and repeated, creating a stable repertoire of recurring themes across product lines. In this creative labor environment the animate minstrels—Felix, Oswald, Bimbo, Mickey, and so on—representing the rebellious products of creative talent channeled into mass production, propagated rapidly. Certainly not the sum total of the panoply of animated characters of the time, but equally certainly the most popular and enduring, these animate minstrels embodied that commodified objection.

The cartoon minstrel, then, simultaneously made and yet seemingly autonomous, exists in a world bounded by a frame within which it attempts to exert its will, and within which that will is thwarted. Although the trickster of the swing-era sound cartoon—Mickey, Bugs, Bimbo—would become increasingly more articulate, its world would become more bounded as it became imbued with a voice necessarily not its own. Imbricated in a world more distinctly separate from that of the animator and the audience, the character would shift its violent opposition to its condition from the cartoon's frame to its contents. Gone were the Fleischer sing-along cartoons that signaled a world outside the frame, and gone was the hand of the animator entering to interfere with the character's autonomy and with the continuity of an increasingly cinematic animated space.[29] The Mickey of *Steamboat Willie* or even of *Trader Mickey* could barely make more than an inarticulate squeak. Yet compared to the more articulate Mickey that was soon to emerge, he had more freedom to challenge the conditions of his making, more opportunity to acknowledge his own existence as a made object—if somewhat less than his silent precursors. There was in silence a lack of voice and also a lack of being voiced; likewise, as cartoon characters gained a voice (the voice of another), they ceased the appearance of autonomously challenging the conditions of their making and their regulation.

To see in something as seemingly trivial and ephemeral as a cartoon short an expression of labor's protest against its own impressment may seem absurd. Likewise, to associate the incredible and real violence against the body of the slave—confinement, torture, and rape—with sadomasochistic performance (and also with cartoon characters) may seem a grotesque trivialization of a horrible inhumanity. It is. And it has been so in American popular culture for generations. As has been discussed in detail elsewhere, blackface minstrelsy was (and is) very concerned with issues of labor, of freedom, and of desire.[30] Nor is the association of sadomasochism with working through issues of labor and power a gesture of petty homology for the sake of mere titillation.[31] For all that

Sacher-Masoch's masochistic Severin in *Venus in Furs* does to protest the involuntary nature of his desires, he also necessarily performs a *willing* subjection when he suffers at the hand of his mistress, Wanda.[32] Of course, unlike Severin, the slave is not free. The fantasy of the slave's (un)willing participation in chattel slavery as being rooted in a core animal self is inflected in the masochist's performative gesture of yielding to his master's will—and serves as a root act of the primal violence that charges sadomasochistic fantasy: the masochist uses his will to tame his will, to become the slave. The slave, though, is (imagined) a slave because his animal urges outpace his will and betray him to his captors. Yet as *Venus in Furs* makes clear, without the figure and fantasy of the slave, the sadist and masochist can find no common ground upon which to build their fantasy, which is entirely taken up with exploring the limits of subjection and free will. Likewise for the minstrel, animate or otherwise, its comic denial of the horror of slavery paradoxically depends on that very horror.

Why would this be so in something as seemingly trivial as early American animation? For the animator of the early twentieth century, minstrelsy—a fading popular performance form—offered a ready-made fantasy of the rebellion of forced labor. In an art that went from artisanal form to full-blown industry in the blink of an eye, the minstrel stood in for the animator as artist for hire, a creator become fabricator on spec, as in the photograph of animators at work on Felix the Cat at Sullivan Studios (Figure 6.15). Animators at the dawn of the industrial age of cartooning were expected to be skilled artists and draftsmen, and to be able to reproduce characters created by others. Continuing characters such as Ko-Ko and Felix became avatars of that impressment, simultaneously thwarted and assaulted, yet rebelliously and deviously fighting back against their owners. Obviously more masochists than slaves—that is, performing the fantasy of "freedom of contract" in which both employer and employee meet as ostensible equals—early animators were willing subjects of an emerging industrial system, subjugating their will and their talents in order to participate, and to get paid. In the process, they made a commodity of their labor power—and displaced and embodied that act in the characters they made, and which they then compulsively punished. For how free, in the capitalist system, is the sale of one's own labor?

With the coming of sound and of films such as *Trader Mickey,* the minstrel trickster increasingly was joined by racist caricatures such as the cannibal king—themselves stand-ins for the profound desire and fear that the efflorescence of African American culture engendered in polite white society.[33] During the silent era of animation, although racist stereotypes abounded within and outside the minstrel tradition, the animated minstrel lacked the syntax-mangling and evasive voice of its brother on the stage. If the animated commodity

Figure 6.15. A shot of animators at the Sullivan studios, circa 1925, suggests that the Fleischer version of endless studio hijinks masked more tedious industrial routines. (The man closest to the camera was Pat Sullivan, the producer, posing as if he were an animator.) From the Al Eugster collection, courtesy of Donald Crafton.

spoke, it did so only in intertitles. If it couldn't speak, it protested by piercing the narrative frame or physically challenging the animator. Whether the animator acknowledged that his marketable skills permitted him only a fantasy of freedom occasioned by the sale of his labor power to the cartoon producer, his creations enacted a fantasy of enslaved labor he had unchained—and then punished with his own hand. Whether for creator or created, a fantasy of consent was proleptic to the violence that was sure to follow, and guaranteed never to redeem a contract made in bad faith. Mickey Mouse may have been ubiquitous, but he was "Mickey Mouse"—a cheap object reproduced endlessly and made valuable only in the subjection of others.

NOTES

Research for this essay was supported by the Social Sciences and Humanities Research Council, and by the Jackman Humanities Institute and Innis College at the University of Toronto. Special thanks to Aubrey Anable for her close reading and thoughtful suggestions, to Stephen Johnson for his editorial expertise and patience, and to Charlie Keil for his unflagging support of the project.

1. An example of a Mickey Mouse short that makes direct reference to minstrelsy is, for instance, *Mickey's Mellerdrammer* (1933). One can also read all of the early Warner Brothers Bosko shorts of the 1930s as intentional minstrel performances.

2. Perhaps the best cinematic example of this nostalgic mythology is *Babes in Arms,* directed by Busby Berkeley (MGM, 1939), which creates a direct line of descent from the movie musical, to vaudeville, to blackface minstrelsy. The radio program *Amos 'n' Andy* (1928–1960) could be seen as the notable exception to this trend. Interestingly, of course, this radio program relied on auditory markers to signal its minstrelsy and, taking place in modern-day Chicago, eschewed the classic minstrel show format. Also significant is that the creators of *Amos 'n' Andy,* Freeman Gosden and Charles Correll, attempted to bring their characters to the screen but failed to extend their otherwise successful franchise to cinema. Also significant is the 1948 premier episode of the television program, in which Gosden and Correll introduced the black actors who would take their places as the living embodiment of the minstrel characters they had created. See Melvin Patrick Ely, *The Adventures of Amos 'n' Andy: A Social History of an American Phenomenon* (New York: Maxwell Macmillan, 1992); and William Barlow, *Voice Over: The Making of Black Radio* (Philadelphia: Temple University Press, 1999).

3. See Daphne Brooks, *Bodies in Dissent: Spectacular Performances of Race and Freedom, 1850–1910* (Durham: Duke University Press, 2006); Jayna Brown, *Babylon Girls: Black Women Performers and the Shaping of the Modern* (Durham: Duke University Press, 2008); Louis Chude-Sokei, *The Last "Darky": Bert Williams, Black-on-Black Minstrelsy, and the African Diaspora* (Durham: Duke University Press, 2006); Arthur Knight, *Disintegrating the Musical: Black Performance and American Musical Film* (Durham: Duke University Press, 2002); Karen Sotiropoulos, *Staging Race: Black Performers in Turn of the Century America* (Cambridge: Harvard University Press, 2006).

4. A portion of that campaign involved reminding fans that the early Mickey had an edge, making the new campaign merely an act of reclamation.

5. Richard deCordova, "The Mickey in Macy's Window: Childhood, Consumerism, and Disney Animation," in *Disney Discourse,* ed. Eric Smoodin (New York: Routledge, 1994), 203–13.

6. Another classic use of the name is the term "Mickey Mousing," which refers to the animation practice of timing the action of animated characters to match the beat of the music, sometimes so much so that it seems almost mechanical.

7. For an overview of minstrelsy, see, for instance, W. T. Lhamon Jr., *Raising Cain: Blackface Performance from Jim Crow to Hip Hop* (Cambridge: Harvard University Press, 1998); Dale Cockrell, *Demons of Disorder: Early Blackface Minstrels and Their World* (London: Cambridge University Press, 1997); Annemarie Bean, James Hatch, and Brooks McNamara, eds., *Inside the Minstrel Mask: Readings in Nineteenth-Century Blackface Minstrelsy* (Middletown: Wesleyan University Press, 1996); and William Mahar, *Behind the Burnt Cork Mask: Early Blackface Minstrelsy and Antebellum American Popular Culture* (Chicago: University of Illinois Press, 1999). For critical readings of minstrelsy in relation to race and labor, see David Roediger, *The Wages of Whiteness: Race and the Making of the American Working Class* (London: Verso, 1991); and Eric Lott, *Love and Theft: Blackface Minstrelsy and the American Working Class* (New York: Oxford University Press, 1993). For compelling readings on race, minstrelsy, and performance in relation to the formation of entertainment in the twentieth century, see Michael Rogin, *Blackface, White Noise: Jewish Immigrants in the Hollywood Melting Pot* (Berkeley: University of California Press, 1996);

as well as Sotiropoulos, *Staging Race;* Brooks, *Bodies in Dissent;* Brown, *Babylon Girls;* and Chude-Sokei, *The Last "Darky."*

8. For examples of the stump speech, see Robert Lewis, ed., *From Traveling Show to Vaudeville: Theatrical Spectacle in America, 1830–1910* (Baltimore: Johns Hopkins University Press, 2003); and Mahar, *Behind the Burnt Cork Mask.*

9. Mickey also makes use of the tune in *The Shindig* (1930).

10. For a discussion of the relationship of the historical figure Walt Disney to the confection of "Walt Disney" produced in the interplay between Walt Disney Productions, its audiences, and its critics, see Nicholas Sammond, *Babes in Tomorrowland: Walt Disney and the Making of the American Child, 1930–1960* (Durham: Duke University Press, 2005).

11. Dennis Childs, "'You Ain't Seen Nothin' Yet': *Beloved,* the American Chain Gang, and the Middle Passage Remix," *American Quarterly* 61, no. 2 (June 2009): 279.

12. Quoted in Alex Lichtenstein, *Twice the Work of Free Labor: The Political Economy of Convict Labor in the New South* (New York: Verso, 1996), 180. See also Debra Walker King, *African Americans and the Culture of Pain* (Charlottesville: University of Virginia Press, 2008), 8.

13. Saidiya Hartman, *Scenes of Subjection: Terror, Slavery, and Self-Making in Nineteenth-Century America* (New York: Oxford University Press, 1997), 31.

14. Ibid., 31–32. For discussion of the intersection of this racial dynamic with the emerging class politics of the nineteenth and early twentieth centuries, see Lott, *Love and Theft;* and Roediger, *Wages of Whiteness.*

15. One could argue that because he is a clown, Ko-Ko isn't a minstrel. But Ko-Ko is a clown within the tradition of animation that favors continuing characters as trickster figures, and that draws on a variety of minstrel tropes (blacking up being one of them) for those characters. Ko-Ko has a white face but performs the minstrel role.

16. See, for instance, Donald Crafton, *Before Mickey: The Animated Film, 1898–1928* (Cambridge: MIT Press, 1982), 169–77.

17. The technical and aesthetic reasons why the introduction of sound would have limited the intrusion of the living animator or his hand in the frame are beyond the scope of this essay. Suffice it to say that the desire to present the cinematic space within which characters lived and spoke as coherent and contiguous militated against the disruption of the frame and space of the animate world.

18. See, for example, Corin Willis, "Blackface Minstrelsy and Jazz Signification in Hollywood's Early Sound Era," in *Thriving on a Riff: Jazz and Blues Influences in African American Literature and Film,* ed. Graham Lock and David Murray (London: Oxford University Press, 2009), 41; and Daniel Goldmark, *Tunes for 'Toons: Music and the Hollywood Cartoon* (Berkeley: University of California Press, 2005), 80–81.

19. Goldmark, *Tunes for 'Toons,* 88–89.

20. See Karl Marx, *Capital,* vol. 1, trans. Ben Fowkes (New York: Penguin, 1976), 125–87; Sigmund Freud, "Fetishism" (1927), in *Sexuality and the Psychology of Love,* ed. Phillip Rieff, trans. Joan Riviere (New York: Touchstone Books, 1997), 204–9. See also Fredric Jameson, "Reification and Utopia in Mass Culture," in *Signatures of the Visible* (New York: Routledge, 1992), for a discussion of the role of mass culture in representing, hence working through, repressed relations. There is an argument for considering the minstrel as a subject masquerading as an object, but space does not permit it.

21. John Randolph Bray, "How the Comics Caper," *Photoplay Magazine* 9, no. 2 (January 1917): 67–70.

22. John Canemaker, "Interview with Shamus Culhane," February 13, 1973, Canemaker Collection, Fales Library, New York University.

23. Willis, "Blackface Minstrelsy," 48–50. For a discussion of voice and access to the Real in film, see Slavoj Žižek, "Grimaces of the Real, or When the Phallus Appears," *October* 58 (1991): 44–68.

24. Jameson, *Signatures,* 23.

25. For an elaboration on this point in the same essay, one that posits the repetitive use of cultural icons as a mass working through of repressed political impulses, see Jameson, *Signatures,* 32–34. See also, of course, Fredric Jameson, *The Political Unconscious: Narrative as a Socially Symbolic Act* (Ithaca: Cornell University Press, 1981).

26. In the case of Warner Brothers, those continuing characters almost always featured a speech impediment. It is beyond the scope of this essay to discuss this peculiar feature of Warner's interpretation of the animate minstrel, except to note that it seems that the impediment is intimately linked to the characters' disruptive power.

27. Even though his first few outings were silent, Mickey is often considered solely as a sound cartoon.

28. See Crafton, *Before Mickey;* and Tom Sito, *Drawing the Line: The Untold Story of Animation Unions from Bosko to Bart Simpson* (Lexington: University Press of Kentucky, 2006).

29. Max Fleischer appeared only once with Betty Boop in 1934, and Walter Lantz also curtailed his onscreen appearances in the 1930s.

30. See Lott, *Love and Theft;* Roediger, *Wages of Whiteness;* and Rogin, *Blackface, White Noise.*

31. Consider Gilles Deleuze, *Masochism: Coldness and Cruelty* (New York: Zone Books, 1989), 91–101.

32. See Leopold Sacher-Masoch, *Venus in Furs* (1879; New York: Zone Books, 1989), esp. 222–26.

33. See Stuart Hall, "Racist Ideologies and the Media," in *Media Studies: A Reader,* ed. Paul Marris and Sue Thornham (New York: New York University Press, 2000), 271–82; and Lott, *Love and Theft.*

7

From New Deal to No Deal

Blackface Minstrelsy, *Bamboozled*, and Reality Television

ALICE MAURICE

Spike Lee's *Bamboozled* (2000) defines itself for viewers from its very first word, spoken in voice-over narration by protagonist Pierre Delacroix (Damon Wayans): "Satire." The film goes on to feature a full-blown minstrel show in which the performers—and ultimately the members of the studio audience—black up. In its goals and methods, you might say that *Bamboozled* takes Lee's typical "in your face" treatment of race relations and puts it "on your face." But while the film does attempt to catalogue the history of blackface performance (and other stereotypical representations of African Americans), it aims its sharpest satire elsewhere, using blackface as a powerful and unsettling device for its larger critique of mass culture. Like the two films that profoundly influenced *Bamboozled,* Sidney Lumet's *Network* (1976) and *A Face in the Crowd* (Elia Kazan, 1957), Lee's film paints a deeply unflattering portrait of television and popular culture. *A Face in the Crowd* (with screenplay by Budd Schulberg) traces the rise to stardom and power of a white southern "country boy" plucked from obscurity,[1] while *Network* offers a prophetic satire about the lengths to which a failing network would go to improve ratings. *Bamboozled* reworks Lumet's film quite explicitly, but its thematic focus and dark commentary on consumer culture owe much to *A Face in the Crowd* (and Lee dedicates *Bamboozled* to Schulberg). By making an industry satire about a television show featuring black performers in blackface, with an African American producer as its main character, Lee tackles head-on issues that could only be either displaced onto white characters or figured through the prop-like use of black characters in the earlier films to which he alludes.[2] What was missing (or only implied) in those earlier films' critiques was a clear sense of the deep entanglement of television and popular culture with the stereotypes and conventions of blackface minstrelsy. By making this legacy a primary focus, *Bamboozled* adds an additional layer of reflexivity to the already recursive show-within-a-film formula.

If we think of the multiple masks of black blackface as reflected in the multiple levels of reflexivity in the film (a film about a television show that features a minstrel show), the film becomes a dizzying hall of mirrors. As one critic put it, "The film is trapped in the unhappy dynamic of disseminating an iconography that it cannot stop destroying, and which it therefore cannot stop producing."[3] But of course that's the point, making this particular comment less a critique than a plot synopsis. If *Bamboozled* is a mise en abyme, its concentric circles of performance are key to its critique, as this structure forces the inclusion of—and in the case of *Bamboozled*, multiple iterations of—the internal audience. *Bamboozled* repeatedly invokes Bert Williams, one of the most successful and groundbreaking performers in the history of the American stage, now largely repressed because of his association with blackface. It makes reference to Williams through photographs and film clips, in one of its monologues on the history of blackface performance, and even by introducing the performers in its minstrel show as "two real coons" (the very phrase Williams and his partner George Walker used to advertise their stage show).[4] In his study of Williams, Louis Chude-Sokei notes how the meaning of his blackface performances shifted when he integrated the Broadway stage, becoming the first African American performer to share the stage with whites when he joined the Ziegfeld Follies in 1910. The mask was mandatory for him there, and it doubly marked his difference. On the black stage, his appropriation of the mask enabled him to reflect on the many layers of identity, but as Chude-Sokei puts it, "the weight of the mask grew in direct proportion to the scale of his success" and "the many faces he balanced were all reduced to one dour visage."[5] Similarly, Man Ray and Womack, the African American street performers featured in *Bamboozled* (played by Savion Glover and Tommy Davidson, respectively), grapple with a question fundamental to their survival: Once packaged for a mass audience, can their performances ever be understood outside the stereotypes imagined by blackface minstrelsy? The film maps the interplay between individual and (racial) group identity onto the relation between performer and audience, with the latter dynamic operating on multiple stages: on TV, in the studio, and behind the scenes. The shifting relations between black performers and the performance of "blackness"—and the consequent shifts in the balance of power—play out not just between the African American producer and the mainstream, white corporate structure but also, crucially, between performer and audience.

Responding to critics who suggest that the movie is too obsessed with minstrelsy and is therefore irrelevant or stuck in the past, Lee notes in his DVD audio commentary that "you don't need to apply burnt cork to be doing minstrelsy in these times."[6] Indeed, *Bamboozled* is very much of its moment—anticipating a "reality TV" craze that was just beginning to take hold when the film was released in 2000.[7] As I will show, by imagining the more insidious possibilities of audience participation, the film predicts the direction of contemporary television's exploitation of identity. Taking the audience as its central image as the movie progresses, *Bamboozled* suggests that the blurring of boundaries between audience and spectacle (the much-touted "convergence")[8] that increasingly defines contemporary mass media mimics the operations of blackface performance. I begin by looking closely at the performer-audience dynamics in the film. In the latter part of this essay, I consider the film in the context of contemporary televisual modes of address associated with "reality television," arguing that the film reveals an affinity in form between blackface minstrelsy and an increasingly spectacular audience participation model routed through consumable identities.

Faces in the Crowd: Collecting an Audience

As in *Network*, the TV network in *Bamboozled* (called CNS) is facing a ratings crisis when the main character, an African American television producer named Pierre Delacroix (changed from his given name, Peerless Dothan), proposes an old-fashioned blackface minstrel show. Although he had hoped the idea would be so preposterous that he would be fired from a job he dislikes (the script here taking a cue from Mel Brooks's *The Producers*), it turns out to be a huge hit for the network. And while Delacroix initially sees a potential for satire and social critique in the show, it doesn't work out that way. *Mantan: The New Millennium Minstrel Show* takes off like a runaway train, spawning merchandise, creating fads, and sanctioning blackface for the masses, and Delacroix is powerless to stop it. As in *Network*, the star of the show, Man Ray, is murdered "live" on television near the end of the film. But in *Bamboozled*, the producer suffers the same fate as his exploited star: Delacroix—who has suffered a breakdown that is represented, in part, by the blackface mask that suddenly covers his own face—is shot by his assistant, Sloan (Jada Pinkett Smith).

When *Mantan: The New Millennium Minstrel Show* premieres to huge ratings, Sloan gives Delacroix a gift: a "jolly nigger bank," the first of what will become an overwhelming collection of disturbing figurines (Figure 7.1). Placing

Figure 7.1. A minstrel bank automaton, Sloan's gift to Delacroix. From *Bamboozled.*

a coin in its hand, she demonstrates its mechanical action: with the press of a lever, the figure lifts its arm and flips the coin into its mouth, while its eyes roll back in its head. As the success of the show grows, so does Delacroix's treasure trove of "Negro collectibles"; the size of his collection, in other words, parallels (and becomes a figure for) the size of his audience. The first piece, the bank, is explicitly tied to Delacroix himself. When Sloan gives him the gift, she notes that it is "appropriate" because "with a successful show, you'll be going to the bank," then goes on to explain that the Negro collectibles remind her of "a time in our history when we were considered inferior . . . sub-human." After she gives Delacroix a coin so he can "give it a whirl," the camera lingers on her face to end the scene, her look suggesting the connections she's making (and perhaps hopes to spur Delacroix in making) between him and the bank. He will become rich, but at a cost: trading in stereotypes, he risks becoming one.[9]

The metaphoric link Sloan suggests is made more troubling—and perhaps even more literal—in the scene that precedes the introduction of the bank. Here Delacroix and Sloan meet with Delacroix's boss, Dunwitty (Michael Rapaport), and media consultant Myrna Goldfarb (Dina Pearlman), who offers the "Mantan Manifesto," a preemptive answer to the expected cries of racism that the show will provoke. Goldfarb ends her list of retorts to the imagined critique (a list including "We employ African Americans in front of and behind the camera") with "And finally, our biggest asset is you, Pierre Delacroix." At this point Delacroix's response unfolds over multiple shots: in medium profile,

Delacroix brings his hand to his chest and says, "Me?" We then cut to a medium shot of Dunwitty, who says, pointing at Delacroix, "Yes, you." Those two shots are then repeated, as are the lines. It is important to note that the actors don't merely repeat the lines; the same *shots* are repeated, so the scene works like an overlapping edit—not quite breaking continuity (because it "reads" as if they were just repeating themselves), but emphasizing the lines and making the exchange seem a little "off." The shots are brief, and the rhythmic editing here underlines the difference between humans actually saying something twice and being made to do so through the recording and manipulation of sound and images. If it seems a little off, it is because the nature of the repetition makes human speech and movement seem unnatural, mechanistic.

In response to Delacroix's confusion, Goldfarb explains why he is their biggest asset:

> *Goldfarb:* The show was created and conceived by you: a nonthreatening African American male. So the show can't be racist because you're black.
>
> *Sloan:* Now, see, that's where you're wrong. He's not black—no, see . . . he's a Negro.

Goldfarb's description of Delacroix sounds like an appraisal of property, but of course that's what it is. He is their asset because they "own" him: he is under contract, and in fact the entire scheme for the show came out of Delacroix's desperate desire to get out of that contract, to escape. Goldfarb's appraisal comes just after the repetition of speech and gesture in the "Me?" "Yes, you" exchange. And so, even before Sloan gives him his first Negro collectible, this scene establishes Delacroix as a "Negro" who seems to repeat himself mechanistically—even moving his arm, in the repeated shot, in a way that prefigures the trick performed by the jolly nigger bank. The bank then freezes this already established image for us, figuring the place Delacroix occupies: he both gobbles up the money associated with the show's success and becomes a very visible symbolic asset in the network's coffers, a token in their collection.

If the bank represents Delacroix, however, it is also the first acquisition in what will become a very large collection. Just after the introduction of his first collectible, the film cuts to a montage. Reporting the success of the show's premiere by referring to other fads like the hula hoop and the yo-yo, Delacroix's voice-over tells us that "the latest, hottest, newest sensation across the nation was . . . blackface!" Spinning magazine covers cut to a series of close-ups of children's blackface Halloween masks and assorted paraphernalia accompanied by the shout "Trick or treat!" We then hear the lines repeated: Delacroix's "Blackface!" is followed this time by a sync-sound long shot of the group of children in masks shouting "Trick or treat!" (again emphasizing repetition and the taking apart and putting back together of image and sound). Coming between these two scenes—the success montage and the "new sensation" montage—the presentation of the bank forms a bridge between the show's status as early ratings success and total pop culture phenomenon. The bank is thus not just a figure for Delacroix. As the first piece in his collection, it is also the representative first member of the growing audience for *Mantan.* From this point on, the collectibles come to function as a kind of doubly internal audience. That is, if the movie's audience is the external audience, then the studio audience for *Mantan* is the internal audience; but if we go behind the scenes, the collectibles form a kind of private, internalized audience, watching Delacroix in his office as the studio audience watches *Mantan.* The tapings of the television show are interspersed through the second half of the film, with each iteration marking the increasing standardization (and commodification) of the show's style, framing, and content—and the subsequent disintegration, despair, and disorder it causes in the lives of its stars and creators. Alternating between the tapings of the shows and scenes featuring Delacroix in various personal spaces (his apartment, his office, and in conversations with his parents), the film extends the parallel between the audience and the Negro collectibles. In the minstrel show scenes, the growing popularity of the program is registered by changes in the appearance and behavior of the studio audience, while the increasing derangement of Delacroix's state of mind is registered by changes in the appearance and behavior of his collection.

The first time we see the minstrel show, we see the taping of the pilot before a live studio audience. The presentation of the show is interrupted by scenes emphasizing Delacroix's loss of control over the content of the show; we also see the first of the performers' "blacking-up" scenes. These become increasingly fragmented as the film goes on, as multiple mirroring, extreme close-ups, and canted angles reflect the growing pain and inner turmoil associated with the mask for Man Ray and Womack. This is particularly marked in the third, and last, of the "blacking-up" scenes. Here the process, from the burning of the cork to the completed mask, accompanied by the film's main theme music, is repeated, but the performers' identities are progressively fractured and confused throughout the scene as the masks appear and the faces multiply. When Man Ray applies his mask, he is framed by his reflection, itself split in two by the makeup mirror. After a dissolve to an extreme close-up of his lips as he applies lipstick, we cut back to his reflection: this time we don't see the performer, only his reflection, framed off to the left side of the screen, with multiple photographs of himself and earlier blackface performers taped to the mirror on the right. In the next shot, Womack stands at the right edge of the screen, appearing to touch Man Ray's reflection—doubled by the split mirror and forming the entire background of the shot—as he issues a quiet command

Figure 7.2. Delacroix surrounded by—or part of—his collection. From *Bamboozled.*

that also happens to be his own character's name: "Sleep and eat." From this quiet and surreal moment, we abruptly cut to the applause of the studio audience: beginning on a pair of white-gloved hands clapping, the camera pulls up to reveal the blacked-up face of a white audience member. This is the first time we see the audience members in blackface, and their jubilation (in contrast to the quiet desperation of the blacking-up scene) suggests that the audience's identity—its identity *as* an audience—is consolidated as the performers' identities (especially Womack's) break down.

The consolidation of the audience becomes even clearer the next (and last) time we see a taping of the show. This time the absolute coherence and conformity of the audience is contrasted to the instability and increasing incoherence of Delacroix's identity. At this point in the film, Delacroix's collection—which has been growing steadily—finally begins to overwhelm him. The figures take up every corner of his office, and in the scene just before the final taping of the show, they take on a life of their own. The scene begins, significantly, with Delacroix calling his mother. Throughout the call, in which his mother expresses her disappointment with him and his show, Delacroix shares the frame with a large smiling figurine that stands on the telephone table and seems to stare at him. (The figure's head is at the same height as Delacroix's.) In the first shot, the two are framed in long shot, with the doll taking up two thirds of the frame, drawing the eye as it stands out against a blank beige wall. The next shot offers a close-up of both heads, with the doll's head now wobbling from side to side, its eyes moving in tandem. The next wide shot reveals more figures, a group of large "lawn jockeys" that stand by the window and occupy screen left. Finally, after his mother offers her withering review of her son—"Peerless, you disappoint me"—we cut back to a shot of Delacroix from a different angle, now appearing to be surrounded by his collectibles (Figure 7.2). He occupies the middle plane of the shot, but he is not quite center screen. Taking pride of place there is the bobblehead that has been the central focus all along. After asking the figure, "What the hell are you smiling at?" he stands up and crosses the room to his desk. As he does so, his head leaves the frame, and the camera does not reframe to compensate. Rather, it just pans to follow him, with the level of the shot missing his head but displaying clearly the lawn jockeys and other collectibles he passes along the way. He sits down at his desk and begins to play with his jolly nigger bank, feeding it coins and touching the lever to make it "swallow" them. With each clink of the coin, we cut to a different part of his collection: individual pieces, groups of related figures ("mammy" pieces, for example), and extreme close-ups of the caricatured faces, especially the goggling, moving eyes.

Beyond the obvious charge that he is getting rich off these stereotypes, the sequence suggests how his success—the success of the show—has helped to propagate them. The minstrel show offers a "live" version of these stereotypical characters, and in this way he has brought these figures (back) to life. Throughout the scene, with its focus on the various sets of moving doll eyes, the collection seems to be watching him. And the potential for the figures to "come to life" plays out fully with the bank. When he turns the figure to face him, he watches as it moves on its own. It makes the coin-swallowing motion once, and then repeats it several times in rapid succession before stopping. The moment is framed ambiguously, as Delacroix struggles to narrate what we have witnessed: "When I thought, or imagined, that my favorite jolly nigger bank—an inanimate object, a piece of cold cast iron—was moving by itself, I knew I was getting paranoid. Did I really see what I saw? Or was I hallucinating?" As Delacroix asks, "Was I hallucinating?" we cut to a close-up of "Honest Abe Honeycutt," the emcee of the minstrel show, complete with a Lincolnesque stovepipe hat. We then get the reverse shot of the audience, from behind Honeycutt, revealing the entire audience in blackface, white gloves, and their standard-issue costumes: they all wear black New Millennium minstrel show sweatshirts (Figure 7.3). In the earlier scene in which the blackfaced audience was first revealed, the sweatshirts also made their first appearance, but that scene focused on individual shots—close-ups and various reaction shots. In this scene, in contrast, the group shot of the audience is followed by group displays of conformity linked to its new group identity. The audience members are in sync—not just with one another but with the show and its goals. In his

Figure 7.3. The audience for *Mantan: The New Millennium Minstrel Show.* From *Bamboozled.*

opening, Honeycutt rocks back and forth, his arm outstretched, and shouts his signature "Ooo-weee!"; the audience responds with the same movement and gesture, shouting, "Ooo-ahhh!"[10] As in *Network,* the scene suggests television as a mass-mediated church, but here, blackface is its communion. Only now do we see Honeycutt enter the crowd "looking for niggers"; each chosen audience member is more than happy to testify:

> *Honeycutt:* "Is you a niggah?"
>
> *Older white woman:* "Yessiree, Bob, darn tootin' I'm a niggah!"

Together, Delacroix's "paranoid" scene and this one point up the film's central concern with the nature of the mass audience. The audience as a group seems to know exactly "who it is," while Womack, Man Ray, and Delacroix become less and less certain of who they are. As the audience appears in blackface for the first time, Mantan and Sleep 'n Eat perform a sketch about an identity crisis (which, according to Lee, was taken from a early-twentieth-century pamphlet on how to put on a minstrel show). Sleep 'n Eat begins the comic dialogue by lamenting, "I don't know who I is."

Bill Brown has noted the haunting effect of Delacroix's collectibles, both in the film's narrative and on the film itself, as a text. In multiple scenes, but especially in the scene just described, the film exploits the play between animate and inanimate suggested by these objects. Discussing these figures as they function in the movie but also in terms of their history as objects, Brown argues that the collectibles represent what he calls the "American uncanny." The uncanny has here to do with the indeterminacy or sliding between "person" and "thing" that these figures embody—a slippage that reminds us of the ways in which slavery depended on that same inability to maintain the boundary between person and thing when it came to African American subjects.[11] In juxtaposing Delacroix's private audience (the figurines and his mother, both acting as a source of disapproving conscience linked to racial identity) with the studio audience (a stand-in or model for the millions of adoring fans watching at home), the film ties the loss of black identity to a stereotyped blackness performed for public consumption. Significantly, it also connects the strangeness of the "animated" inanimate objects with the nature of the "live" recorded performance. The "live studio audience" is crucial to constructing the televisual "liveness" associated with programs that are prerecorded and mediated for the television audience (and are thus more dead than "live").[12] And so in the film's use of the Negro collectibles, the indeterminacy between person and thing that Brown locates in the "American uncanny" is a reference not just to the repressed memory of slavery but also to the definitive conditions of mass culture, and of television in particular.

The film highlights the various layers of mediation between the performance of the show, taped before a "live studio audience," and the final televised product. We first see the taping of the pilot, entirely within the studio context, and then we see the show's premiere, both "live" in the studio and through the mediation of the TV screen as various members of the cast and production team watch at home. It is important to note that when we watch the show "on TV," we also see the commercials (parodies including ads for "Tommy Hilnigger" and "Da Bomb" malt liquor) as well as the credit sequence which frames the show proper with animated versions of Mantan and Sleep 'n Eat, further caricatures of the already exaggerated features of the minstrel mask. In his audio commentary for the DVD, Lee notes that he "felt it was very important to include the audience; because the audience is America, the America that is watching this show, the America that is embracing this show." But of course the live studio audience's relation to "America" is more complicated than that: the studio audience does not merely represent the home audience (and "America"); it models how to *be* an audience, how to feel about the show. The audience imitates the studio audience, and so, when the studio audience wears blackface, it is instituting a double mimicry: the television audience must mimic the members of the studio audience (who cue our laughter and other reactions), and that studio audience also okays (makes acceptable) the mimicry of "blackness" via blackface. The studio audience is hardly originary, however. The film emphasizes the already "automatic" and "produced" nature of its response by focusing on the applause signs in the studio. Together the Negro collectibles and the studio audience represent the full cycle of mechanical gesture and automated response. The studio audience stands in for the home audience but also for the missing liveness of the show; the audience's responses make those at home less spontaneous and thus more imitative and automatic.

But what does this culturally specific iteration of the troubled boundary between animate and inanimate (the condition of being "life-like") say about Delacroix—positioned, as he is, between these two audiences, between his two collections? The Negro collectibles resemble both performer and audience; they dance, swallow coins, and so on, on the one hand, and they (appear to) watch, on the other. In this sense they seem to give tangible form to W. E. B. Du Bois's notion of "double consciousness."[13] As a collection, they increasingly surround Delacroix, encircling him until he is one of them. (In his final breakdown scene, he wears a blackface mask.) The scenes featuring the collectibles are increasingly expressionistic; they come alive as Delacroix loses his grip on reality. (When the bank comes to life a second time, there is no ambiguity: the cast iron figure is replaced by a 3D animation.) His affinity with the bank is established early on, but the line between collector and collected—possessor and possessed—is fully crossed by the end. In his essay on collecting, Walter Benjamin notes the collector's "very mysterious relationship to ownership."[14] Of course, Benjamin is envisioning a willing collector, a loving collector, and his musings in "Unpacking My Library" would seem to have little to do either with Delacroix (a reluctant collector) or with Negro collectibles (whether collected for their original purpose or as "racist kitsch"). But Benjamin insists, if playfully, on the dialectic of freedom and imprisonment inherent in the act of collecting: "The most profound enchantment for the collector is the locking of individual items within a magic circle in which they are fixed as the final thrill, the thrill of acquisition, passes over them."[15] Yet locking up the collected items (books in Benjamin's case), amounts to freeing them. Even slavery comes up, as he imagines the collector "rescuing" a book from the marketplace, "giv[ing] it its freedom, the way the prince bought a beautiful slave girl in *The Arabian Nights*. To a book collector, you see, the true freedom of all books lies somewhere on his shelves."[16] Benjamin, too, animates his inanimate objects—and in the process, (in)animates himself. The objects don't "come alive" in the collector; he "lives in them." If even Benjamin's happy collector disappears, at the end of the essay, inside the "dwelling" he has built "with books as building stones,"[17] whither Delacroix, a man surrounded by objects that, in a sense, African Americans have been forced to live with/in? Benjamin's collector "studies and loves" his objects not for their usefulness but "as the scene, the stage, of their fate."[18] Delacroix has both locked his collection up (in his office) and set it free (by bringing it to life in the minstrel show). In the end, however, his office becomes the stage of his fate just as the minstrel stage becomes Man Ray's "fate."

While the film suggests that Delacroix gets what he deserves, his fate links him to the performers Man Ray and Womack, who are portrayed much more sympathetically. As they are locked onstage—even after he leaves the show, Man Ray is forced to "dance" as the Mau Maus shoot him—Delacroix is trapped in his office, seemingly held captive by his collection. As he smashes the objects just before he is killed, he shouts, "Leave me alone!" When Sloan shoots him, he too becomes a broken figure. Many have criticized the film's portrayal of Delacroix, and the violent ending is typically understood as the film "crumbling into melodrama" under its own weight.[19] But for Delacroix, Womack, and Man Ray, the stage has been set by blackface minstrelsy and other appropriations and commodifications of blackness. When they take their (literal or metaphoric) places on that stage, it becomes the stage of their fate.

Facing the Crowd: Animating the Audience

I want to return for a moment to that first audience: the one that watched the taping of the pilot for *The New Millennium Minstrel Show.* These audience members are unsure how to react until they see others laughing. In particular, we get shots of white audience members looking around at black audience members, searching, it seems, for permission to laugh at racist humor. They get it, and soon everyone is laughing. This move from displeasure (or at least discomfort) to pleasurable release is reiterated backstage. During a later performance (the first before the blackfaced audience), Delacroix breaks into uproarious laughter, screaming, both hands to his chest, as Dunwitty congratulates him. "You couldn't hold out any more, could ya," he says as they exchange a high five. Only moments later we cut to the disgusted, disapproving expressions of the Mau Maus as they watch the show on television. When one of them starts laughing, the group turns on him; he shrugs his shoulders: "That shit's funny to me." Interestingly, the bit they're laughing at features Sleep 'n Eat singing a country-style song with the refrain "You ain't never seen no nigger playing a funky fiddle." According to Lee's commentary, this was entirely created by the performer, Tommy Davidson. He notes that the act is from Davidson's stand-up routine and claims that this moment was "impromptu . . . Tommy just broke out."

The spontaneity of the laughter seems to be tied here to the spontaneity of the performance itself. The complexity of the relation between black performance, creativity, and improvisation on the one hand and the stereotyped, racist frame of minstrelsy on the other is borne out here in a way that is richer than the film is sometimes given credit for. But if laughter is aligned with spontaneity, it is also associated with a troubling automatism. The shot of the white audience member looking for cues from the black audience members reiterates, on a racial level, the function of the applause sign (for the studio audience) and the function of the studio audience itself (for the home audience). These moments seem to suggest that laughter is the "natural" response to the material, but "natural" is not an undifferentiated term here. Do the white audience members laugh because that's what they would do if they weren't inhibited by social acceptability (which might function only in the presence of nonwhites)? Do the African American characters laugh "despite themselves"—that is, even though they may be disgusted by, and suffer because of, the "misrepresentation" performed by minstrelsy? The productive tension between laughter as natural or spontaneous and as an automatic response culminates in Delacroix's final lines of narration. As he lies bleeding to death, his blacked-up face is streaked with tears. His voice-over, recounting his thoughts "as the very life oozed out of [him]," reminds us that he has been only "life-*like*" the whole time: his narration is posthumous.[20] After a long montage sequence covering both blackface and stereotyped black performers in Hollywood films and animation, we cut to Delacroix's dead body, followed by the film's final images: a series of close-ups of Man Ray (as Mantan) as he performs in blackface, smiling the wide, iconic minstrel smile. "As my father always told me, always keep 'em laughing," Delacroix narrates as we linger on that minstrel face that keeps performing for us, and then, on cue, Delacroix laughs—a polite, unconvincing laugh that gradually becomes louder, harder, until it reaches that point where it's difficult to distinguish the sound of laughing from that of crying. But he is joined, and soon drowned out, by a laugh track, as Mantan continues to smile in a way that suggests just how painful it can be to *keep* smiling—to keep 'em laughing.

The mixture of laughter and tears, of "real" laughter with canned, evokes the cultural seriousness of humor and the force it can exert. Film and cultural critics often recognize (and decry) the manipulation of "weepies"; as Linda Williams and others have noted, the violence and invasiveness of the sentimental film are denoted in the term "tearjerker."[21] Though not included among Williams's exemplary "body genres" (horror, melodrama, porn), comedies, too, provoke a bodily response: laughter. (They may even provoke tears if we laugh hard enough.) Yet we don't use the term "laughjerker," perhaps only because we perceive laughter as pleasurable, in contrast to crying (though of course that's to mistake a sign of pleasure for the experience of pleasure). But if a film like *Bamboozled* offers comedy that most would prefer *not* to laugh at (at least not in public), then I think it's fair to say that *Bamboozled*, at least in its minstrel show segments, is a laughjerker. Having laughter "jerked" from us may force us to confront our own racism and/or the still pervasive racism of the culture. If you are a victim of these stereotypes, or just one who wants to forget them, then comedy can be every bit as manipulative as a sentimental melodrama. In this sense, when Delacroix can't "hold out" any longer, when he succumbs to laughter, it is a real surrender: to the crowd, to commercial success, to the white power structure, to be sure—but also, crucially, to "the pleasure that the stereotype urges upon us."[22]

The minstrel shows form the center of the film, and while the meticulous, even loving detail with which Lee renders these segments—which function like the "numbers" that interrupt the narrative in a Hollywood musical—may seem perverse, it is crucial to the film's portrayal of (and effect on) the audience. The minstrel show sequences telescope the history of American popular entertainment, a lineage that runs from minstrelsy through the variety stage and the Hollywood musical. These sequences borrow or adapt material from late-nineteenth- and twentieth-century minstrelsy, calling to mind a host of stage, screen, and (in the case of *Amos 'n' Andy*) radio acts linked to both white and black blackface performers. As Arthur Knight has pointed out, *Bamboozled* offers the reverse relation between the musical performances (the "show") and the backstage plot: rather than the success of the show paralleling the success of a romantic couple, here the success of the show tears relationships apart.[23] The way the film frames the minstrel shows—by always presenting them through their performance before a live studio audience—reiterates the way the early Hollywood musicals (almost always "backstage" musicals) used an internal audience to refer to the experience of "live" theater for the film audience. As Rick Altman has shown, the early backstage Hollywood musicals established a pattern in terms of how the musical numbers were shot. These numbers were not yet "integrated" into the narrative. Rather, they were performed onstage and often presented, at least in part, frontally, positioning the movie spectator in an "ideal" third row of a theater audience.[24]

In the backstage musical, then, the numbers are set apart from the rest of the narrative, to some extent because of the demarcated performance space, the mode of address, and the inclusion of an internal audience. Lee takes this a step further, adding a layer of differentiation to the boundary already created by the proscenium stage by filming the minstrel show on 16 mm film, while the rest of the movie is shot on digital video.[25] Thus the minstrel show is also set apart visually from everything else; even the studio audience's reactions are shot on video, creating a markedly different look and feel for the performances. Despite the artifice of the sets and the anachronism of the costuming and comic material, there's something "real" about these scenes. Although the video aesthetic (especially as produced with small, consumer-market mini-DV cameras, as in this film) has become associated with increased "realism"—whether through documentary-style, home video surveillance footage or other spontaneous or hidden camera effects—the cinematography of the minstrel shows offers a different kind of "real." In addition to the saturated colors and theatrical lighting, this "real" has everything to do with embodiment: the dripping sweat on a performer's face, the emcee's spit arcing out toward the audience as he speaks, the thumps and taps of bodies onstage all evoke the sense of presence associated with stage performance. This presence, combined with the spontaneity of the performances within the filmic context, achieves a kind of "liveness" that differentiates itself from the televisual liveness that the film critiques.[26]

The feeling of live performance that the film, like early musicals, tries to re-create extends beyond the attempts to re-create the conditions of stage performance. As noted earlier, traditional musicals—and, more generally, films that contain stage performances—emulate the feeling of live performance in part through direct address. The performance, presented frontally, positions us like a "live" theater audience. By using the (supposedly) bygone, denigrated, disreputable form of blackface minstrelsy, however, *Bamboozled* goes beyond direct address to *activate* the audience to become aware of itself as a group. While the film engages, elsewhere, in various kinds of distancing techniques (for example, jump cuts, overlapping edits, self-referential dialogue), the minstrel show operates somewhat differently. It creates awareness not by disengaging us but by engaging us. By including these minstrel shows, the film provokes an experience that speaks to the fact that the audience is composed of different people with different backgrounds that engender different reactions to this material. It invites a differentiated viewing experience—even as it is enmeshed in a film that denies that there can be such a thing, or that questions the possibility of such a thing in a mass medium.

It may seem banal to say that this film "watches" differently depending on who watches it, and also depending on where and how it is being watched—after all, that's true of all films. But that's not what all films intend. Mainstream films intend, or assume, a common denominator, a generalized reception. (And the differences and hierarchies constructed by that "generalized reception" have of course been widely theorized.) This film not only intends a differentiated experience—and not only provokes it through its racially charged subject matter (as many Spike Lee films do)—but thematizes it as well, in part by reflecting the movie audience's experience through its multiple uses of the internal audience. When I teach this film, I often lament the fact that many of my students will watch it on DVD alone or in small groups. This is not because I feel they are missing the "big screen" experience, but because they are missing the "big group" experience of the movie theater. I first saw *Bamboozled* in a movie theater in Manhattan filled to capacity with a diverse audience. To some extent we exhibited the same behavior as the first studio audience in the film: uneven laughter, heads swiveling, nervous checking around. Having that experience, and seeing it reflected on screen by an audience that would end the film in blackface, gave this viewing a specificity typically associated with live performances; the usually deadened movie audience came alive, if only momentarily. I'm suggesting that the film brings its "ideal audience" to life not by provoking loud, uniform laughter, or even merely through the shock value of blackface, but rather by making the individuals who compose an audience aware of the group and vice versa. The minstrel shows in the film crackle because they look different, because they include great dancing and impromptu humor, to be sure. But they also crackle because they keep the audience off balance, making it unsure how to behave. The discomfort comes, in other words, from not knowing what kind of audience to be. This is the opposite of the progression traced by the film's internal audience, which *finds* its identity by watching the minstrel show and by adopting blackface: the mass-mediated minstrel show addresses its audience as "niggahs," and the audience complies. This is yet another way the film focuses on the audience as a privileged and contested site, a site where the dialectic between pleasure and unpleasure, between "oppositional spectatorship" and conformity plays out.[27] In so doing, the film takes the audience as its anti-group identity just as Delacroix is its antihero: the audience offers a frightening, mass-mediated spectacle of group identity that hovers over the (inherently unstable and questionable) authenticity of "race" as a group identity.

During the scene in which Honeycutt goes into the studio audience "looking for niggers," Lee's DVD audio commentary is limited to a simple, sarcastic exclamation: "Audience participation!" When the audience "participates" in blackface, it melds the "culture industry" model of consumption and uniformity with a more sinister sense of audience as mob. The entertainment served up on *Mantan* leads directly to Man Ray's murder; in this sense, the convergence of audience and media spectacle is akin to the convergence of the crowd and the law in the lynch mob. The blacked-up crowd threatens to engulf the black performers in *Bamboozled*. As the phenomenon spreads, there is no escape; with the whole world a participatory audience, leaving the stage is impossible. In addition to wearing blackface, the audience participates with the show primarily by interacting with the emcee, Honest Abe Honeycutt, who engages them in call and response in order to warm them up (as most television shows taped before a live audience do) for the main event. As mentioned earlier, Honeycutt's signature "Ooo-weee" shout recalls the Andy Griffith character Lonesome Rhodes in *A Face in the Crowd*. I want to return to that film for a moment to show how it contains an implicit critique of blackface minstrelsy which also informs *Bamboozled.* Both films suggest that minstrelsy is the repressed element in the mixture of authenticity and automatism that constructs the mass audience.

A Face in the Crowd links the poor white southerner Larry "Lonesome" Rhodes to African Americans from its very first scene, alluding to the way race relations informed American popular and mass culture. When Marcia Jeffries (Patricia Neal), producer of a radio show called *A Face in the Crowd,* goes looking for interesting "real" people in an Arkansas jailhouse, she finds Lonesome Rhodes.[28] The African American prisoners in the scene are doubly jailed—segregated from the white prisoners in cells within the cell. When Marcia asks if anyone might sing a song, the sheriff looks to one of the black prisoners, who responds, knowingly, "Just because I got black skin, I ain't no minstrel man."[29] Instead, Rhodes is the "minstrel man" who travels with his "mama guitar." In honor of making a deal with the sheriff in return for performing for the radio show, he sings a rousing rendition of a song called "Free Man in the Morning," stopping to ask another of the black prisoners, "How 'bout you, you got any objection to being a free man in the mornin'?" To which the prisoner replies, his arms poking through the bars, "No, sir." But of course he won't be free, just as he would not be chosen to be a radio personality in Arkansas, as Lonesome Rhodes will be.

As his success and fame grow, overt references to this link disappear, and the only African Americans present on screen are servants. At the end of the film, after Rhodes has suffered a public embarrassment, he sits alone at a dining table that has been set for a banquet. His powerful white guests have all stood him up, as they no longer want to be associated with him. He complains on the phone to his tortured gal Friday, "All of a sudden, I'm poison!" At this point he looks around at the servants (all African American) who stand at attention around his empty table, as if to denote his realization that his new status as social outcast makes him "like them." But this is momentary and apparently untenable. His power is tied to his audience, and so he imagines regaining that power by adopting a new audience. He tries to turn the servants' judgmental stares into the gaze of adoring viewers. "I'll make you love me," he tells them, and then goes to one of the servants and commands, "Say you're gonna love me!" When he doesn't, Rhodes reaches out and manipulates the man's face in an attempt to make him mouth the words, repeating, "Say you're gonna love me!" (Rhodes has foreseen the "problem" posed by dependence on a live audience. He is also the inventor of a machine that emits canned responses, like laugh tracks, and he is holding forth to its approval by the time his producer arrives.) In one sense, then, this moment serves as a commentary on how

Rhodes sees his audience, which is itself just an extension of the way audiences are positioned by commercial media: as something to be collected, owned, told what to say, how to act, and, most important, what to buy. But it also seems to be a sly reference to blackface minstrelsy: working the black servant's face like a puppet master turns out to be much less effective and successful than putting on the burnt cork mask and thus literally putting words in (imaginary) blacks' mouths.

Michael Rogin has discussed the image of the exaggerated minstrel mouth—from the "wide-open, maternal or infantile blackface mouth" of Al Jolson in *The Jazz Singer* to the free-floating signifiers showing up "everywhere," including restaurants featuring "mammy" signs or where customers would enter through the minstrel's mouth.[30] Taking a page from *Dixie* (the 1943 musical about the early minstrel performer Dan Emmett), *Bamboozled* uses the open minstrel mouth as a stage backdrop through which Mantan and Sleep 'n Eat make their entrances. A profoundly ambivalent image—the minstrel mouth may be ever smiling, but an open mouth may also be all-consuming—the mouth as entryway reiterates and racializes the relation between spectator and spectacle, consumer and product. This is a convenient way to figure the tangled web of cultural appropriation and racial transgression in blackface minstrelsy, especially in its origins as a northern white urban form. As many scholars have noted, the "origins" of blackface have long been debated; most contemporary commentators cite the way the black origins of minstrelsy became part of the lore, part of its claim to authenticity. As Eric Lott notes, the various (and likely mythical) origin stories of blackface minstrelsy usually pivot on a similar event or transaction: T. D. Rice sees or hears a black man singing, recognizes his song as something unique, and then appropriates it (steals it or, in some accounts, pays for it), puts on the black mask, and performs. Thus the hugely popular "Jump Jim Crow"—a song and dance routine that spreads "like contagion" across American and Europe—is born.[31] And so the blackface minstrel is first a spectator. When he dons the mask and jumps Jim Crow, it's akin to saying, "I saw a Negro perform this, and now I'm performing it for you." He claims a kind of participant observation. The performer is the primary audience, who then models both an imaginary blackness (marked as "authentic") and ideal audience behavior: participation through racially transgressive imitation. In essence, to cross the boundary between spectator and spectacle is (imaginatively) to cross racial boundaries. If blackface minstrelsy became a commodity in the nineteenth century, what was also commodified was a mode of spectatorship associated with racialized, alienable identities.[32] In the next section I consider the way this transaction has morphed in our current media landscape, reflecting and extending the audience-spectacle dynamic imagined in *Bamboozled.*

"No Deal" Blackface

With its inclusion of Negro collectibles, old photographs, and archival footage, *Bamboozled* attempts to offer a history lesson. But it is equally of its moment, a film about the state of contemporary popular culture including several nods to the nascent (at the time of its release) boom in so-called reality television. *Bamboozled* was released in 2000, the same year that *Big Brother* and *Survivor* premiered in the United States. It updates *Network*'s satirical plot of a television anchor who threatens to commit suicide on TV (and who is eventually shot, live, on the air), by serving up Man Ray's murder via a streaming video on the Internet (taped by the Mau Maus and obligingly picked up for broadcast on TV by CNS). *Bamboozled* gestures toward the intensification of audience participation and the contortions of television programming brought on by technological and economic shifts in the media landscape: the increasing power and reach of the Internet, widespread popular access to video imaging, multiple platforms for distribution, the turn to "reality" genres in television, and the modular, ready-made formats through which they are packaged for a global audience.[33] Part of the power of Lee's film derives, of course, from its own "real" or "documentary" elements. The minstrel shows are not wild exaggerations; they are, in a sense, historical reenactments, backed up by the archival footage (and the racist figurines) collected in and by the film. The seeming exaggerations, the heart of the satire, come from the responses the film imagines to the resurrection of blackface: that contemporary audiences would "buy" something as offensive as blackface is exactly what Delacroix cannot foresee. Likewise, the film's satire seemed, in 2000, more a commentary on Hollywood's treatment of African Americans and a skewering of certain elements of hip hop culture than an accurate predictor of future trends. But the film's prescience—especially in terms of its depiction of the audience—is made clear by current trends in reality television. In particular, if we look at how certain programs envision, address, and include the audience, the blacked-up audience of *Mantan* begins to look less like a metaphor and more like an industry model. *Bamboozled* suggests that contemporary popular culture still thrives on the stereotypes and racial humor of blackface minstrelsy—saying, essentially, that this kind of racism is forgotten but not gone. Looking at current television practices reveals the multiple ways that racialized identities fuse the production of "reality" with the rhetoric of the participatory audience, not quite bringing back the minstrel mask, but diffusing it in a number of surprising iterations.

"Reality television" is a blanket term that serves at once to exaggerate the novelty of the programs marketed under this rubric and to elide the variety of genres contained within it. When scholars take up this term—especially those who wish to link reality television to major social and cultural shifts associated with new media technologies—they typically privilege what is sometimes referred to as the surveillance genre. As a result, *Big Brother* and other programs that follow "real people" in a constructed version of everyday life receive a large share of critical attention.[34] Much less has been said about the game show, despite the fact that so many reality shows, even those pitched primarily as dramas, soap operas, and romances, ultimately function as some form of competition. While reality TV comes in a multitude of forms, many of these—especially those that are marketed globally—are merely variations on this longtime staple of broadcast radio and television. In numerous ways, game shows condense and epitomize the way "reality television" discourse constructs its audience. And so I want to consider how the depiction of the audience that I have traced in *Bamboozled* relates to current television practices by looking at the worldwide hit game show *Deal or No Deal.*

Deal or No Deal was created by Endemol, the Dutch company that attained global success with *Big Brother* and went on to become one of the largest and most successful producers of reality shows or, as the company's marketing materials would have it, "non-scripted program formats." *Deal or No Deal* premiered in the United States in 2005 and by 2009 was appearing, with slight variations, in sixty countries around the world.[35] *Deal or No Deal* is basically a slick twenty-first-century reimagining of *Let's Make a Deal,* which aired in the United States in the 1960s and 1970s, in both primetime and daytime slots. That show, created and hosted by Monty Hall, featured various kinds of small deals made between host and audience ("I'll give $50 to anyone who has a hard-boiled egg"), in addition to the climactic deal in which contestants could keep whatever they'd already won or trade it for a prize hidden behind one of three numbered curtains, the risk being that they could wind up with anything from a new car to a billy goat. Rather than numbered curtains, *Deal or No Deal* offers the contestant twenty-six numbered cases (held by female models), each containing an amount ranging from one penny to $1 million. The contestant chooses one of these cases to keep at the start of the game, and then proceeds to reveal the amounts contained in the remaining cases, in hopes of improving the odds that the initial case contains a high dollar amount, thereby provoking the "banker" to offer greater and greater sums of money for it.

Premiering in 1962, *Let's Make a Deal* arrived after the quiz show scandals of the 1950s. In his history of American quiz shows, Olaf Hoerschelmann notes that *Let's Make a Deal* was a particularly successful and representative example of the way quiz shows were reworked in order to distance them from those scandals. To that end, the program's greatest innovation was in reorienting the relationship between the stage and the audience. While in the earlier shows, the camera focused on the host and contestants onstage, maintaining a sharp division between the audience and the participants, *Let's Make a Deal* made the audience section "the real stage." As Hoerschelmann describes it: "The center of events in the show is the dealing area, which is in the middle of the audience section. The actual stage of the studio is used only for display of larger prizes, which are hidden behind curtains. The camera continuously moves in and out of the audience section, alternately being a part of it and facing it. . . . [T]he camera (sometimes handheld) enters the audience to focus on the host making deals with the audience members."[36] In *Deal or No Deal,* the prominence of the traditional stage is back, along with dramatic lighting, bombastic music, and relatively elaborate sets and other stage business. But the spirit of making the audience section "the real stage" remains. Rather than taking the camera out into the audience, *Deal or No Deal* finds a way to "stage" the audience: by representing the studio (and home) viewers with multiple onstage "audiences," the show incorporates and thematizes the act of watching in various ways as part of the game.

The contestant in *Deal or No Deal* stands onstage with the host, comedian Howie Mandel. Their backs turned to the studio audience, contestant and host face the twenty-six female models who hold the numbered cases, metal briefcases of the sort seen in movies featuring large sums of money being carried through airports. The models, cases positioned beside them, stand on risers, which mimic, to some degree, the raked seats of the theater audience. Another mini-audience stands off to the side of the contestant: three supporter-cheerleaders, typically friends or family. Finally, "the banker" watches all the proceedings from a glass booth above the stage and proposes various deals (money offered to get the contestant to stop playing) by phone in a series of calls to the host. We never hear the banker's voice or see his face; only his silhouette is visible. Through these multiple audiences, the home viewer sees several different models of spectatorship turned into spectacle: the sadistic-voyeuristic gaze of the banker as he dangles money before the contestant; the "chorus" of friends and family offering support and advice, which no doubt echoes what the viewers are urging at home; the traditional theater audience represented by the live studio audience; and finally the simultaneous look and "to-be-looked-at-ness" (to use Laura Mulvey's phrase) of the models,[37] whose bodies function prominently in the show's mise-en-scène. Forming a kind of human game board, the models also act (as we will see shortly) as a kind of mirror. *Deal or No Deal* thus effectively stages (and plays with) the way the audience in reality TV "seems to be everywhere, more visible than ever."[38] Audience participation—especially as a model for identifying and bringing consumers to sponsors—is as old as broadcasting itself. But what Su Holmes has called the "restaging of participation" has crucially to do with staging identity.[39]

First, the contestant's identity is tied to some tangible, recognizable, or easily visualized trait. A contestant might be summed up as anything from "Laker fan" (the cue for basketball and the Los Angeles Lakers to determine the show's theme and set design) to "southern belle" or "single mom." Physical traits, personal struggles, fantasies, and ethnic background all become fair game for the show's narrative arc, theme, and mise-en-scène. Through costuming and other gimmicks, the models reflect the chosen theme or identity trait, becoming a multiplying mirror in which the contestant sees a kind of mass-produced version of himself or herself. In other words, the models do just that: they "model" the contestant's identity and/or desire for the contestant, and in so doing they serve as a model audience, fully identified with and sympathetic to the contestant, cheering him or her on. The simultaneous modeling of contestant and audience is enabled, in part, by the translation of the contestant's identity into scenic display. This ping-ponging—between spectator and spectacle, individual and group, real live bodies and uniform, reproducible images—is central to the show's form and to its mode of address. In other words, it's a key part of the game. I would suggest that the models offer a particularly delirious play on the notion of "convergence"—the merger of viewer and "show" associated with a newly empowered, participatory audience—that is the primary fantasy offered up by "reality television."[40]

Consider both the textual and extratextual function of the models. They figure prominently in the show's on-air program and its many Internet-based extras. Although the models wear identical costumes (usually skimpy dresses) on the show, and come complete with price tags (the dollar amounts contained in the cases), the producers do their best to disavow their objectification. While the contestants call on them by number (the number of the case they hold), the host and the producers refer to them by their names. And their purported humanity is supplemented by NBC's official website for the show, where viewers can learn more about each model and watch them participate as "actresses" in send-ups of current television dramas and comedies (only those aired on NBC, of course). Yet their status as identical objects on display trumps all these efforts. One brief example shows how the models' function melds their status as uniform display and as reflectors of the contestant's identity. In one episode from the prime time show's third season, the producers aim to surprise the contestant by replacing one of the models with the contestant's sister. She is of course dressed identically to the other models. When the contestant repeatedly fails to notice, the host tries to direct her attention by asking, "Does number 21 look like a good case to you?" Despite peering at "number 21" for several seconds, neither the contestant nor her mother in the cheering section recognizes the sibling. Finally the host implores, "Look at the *model* that's holding the case!" Only then does the contestant recognize her sister. The models are just cases after all; their individuality does not figure in the contestant's viewing practices. Instead, the show's collection of "identical" models overwhelms even family relationships.

The models serve as setting, like the kaleidoscopic chorus girls in Busby Berkeley musicals. The coin-wearing dancers in the ironic "We're in the Money" number from the depression-themed *Gold Diggers of 1933* come to mind—only here the imaginary money (the suitcases) the models hold represents real dollars to be won. The big difference, of course, is that the models don't dance or sing; in fact they rarely move, except to open the cases and to enter and exit the stage. In this sense, the presentation of the models collapses the store window display, the theater audience, and, significantly for our purposes, the doll collection. They dress identically, and, like any good collection, are displayed on risers. The show—and the contestant—plays with them. The show does so by dressing them in different doll-like dresses and hairdos—and by removing and replacing them, as in the example just cited. And the contestants often wind up crossing the imaginary boundary separating them from the models, touching the cases (and sometimes the models, as if rubbing a talisman for luck), standing next to them, and so on.[41] The boundary is imaginary because both the contestant and the models are onstage, but these moments look transgressive, and that's the point. By moving back and forth between the contestant's position (near the podium and the host) and the models' risers which form the backdrop for the set, the contestant stages the permeability of the boundary between spectator and spectacle, and between audience and participant. Together the identity-based themes, the multiple representations of the audience, and the regular crossings that stage the permeability of an already false boundary combine to create a dynamic that becomes particularly revealing when race or ethnicity is foregrounded.

The similarities between this dynamic and the one imagined in *Bamboozled* become clearer when the already exaggerated, even stereotypical alignment of the contestant with a recognizable trait becomes racialized. Such was the case with season two contestant Antaie Greer, an African American woman from Tennessee. Greer's story, told at the beginning of the show, aligns her squarely with the game show version of extreme financial need and deprivation: she states that she wants to win enough money to purchase power locks and windows for her car. She sets the show's theme with her mantra "It's all about the 'fro," referring to her hair, to which she points repeatedly as a good luck charm as the game progresses. Not missing the opportunity, the producers "surprise" the viewers by coming back from commercial to reveal an empty set—that is, the models have disappeared. When they return, striding back on set in time with the music, they are all wearing pink " 'fro" wigs—all but one, an African American model, Haylee Marie Norman, who sports her own "real" Afro (Figure 7.4). The now sharp distinction between her and the pink-haired models serves as both a distraction and a focal point for the rest of the show, as she is featured in a number of close-ups. Much rubbing and touching of hair ensues, as Antaie, to an even greater extent than other contestants, crosses the imaginary onstage boundary and joins the models several times, getting very close to them as she chooses her cases (Figure 7.5). She admires and rubs their hair, and the models return the favor. Her continued success inspires her to lead the studio audience in a rhythmic chant of "It's all about the 'fro," and when she gets a $402,000 offer from the banker (which she accepts), he declares that he has been "defeated by a hairdo." Cut to the shadowy figure in the booth, wearing his own pink wig.

The choice of pink is strategic, as it seems to save the "all-in-good-fun" symbolic sympathy with Greer from any whiff of racial stereotyping or minstrel-like mimicry. It is hard to imagine the models wearing more "realistic" Afro wigs. Haylee Marie Norman, meanwhile, excessively signifies for the remainder of the episode; not only does the camera find her more often than usual, but also Greer never chooses her case, so as the number of pink-haired models dwindles over the course of the game, Norman's presence takes on greater prominence. As Greer makes her fateful choices, pacing about the stage, swooning, dropping to her knees more than once as the pressure builds, the producers cut to Norman for reaction shots. And when Greer eventually says, "Deal," accept-

Figure 7.4. *Deal or No Deal*'s models display their solidarity with the contestant.

Figure 7.5. Contestant Antaie Greer becomes part of the display. From *Deal or No Deal.*

ing the offer of $402,000, she runs up and hugs Norman, who is one of only two models left onstage at that point. When the remaining models reveal the amounts in their cases at the end of the show, as they always do, it turns out that Norman's case carries the $750,000 prize, the largest amount left; this is greeted as amazing by the host, and Greer and Norman hug again. Thus, while the pink wigs (and matching pink frocks) make this game of dress-up only a soft version of racial disguise, referring to it with an obviously silly effort, the uniformity of the models actually ends up throwing racial identity, and especially a black identity tied to the performance of authenticity, into high relief.

As Endemol bills it, the show is "part game show, part psychological thriller";[42] the thrill comes from watching as the contestants' "psychology" drives them from hope to greed and back again, as the banker's offers punctuate the game with appropriate amounts of psychological torture. The scene tells us that the contestant controls her own destiny (a big red button sits on the podium, and the contestant can stop the game by taking one of the "deals" offered by the banker), even as we watch her being tantalized with offers of money that, we are meant to understand, she would never see in her lifetime. Once this dynamic is established, the decor, which is really the multiplied audience—which is itself really an externalization of her own identity—threatens to overwhelm her. Over the course of Greer's episode, she falls to the ground more than once. If we think of the models, again, as a doll collection, we can see this as a "happy" version of the collection that overwhelms Delacroix in *Bamboozled.* Engulfed by the stereotypes that, multiplied and proliferated, become his audience, Delacroix goes crazy. Greer merely goes home rich, but first she must give way to the madness of being represented and reproduced by and as the audience. In her post-win interview Greer sums up: "I came from nothing; I had nothing. Now my life can change; it can be better. I don't have enough money to pay my rent; I don't have enough money to eat. And now for me to have this opportunity—it's just overwhelming, it's overwhelming. . . . When the models came out in their pink dresses and pink 'fros, that was absolutely great. The crowd was up, cheering, 'It's all about the 'fro'—it was just crazy. It was just *about the 'fro.*"[43]

The Antaie Greer episode aired in 2007; that same year the *Deal or No Deal* models tried on other identities, taking this talent offstage and into the streets for a special *Entertainment Tonight* "investigation." Two of the models (Brooke and Leyla) donned "fat suits" and took to the streets to "see how it feels to live like 66 percent of America, overweight and often mocked by strangers."[44] Taking on an "extreme" disguise, the models participated in a mini–"reality show" of their own, while also managing to represent "66 percent of America," many of them likely viewers of *Deal or No Deal.* If it wasn't entirely clear that identity was on the trading floor in *Deal or No Deal,* NBC's short-lived game show *Identity* made the (just barely) latent manifest. Premiering in 2006, *Identity* offered a guessing game akin to classic television game shows such as *What's My Line?* and *I've Got a Secret.* The network describes the game as follows: "In this intense game of impulse and reasoning, each new contestant faces 12 new strangers and a list of 12 new identities. The game unfolds as the contestant picks an identity—ranging anywhere from a profession to a shoe size—and tries to match it with one of the 12 strangers. The amount of money the contestant accumulates increases with each correctly identified stranger. If all 12 are matched up correctly, the player is rewarded with the top prize of $500,000."[45]

The show's set design owes much to that of *Deal or No Deal:* here, the various strangers/identities stand on a series of raised platforms dressed either to or against "type"—so, for example, the identity of a tall blonde woman in a bikini may turn out to be "I.Q. of 200." This show throws out the numbered suitcases but keeps the models; only here, difference is privileged over uniformity. While the models on *Deal or No Deal* "represent" the contestant by donning accessories such as pink Afro wigs, these twelve strangers are "representative." They model differences in identity, but they also model difference within identity, pointing up the assumptions we make about people on the basis of external characteristics and, in the best-case scenario, reflecting and defying audience expectations. But it doesn't always turn out that way. Some people play to type—otherwise it wouldn't work as a game—and the process of defying types in some ways reinforces them. Like a number of shows that take the subtext of identity and difference running through many "reality" programs and make it the main focus, *Identity* did not become a big hit. Its run was short-lived, and it soon went "on hiatus."[46] But the occasional focus on these issues—and the occasional eruption, in televisual "reality," of race (and to a lesser degree sexuality) into heated, even violent displays—reveals the way race difference, and specifically the specter of race-based authenticity and conflict, ultimately underpins the role that consumable identities play in the efforts of these programs to construct, figure, and address the audience.

Reality TV breaks into "real" reality when race-related conflicts arise—typically either overtly contrived or subtly provoked by the shows' producers. Two examples that made off-the-entertainment-page headlines: the *Survivor* "experiment" in which the producers divided "tribes" by ethnic group, and the trials and tribulations of reality television star Jade Goody. In the 2006 iteration of the former, *Survivor: Cook Islands,* the racial angle sparked a fair amount of controversy. In the latter example, Goody, who rose to fame as a contestant on the UK version of *Big Brother* (2002), fell out of favor when, in 2007, she hurled racially charged insults at Bollywood actress Shilpa Shetty, a fellow contestant on *Celebrity Big Brother,* sought redemption by appearing on *Bigg Boss* (the Indian version of *Big Brother*) in 2008, and generally parlayed her reality television fame into a career. Her battle with cancer was also televised, and her death was covered by major news organizations.[47] In a way, a show like the Antaie Greer "It's all about the 'fro" episode of *Deal or No Deal* underwrites the rest. It represents an outburst of the racialized logic that underpins the play with exchangeable identities, fusing it with "real" emotion by way of an authenticity equated, in stereotypical fashion, with "real" blackness. The seeming paradox between an identity that is eminently alienable and performative and one that guarantees authenticity is the ultimate "reality television" fantasy. It also happens to be the model commodified by blackface minstrelsy.

Deal or No Deal emphasizes the personal stories of the contestants, typically positioning them in terms of financial hardship, brave struggle, unexpected calamity, or heroic actions. In this way the show relies heavily on the rhetoric of the "American Dream." While the "deal" of the title refers to the way the game plays with financial dealings (offers, negotiations, the control of the market by a shadowy "banker" figure), it also suggests echoes with the New Deal of the Roosevelt era. Although the individual is here reliant on a game of chance rather than government programs, the sense that a contestant—a deserving but perhaps struggling citizen up against unseen economic forces—can change his or her life and start anew is emphasized in every episode, as part of a narrative that both establishes why the contestant deserves the money and why the risk she or he takes with each utterance of "no deal" is especially high.[48] The emphasis on coincidence is also typical of the show, which adds drama to the way luck is transformed into fate, especially when tied to personal narratives, family history, and the rags-to-riches formula.

Tracing the permutations of blackface performance in Hollywood films from the 1930s and 1940s, Michael Rogin describes how "New Deal blackface" offered "regression as national integration."[49] Whereas *The Jazz Singer* had proffered blackface as an assimilation tool for immigrants, Rogin argues, depression-era blackface musicals depicted the ability to disguise one's identity (via blackface) as part of the narrative of self-making that was inextricably linked to an American identity envisioned as a communal white identity.[50] At the beginning of a new century, amid the financial collapse that some have called "the Great Recession,"[51] we might think of the contemporary model as "No Deal blackface." In *Deal or No Deal*, the faint echoes of the New Deal give way to the repeated refrain "No deal," for if a "deal" is made, after all, the game ends. In the audience dynamic imagined by *Bamboozled* and perhaps realized in reality television, however, the "deal" itself is no simple transaction. In place of a simplified, nostalgic patriotism tied to blackface and entertainment, multiple forms of identity exchange are imagined through the negotiations between, and mergers of, audience and spectacle. What is on display here is the endless exchange itself, the ecstatic spectacle of the individual dissolving into the mass. As in Honeycutt's call and response to the blacked-up audience of *Mantan's New Millennium Minstrel Show*, this is mass culture as communion. *Bamboozled* poses the problem of individual versus group or racial identity via multiple internal audiences, tying the collector and his collection to the performer-audience relation in mass culture. *Deal or No Deal* offers this very "problem" as vertiginous spectacle.

In the era of "No Deal blackface," I would suggest, various kinds of soft racial disguise compete with other bartered identities and traded "realities," replacing narratives of upward mobility with a kind of endless back-and-forth that reproduces appropriation as participation. In this context, race difference is still the gold standard: the racialized performance of identity is simultaneously "no big deal" and the heart of the deal. What is really at stake in the game is the backing that promises something essential. When actual racial disguise and/or racial conflicts appear, they fulfill the promise of the ultimate deal: the merger of authenticity and iterability so important to the audience-centered rhetoric of reality television. The performers and audiences in *Bamboozled* are caught between mimicry and hallucination, the blackface mask disguising mechanistic, automatic responses as spontaneous and "live." Even in the contemporary televisual model, an imagined blackness can still make up for the lost liveness that television strives for—and that "reality television" attempts to reanimate.

NOTES

I thank Stephen Johnson for organizing the Burnt Cork symposium and for inviting me to contribute to this volume. He has been inspiring throughout. Thanks also to my fellow participants in the Burnt Cork symposium; their comments have helped to shape this essay. Thanks also to Marlene Goldman and to the participants in the Altered States of Mind symposium, held at the University of Toronto in 2008, at which I presented an early version of this piece.

1. The film is generally hailed as a deeply collaborative effort between Schulberg and Kazan, who also collaborated on *On the Waterfront* (1954).

2. I will have more to say about resonances with *A Face in the Crowd* later in this essay.

3. Tavia Nyong'o, "Racial Kitsch and Black Performance," *Yale Journal of Criticism* 15, no. 2 (2002): 383.

4. For an account of the complexities of the West Indian immigrant playing the "coon," see Louis Chude-Sokei, *The Last "Darky": Bert Williams, Black-on-Black Minstrelsy, and the African Diaspora* (Durham: Duke University Press, 2005).

5. Ibid., 25. Chude-Sokei emphasizes the plural nature of black blackface, arguing against the tendency to collapse the multiple forms of black blackface into the singular, shameful image of the blackface minstrel. He discusses the way the minstrel mask worked as cover for the "radical formal departures" (32) from traditional minstrelsy and opened up a space for multiple layers of irony and self-consciousness in the performances of Williams and Walker.

6. Audio commentary, *Bamboozled,* DVD, directed by Spike Lee (2000; New Line Home Entertainment, 2001). All quotations from the film, including the audio commentary, are from this source.

7. The two shows most associated with beginning the trend toward the dominance of "unscripted" programming on television are *Survivor* (CBS, Mark Burnett Productions) and *Big Brother* (CBS, Endemol), both of which premiered on U.S. television in 2000 after having already had successful runs in the UK and Europe.

8. On this industry term that refers both to the melding of multiple media formats and outlets and to the consequent blurring of the boundaries between producers and consumers, see Henry Jenkins, *Convergence Culture: Where Old and New Media Collide* (New York: New York University Press, 2006).

9. Bill Brown traces the history of these cast iron banks in "Reification, Reanimation, and the American Uncanny," *Critical Inquiry* 32, no. 2 (Spring 2006): 175–207. He notes that "the Jolly Nigger bank was understood as the materialization of an actual practice" (189) and mentions that a human version of the bank makes an appearance in Melville's *Confidence Man.* This practice holds pride of place in the history and mythology of blackface minstrelsy as well. Eric Lott recounts how this figure of the black man opening his mouth to receive pennies makes its way into one of the oft-repeated origin stories of blackface minstrelsy, with an account of T. D. Rice's first blackface performance that involves a mythical meeting between Rice and a black man named Cuff, who is described, in an 1867 article in the *Atlantic Monthly,* as a free laborer in the North "who won a precarious subsistence by letting his open mouth as a mark for boys to pitch pennies into." Robert P. Nevin, "Stephen C. Foster and Negro Minstrelsy," *Atlantic Monthly* 121 (1867): 609–10, cited in Eric Lott, *Love and Theft: Blackface and the American Working Class* (New York: Oxford University Press, 1993), 18.

10. The "Ooo-wee" alludes to Andy Griffith's character (Lonesome Rhodes) in *A Face in the Crowd;* it is his signature "country boy" shout.

11. Brown, "Reification," 199.

12. There is a great deal of critical work on the importance of the rhetoric of liveness to televisual discourse, and on the connections between the "live" and the "real" in television. See, for example, Jane Feuer, "The Concept of Live Television: Ontology as Ideology," in *Regarding Television,* ed. E. Ann Kaplan (Frederick, Md.: University Publications of America, 1983), 12–22; Stephen Heath and Gillian Skirrow, "Television: A World in Action," *Screen* 18, no. 2 (Summer 1977): 7–60; Mary Ann Doane, "Information, Crisis, Catastrophe," in *The Historical Film: History and Memory in Media,* ed. Marcia Landy (New Brunswick: Rutgers University Press, 2001): 269–85; and Mark Williams, "History in a Flash: Notes on the Myth of TV 'Liveness,'" in *Collecting Visible Evidence,* ed. Jane M. Gaines and Michael Renov, Visible Evidence Series, vol. 6 (Minneapolis: University of Minnesota Press, 1999), 292–312.

13. W. E. B. Du Bois, *The Souls of Black Folk* (Chicago: A. C. McClurg & Co., 1903).

14. Walter Benjamin, "Unpacking My Library," in *Illuminations,* ed. Hannah Arendt, trans. Harry Zohn (New York: Schocken Books, 1969), 60.

15. Ibid.

16. Ibid., 64.

17. Ibid., 67.

18. Ibid., 60.

19. Stephen Holden, "Trying on Blackface in a Flirtation with Fire," *New York Times,* October 6, 2000. Responses to the violent ending seem similar across the board. For a variety of scholarly reactions to *Bamboozled,* including reviews and a roundtable discussion, see *Cineaste* 26, no. 2 (March 2001).

20. Lee notes the parallel with *Sunset Boulevard* here. See Gary Crowdus and Dan Georgakas, "Thinking about the Power of Images: An Interview with Spike Lee," *Cineaste* 26, no. 2 (Spring 2001): 4.

21. See Linda Williams, "Film Bodies: Gender, Genre, and Excess," *Film Quarterly* 44, no. 4 (Summer 1991): 2–3.

22. Nyong'o, "Racial Kitsch and Black Performance," 371. Arthur Knight notes the way this final moment echoes the end of *Sullivan's Travels,* when the director affirms the importance of making people laugh, of making them forget their troubles, in his words, accompanied by a montage of audience members (all white) laughing. See Arthur Knight, *Disintegrating the Musical: Black Performance and the American Musical* (Durham: Duke University Press, 2002), 261. I would add another resonance, with a film that offers a more ominous portrait of mass culture: King Vidor's *The Crowd.* That film ends with a famous overhead shot of its titular subject, envisioned as a theater audience, rocking back and forth with laughter. The anonymity and sameness of the audience is offered as both symptom of and cure for the anonymity and sameness of the modern condition.

23. Although, as Michael Rogin argues, this reverse trajectory is also part of the twinned legacies of *The Jazz Singer,* which, he argues, spawned both the musical and the racial problem film. He also notes that later musicals that use blackface (*Holiday Inn,* for example) reverse the usual parallel between show and romance, as the "fakeness" of the "show" becomes tied to the inauthenticity and deceit that threaten the relationship. See Michael Rogin, *Blackface, White Noise: Jewish Immigrants in the Hollywood Melting Pot* (Berkeley: University of California Press, 1996), 159–208.

24. Rick Altman, *The Film Musical* (Bloomington: Indiana University Press, 1988), 200–250. Altman traces the typical progression of such a scene: early shots would establish the stage and the audience, including audience reaction; then as the scene progressed, frontal

shots of the performers onstage would cease to include the internal audience; and finally, close-ups and shots of the performers from multiple angles and positions would follow. In this way, the audience within the film suggests the "live theater" experience, cues us or acts as our proxy, and then we take the place of that internal audience.

25. See his audio commentary on the DVD of *Bamboozled.*

26. It is arguably impossible, even hypocritical, for the film to position itself this way, as it is part of the mass media. But it does gesture toward self-critique when Lee is mentioned by name by Dunwitty, when the performers' own work is referred to, and possibly in the TV commercials, which call to mind Lee's own work starring in and directing commercials. On the complicity and possible critiques of Lee's own previous work, see Knight, *Disintegrating the Musical,* 245–46. But the tension in trying to make a film that critiques mass culture is revealed by Lee's audio commentary, in which he supplements the "realness" and spontaneity of the minstrel show performances not only by noting their improvisatory nature but also by authenticating the "real" emotions of the performers as they blacked up. As one such scene shows Womack crying, Lee adds, "Those are real tears right here."

27. For influential takes on "oppositional spectatorship," see Manthia Diawara, "Black Spectatorship: Problems of Identification and Resistance," in *Black American Cinema,* ed. Manthia Diawara, AFI Film Readers (New York: Routledge, 1993) 211–20; and bell hooks, "The Oppositional Gaze," ibid., 288–302.

28. Her radio show is based on *Vox Pop,* a popular radio show that originated on KTRH in Houston in 1932 before moving to the NBC radio network from 1936 to 1948. The show featured man-on-the-street interviews, which were conducted by host Parks Johnson. For a discussion of how this program contributed to the way radio and later television would construct audience participation, see Olaf Hoerschelmann, *Rules of the Game* (Albany: SUNY Press, 2006), 43–50.

29. *A Face in the Crowd,* DVD, directed by Elia Kazan (1957; Warner Home Video, 2005). All quotations from the film are from this source.

30. Rogin, *Blackface, White Noise,* 176–77.

31. Lott, *Love and Theft,* 56–57.

32. For blackface minstrelsy as a nineteenth-century commodity, see William Mahar, *Behind the Burnt Cork Mask: Early Blackface Minstrelsy and Antebellum American Popular Culture* (Urbana: University of Illinois Press, 1999).

33. For discussions of the changing business and audience models in television, see Ted Madger, "The End of TV 101: Reality Programs, Formats, and the New Business of Television," in *Reality TV: Remaking Television Culture,* ed. Susan Murray and Laurie Ouellette (New York: New York University Press, 2004), 137–56; and Jenkins, *Convergence Culture.*

34. See, for example, Mark Andrejevic, *Reality TV: The Work of Being Watched,* Critical Media Studies (Lanham, Md.: Rowman and Littelfield, 2003).

35. According to Endemol's corporate website; see "Our Shows: Deal or No Deal," www.endemol.com/what/deal-or-no-deal.html. The list of programs produced by Endemol includes some of the most successful reality and game shows, including *Big Brother, Deal or No Deal, Fear Factor,* and *Extreme Makeover,* among others.

36. Hoerschelmann, *Rules of the Game,* 105.

37. Laura Mulvey, "Visual Pleasure and the Narrative Cinema," *Screen* 16, no. 3 (1975): 6–18.

38. Su Holmes, "'The viewers have . . . taken over the airwaves?' Participation, Reality TV, and Approaching the Audience-in-the-Text," *Screen* 49, no. 1 (Spring 2008): 14.

39. Ibid., 15.

40. For a more positive take on the newly "empowered" participatory audience, see Jenkins, *Convergence Culture.*

41. It's worth noting that in some versions of the show in other countries, and in the daytime version in the United States, the models are replaced by audience members; one contestant is chosen from among them to play, and the rest stay on to hold the cases.

42. "Our Shows: Deal or No Deal."

43. This interview can be viewed on the show's official website, www.nbc.com/Deal_or_No_Deal/video/clips/antaie-greer/79331/.

44. "ET's 'Deal or No Deal' Fat Suit Investigation," *ETOnline,* November 7, 2007, www.etonline.com/news/2007/11/55484/.

45. "Identity Game Show: About," www.nbc.com/Identity/about.shtml.

46. In 2009 the NBC website listed the show as "returning soon," but there were no specific dates for its return. By 2011, the show no longer had a functioning webpage on NBC's site.

47. Henry Jenkins provides a useful compendium of reaction to *Survivor*'s "race wars" on his blog, www.henryjenkins.org/2006/08/survivor_the_race_wars.html. For Jade Goody, see http://en.wikipedia.org/ wiki/Jade_Goody#2007: _Celebrity_Big_Brother_5_; and Sarah Lyall, "Jade Goody: British Reality Television Star, Dies at 27," *New York Times,* March 27, 2009.

48. The resonance with the Great Depression and the New Deal became even clearer in the economic climate of 2008–9, when subprime mortgages, shady financiers, toxic assets, and failing banks dominated the headlines. In one episode that became exemplary (the show's host, Howie Mandel, refers to this particular episode repeatedly in interviews and publicity materials), a contestant told the story of his father, who had emigrated to the United States from Korea carrying "a bag with $750 in it." It was revealed, after the contestant had won a large sum of money, that the case he had initially chosen (which is always revealed at the end to demonstrate whether the contestant has "made a good deal") contained $750. This spurred Mandel to give the case to the contestant's father, who was sitting in the audience, and to declare that this was an example of the "circle of life." I saw this episode when it first aired, and my description relies partly on my own memory and on Mandel's recounting of it on the *Deal or No Deal* website; see "Deal or No Deal Game Show: Host Howie Mandel Profile and Bio," www.nbc.com/Deal_or_No_Deal/howie/.

49. Rogin, *Blackface, White Noise,* 175.

50. Ibid., 159–208.

51. The *New York Times* charted the increased use of "great recession" to describe the economy in one of its online blogs. See "Great Recession: A Brief Etymology," *New York Times,* March 11, 2009, http://economix.blogs.nytimes.com/2009/03/11/great-recession-a-brief-etymology/.

8

American Ghetto Parties and Ghanaian Concert Parties

A Transnational Perspective on Blackface

CATHERINE M. COLE

Ralph Ellison identified the minstrel mask as "an inseparable part of the national iconography," and he is certainly not alone in seeing minstrelsy as a quintessentially American form.[1] How deeply embedded blackface is in our national psyche is perhaps nowhere more evident than the transformation of Jim Crow from a fictional nineteenth-century stage character to the rubric for legislation that enforced racial segregation in schools, public places, and public transportation for eighty-nine years. No other single performance tradition in U.S. history has had the same scope, popularity, volatility, and problematic endurance. The genre's characteristic blackened face makeup, whitened lips, exaggerated gestures, malapropisms, derogatory accents, and cartoonish dress have morphed and been transformed from the earliest manifestations of blackface in places like the Catherine Market in the Seventh Ward of New York City in 1820 to more recent iterations such as Spike Lee's film *Bamboozled* in 2000 or indeed the "Compton Cookout" party staged by fraternity boys at the University of California, San Diego, in 2010—a subject to which I shall return.

Minstrelsy's historiography has likewise morphed from the breathy fetishism and nostalgia of collectors and aficionados and the pained ambivalence of writers such as Paul Laurence Dunbar and W. E. B. Du Bois in the early twentieth century to the ethical criticism of writers such as Ralph Ellison and Robert Toll, who read minstrelsy as both reflective and constitutive of the material realities of slavery and racial segregation. More recent scholarship by Eric Lott, W. T. Lhamon Jr., and Saidiya V. Hartman, among others, has attempted to move beyond the extremes of uncritical celebration and moral condemnation to analyze precisely *how* blackface operated, what cultural and political work it did, and how it worked on both its producers and its consumers during very particular moments of our national history.[2] Yet for all the richness of this historiography, blackface scholarship to date has tended to be nationalistically myopic. How would our appraisal of blackface change if we were to take account of its rather astonishing transnational reach?

The map of minstrelsy's global circulation in the nineteenth, twentieth, and twenty-first centuries includes such disparate locations as Australia, Brazil, Britain, Colombia, Cuba, colonial Ghana (Gold Coast), Jamaica, Puerto Rico, South Africa, and Trinidad.[3] In South Africa, blackface has deep historic roots dating back over 150 years. Blackface in South Africa has for over a century been commonly performed among the Cape Coloreds, a Creole population that includes Dutch, Indonesian, Malaysian, Bantu, and Khoisan ancestry, who have been performing the annual "Coon Carnival" or "Kaapse Klopse" ever since the arrival of the traveling Christy's Minstrels on South Africa's shores in 1862. Blackface was also adopted among the black Zulu population in South Africa, and one can see vestiges of blackface in the dance and musical genre known as *isicathamiya,* a form made famous in the choreographed line dancing, hand gestures, and a cappella harmonies performed by the Afropop troupe Ladysmith Black Mambazo.[4] An even earlier manifestation of blackface outside American soil took place in Cuba in the form of *negritos,* performers who appeared as early as 1812, concurrent with the earliest history of American minstrelsy.[5]

These global examples of blackface share one common denominator: colonization. But just how common is this denominator? Spanish colonization of Cuba is quite different from Dutch and British colonization of South Africa, and American (and to some extent Cuban) colonization of Puerto Rico is not to be confused with British colonization of the Gold Coast. Could a transnational appraisal of blackface lead us to conclude that blackface, rather than being a quintessentially American form, is rather a quintessentially colonial one? And what would be the implications of such a claim? Louis Chude-Sokei has taken us the furthest in thinking of blackface as a transnational sign, a mask that even within America has had a radical transnational polyvalence when one considers the history of Bert Williams, one of the most famous black performers of late-nineteenth- and early-twentieth-century America. Williams was not actually African American but rather a West Indian immigrant from the Bahamas. "For the foremost 'exponent' of the 'darky' to not be African American, well, that was no doubt a fascinating political and cultural scenario," observes Chude-Sokei, "particularly since it was through his double black mask that a revived African American dialect poetics was being proffered."[6] Williams's polyphony of masking through burnt cork, his mask behind the mask behind the mask, and his identity as a West Indian minority within the African American minority of the Harlem Renaissance are vividly depicted by Chude-Sokei, who works against a long historiography that would flatten and erase Williams's Caribbean difference. Chude-Sokei's book *The Last "Darky"* also contains a chapter titled "The Global Economy of Minstrelsy" which refers to blackface in Ghana, Jamaica, Trinidad, and South Africa, thereby gesturing toward an interpretation that could encompass the polyphonic dimensions of blackface when viewed outside of America's privileged racial binary of black and white. Chude-Sokei concludes, "Minstrelsy, then, especially when separated from the bichromatic cultural politics of the United States, registers on multiple levels within a polyglot community still under formal colonial control."[7] The colonial experience is certainly central to any consideration of the global economy of blackface, as the form both traveled and found fertile soil throughout the circuits of empire.

In my book *Ghana's Concert Party Theatre* I analyzed one instance of this global economy of blackface: the appearance of the concert party theatrical form in colonial Ghana in the early twentieth century, a popular theater genre that included appropriations of American sources such as Al Jolson films and a radical reinterpretation of foreign signs within local Akan-dominated discourses that were often far more focused on issues of class, ethnicity, education, and gender than they were on issues of race. In this essay I turn to a more recent example of blackface on American soil: the penchant for racially themed parties in the semiprivate spaces of fraternities on American college campuses. These "ghetto parties" include cross-racial and cross-ethnic impersonation, including the donning of blackface. What concert parties and the so-called ghetto parties share, aside from the word "party," is a close connection to sites of education and the social mobility such education promises and engineers. But whereas the Ghanaian concert party adapted a process of performed enculturation which some Africans experienced in exclusive colonial schools and then turned this theater of impersonation into a public spectacle consumed by the masses, contemporary American fraternity ghetto parties privatize a performance of racial difference that is otherwise disavowed in contemporary curricula and in polite, politically correct society. What happens if we read these contemporary manifestations of blackface together? In both instances one sees familiar dynamics: a simultaneous invocation and denial of political meaning; an intersectional masquerade of race, gender, class, and ethnicity; a compression of identity signifiers so potent that no matter what performers or spectators say, the "troubling parts" in densely layered performative invocations keep "grinding against one another."[8] And in that grinding, we hear the rhetoric of upwardly mobile promise grate against the reality of economic disparity.

Ghana's Concert Party

Images of blackface as practiced in colonial Ghana readily evoke American referents (Figure 8.1).[9] Yet what blackface signified in West Africa either in, say, 1922, when it was introduced in this British colony, or in 1957, when the Gold Coast became the first modern African nation-state to achieve independence, demands a careful and precise excavation of local meanings. One must hold in abeyance the politically overdetermined, Americocentric baggage of blackface. Blackface in colonial Ghana operated within a zone of contact between the Fante, Nzema, and Ga ethnic groups located in the southern regions of Ghana; the Twi and Hausa speakers located to the north; and more distant outsiders who arrived on the Guinea coast by boat, such as Liberians (especially Kru), Nigerians (especially Yoruba), Sierra Leoneans, and Ivorians, who were traders, laborers, clerks, fisherman, and seafarers, as well as foreigners from farther away, such as Belgian, Dutch, Lebanese, and British merchants, civil servants, and missionaries. The cities that gave birth to the concert party, such as Axim, Sekondi, Takoradi, Cape Coast, and Accra, were all coastal towns that had long been marked by a complex history of contact with outsiders, whether those outsiders came from Europe, Lebanon, or America or elsewhere in Africa, including repatriated African slaves who had gone through the so-called Gate of No Return of the Middle Passage only to return as colonists themselves in Liberia in the nineteenth century.

"No town in West Africa provides more contrasts in material progress, more wide divergences between the old and the new, more demonstrations of the past and the present," noted *The Red Book of West Africa* about the city of Accra, one of the thriving urban centers of the Gold Coast, in 1920.[10] It is precisely in such a cultural milieu that the concert party was born. The adoption of a performance form that played with mimicry and difference within a heterogeneous cultural context marked by newly acquired socioeconomic mobility, vast power asymmetries, political and economic colonization, migration, and profound cultural, political, social, and economic transformation is quite reminiscent of the birth of minstrelsy on American soil. The Gold Coast of the 1920s was much like nineteenth-century New York as described by W. T. Lhamon Jr. in *Raising Cain: Blackface Performance from Jim Crow to Hip Hop*. Living side by side in New York City's Catherine Market, the site where Americans first witnessed the "jumping" of Jim Crow, were both free and enslaved blacks,

Figure 8.1. Bob Johnson, "Ghana's Ace Comedian," wearing his signature costume. Courtesy of Efua Sutherland.

European immigrants from Ireland and France, fruit sellers, fishmongers, sailors, butchers, and evangelists. "In the 1820s and 1830s everyone is looking askance, trying to figure out where they stand in relation to everyone else," says Lhamon. "The challenges of different cultures living cheek by jowl, as along Catherine and Chatham Streets and in the Five Points, winds up by several notches the mixing of behavioral cues, making everyone the more conscious of gestures and signs, and of cultural presentation in general."[11] The same was true of the cities where blackface minstrelsy first took root in the Gold Coast. Urban areas along the shore were nodal points in vast networks through which indigenous Fante and Ga populations encountered, experimented with, and adopted behaviors, languages, clothing, and music inculcated from the larger world, including *aburokyir* (overseas), as well as neighboring African countries to the west, north, and east.

Kobina Sekyi's play *The Blinkards,* first performed in 1915 and set in Cape Coast, vividly describes a world in which interpersonal relationships dramatized the conflicted relationships Africans had to traditional and imported customs. "We were born into a world of imitators," complains one character, Mr. Brofusem, summing up in one phrase the obsession with copying that propels much of the play's action and, indeed, explains his own name.[12] In many of the disparate locations where blackface has been found throughout the world, one can imagine echoes of Mr. Brofusem's remark being uttered. "We are born into a world of imitators" could very easily have been said in the Puerto Rican radio comedy *El tremendo hotel* created by Ramón Rivero. During the 1950s this show lampooned the Spanish and aristocratic pretensions of the hotel owner, Don Nepo, while staging a complex "CubaRican" identification of its blackface-clad trickster, Calderón.[13] Such multifarious enactment of pretension, aspiration, and imitation within a world that is both radically hierarchical and culturally heterogeneous is emblematic of blackface as it has circulated and transmogrified globally.

The concert party form as it developed in the British West African colony of the Gold Coast had a complex heritage that combined Akan folklore, British music hall traditions, and American vaudeville. My book *Ghana's Concert Party Theatre* is a history of the concert party from its inception though the early years of Ghanaian independence, and the scholar David Donkor has conducted research that analyzes the more recent history of the form.[14] For the purposes of the present discussion I focus on the 1920s and 1930s, a period when the concert party form went from being an amateur entertainment enacted by schoolboys to a primary source of income for professional performers. Notable here are the transnational connections that gave rise to the form as well as the concert party's coalescence into a standardized trio for three stock characters that show both a clear continuity with American sources and profound modifications that rendered the form locally legible and relevant. What made the concert party so distinctive and popular in colonial Ghana was how it spoke at once to very particular local concerns and to a larger sense that the boundaries of this locality were no longer so tightly circumscribed, that this place was becoming part of a much larger global discourse with people from beyond the horizon.

In the 1920s, amateur theatricals arose in coastal cities of what was then the Gold Coast in venues such as the Accra Palladium cinema, the Mikado cinema hall in Nsawam, and the Optimism Club in Sekondi. Augustus Alexander Shotang Williams was one of the first practitioners of the concert party (Figure 8.2). In 1995 I interviewed Williams, who at the time was ninety-two years old. Williams's grandfather was Nigerian, a Yoruba civil servant from Abeokuta who had immigrated to the Gold Coast in the nineteenth century to serve in the British colonial administration. So Augustus Williams was "foreign," or at least had significant foreign parentage, though his mother was Ga, the ethnicity indigenous to Accra. Like minstrel performers from elsewhere in the world, Williams was of mixed race, both an insider and an outsider in the urban nexus of Accra. Both Williams's grandfather and his father worked as British civil

Figure 8.2. Augustus Williams in blackface, circa 1922. Courtesy of A. S. Williams.

servants, and the family was therefore relatively well positioned socioeconomically. Nevertheless, one should not read too much into the Williamses' "elite" status, for the colonial hierarchy was carefully crafted to exploit the indigenous knowledge and language skills of Africans whom it admitted to its ranks without giving them liberty to ascend far within the colonial administration. Augustus Williams, born in 1903, grew up in Accra, where he would patronize cinema halls such as Azuma House and Merry Villas to watch "cowboy pictures" as well as films of people from America dancing. "I see people who dance . . . and I was a dancer. So I tried to copy them," Williams told me.[15] He also read magazines and books on dancing from abroad. In magazines, he saw cartoons that included images of blackface, with its characteristic darkened faces and whitened lips. All of this he studied and imitated.

Like the characters in *The Blinkards*, Williams lived in "a world of imitators," and he himself was especially keen to imitate things he had seen. Williams copied dances from movies and sartorial styles from magazines, just as he copied the English manners, comportment, and modes of speech he was learning at the Government Boys' School. Williams also studied performers who visited

Accra from overseas. He remembered a man named Gene Finerman, a white American tap dancer brought to the Gold Coast by way of London. "Oh, that man," Williams recalled, "he's a good tap dancer! A-1! Tap dances! I try to copy it." Finerman apparently recognized Williams's talent and went about training him. "When he saw that I could tap-dance," said Williams, "now he started showing me. Even sometimes he marked the floor with chalk. And I do the same thing: copy, he said, moving his feet on the floor to show the motions of tap dancing. "Ta-ta-ta-ta-ta ta ta ta-ta." Williams vividly remembered his training sessions with Finerman, which must have occurred around 1920, when Williams was seventeen years old. Finerman not only brought the American popular style of tap dancing to the Gold Coast but also brought blackface. Finerman had "all these colored paints mixed up with Vaseline in bottles, jars," said Williams. While backstage, Finerman "would sit down with his towel" and paint his face and mouth. Williams recalled that the owner of the Palladium Hall, where Finerman performed, was a Mr. Ocansey, who specialized in imports, specifically cars, but he was also a cultural broker who imported performers from other lands. He brought to the Gold Coast two performers from Liberia named "Glass and Grant," a man and a woman who were Kru, an ethnic group from coastal Liberia. Kru people were often seen in the Gold Coast as sailors and migrants along the West African shore. Mr. Ocansey told Williams that Glass and Grant were American, which confused Williams because he was not aware of Liberia's history of having been founded by repatriated American slaves. Grant was a tall, slim woman who had a very light complexion, which may have meant that she was a mixed-race descendant of slaves from the Liberian coast. Glass and Grant as well as Gene Finerman modeled for Williams vaudeville performance styles that combined dancing, especially tap dancing, and face painting. Williams did his best to study every move of these visiting artists and then surpass them as he strove to win the affections of the audience. The popularity he garnered with local audiences, who would cheer him with shouts of "Gus!" on his way to the theater, was for him a validation of his talent. "It's a gift which God gave me," said Williams. For Williams, black face paint with white lips had nothing to do with race. He saw his whole act as pure entertainment.

Williams eventually teamed up with a schoolmate named Marbell to form a comic duo modeled on the Liberians Glass and Grant (Figure 8.3), and together they enacted various vaudeville scenarios and songs they had seen in films. Williams and Marbell's vaudeville-inspired act revolved around impersonating foreign characters and manners, and this comic imitation struck a chord with colonial audiences in the Gold Coast. Soon other local performing groups sprang up in a number of coastal cities, each with its own variations on common

Figure 8.3. The comedy team of Williams and Marbell, who performed at the Accra Palladium in the early 1920s. Courtesy of A. S. Williams.

themes. During the 1930s, one could see shows like Williams and Marbell's act in cinema halls, social clubs, and schools in places such as Nsawam, Sekondi, and Axim. Archival sources don't tell us much about the identity of the spectators for these shows, but oral history, ethnography, and archival newspaper sources suggest that they were from the intermediate classes—those who had at least enough expendable income to pay the gate fee, modest though it was. Many spectators had some exposure to English through formal education. And in a few venues, such as the Palladium, there was a stratified gate fee that created a class differentiation within the house in terms of seating. Some venues were exclusive private clubs, such as the Optimism Club in Sekondi, where only clerks, lawyers, and merchants could be members. But when concert parties were performed at the Optimism Club, this elite private space became public, as concert party attendance was open to all. According to Lawrence Cudjoe, who served as rector of the Optimism Club in 1994, "Once a concert was going to be staged there, anybody could buy a ticket and attend."[16] Thus, concert parties played a democratizing function in these elite social spaces. They took place on the cusp between classes, often literally enacted in spaces that demarcated (and in fact created and intensified) socioeconomic differentiation, whether the performance was held at an exclusive elite club that opened its doors to the general public for one concert party show or in a primary school that was itself a mechanism for instilling and inculcating new means of social mobility and class differentiation among Africans.

The history of the concert party from the 1920s to the 1960s is a story of gradual indigenization as shows moved from the intermediate to the working classes, traveled from the cities into the rural areas and from regions of the coastal south into the hinterland and the north. Audiences throughout most of the history of the concert party were almost exclusively African. So although the concert party was very much a colonial form, it was largely unknown to white British colonists. During the early years of its history, the concert party was performed in English. But gradually shows incorporated local languages, especially Fante. Concert parties became especially popular with members of the working class, particularly those who worked in the gold mines. Shows provided organized entertainment that fit well within the structured division between working hours and leisure time for migrant laborers who were separated from their families. In a colony with limited literacy rates and media networks, the concert party functioned as a kind of living newspaper, carrying information about the coast to other parts of the colony. By watching these shows, audiences learned about the styles of dress, comportment, language, and manners (and conflicts) that transpired in the households of coastal city dwellers who adopted English behaviors and customs. Spectators of concert parties were always raucous, for audiences routinely talked throughout the shows and commented loudly on the action and characters. Concert parties thus provided a public forum for conversation about social changes that were dramatically impacting cities, towns, and villages throughout the Gold Coast, particularly as these affected domestic arrangements and daily life. The shows also made the customs and behaviors that were granting some Africans unprecedented socioeconomic mobility in a rapidly transforming economy accessible to a far larger constituency of working-class and agrarian Ghanaians.

Over time the features of the concert party form crystallized and coalesced into a standardized trio of characters, who reveal much about the ways that imported signs such as blackface became locally legible. During the 1930s the concert party saw a recurring trio of stock characters: the Gentleman, the Lady, and the Houseboy. The Two Bobs and Their Carolina Girl was the first concert party trio to become professional, that is, the first to make touring concert shows their sole source of income. A photo taken around 1934 (Figure 8.4) is the earliest picture of a concert party trio that I have found. The Gentleman

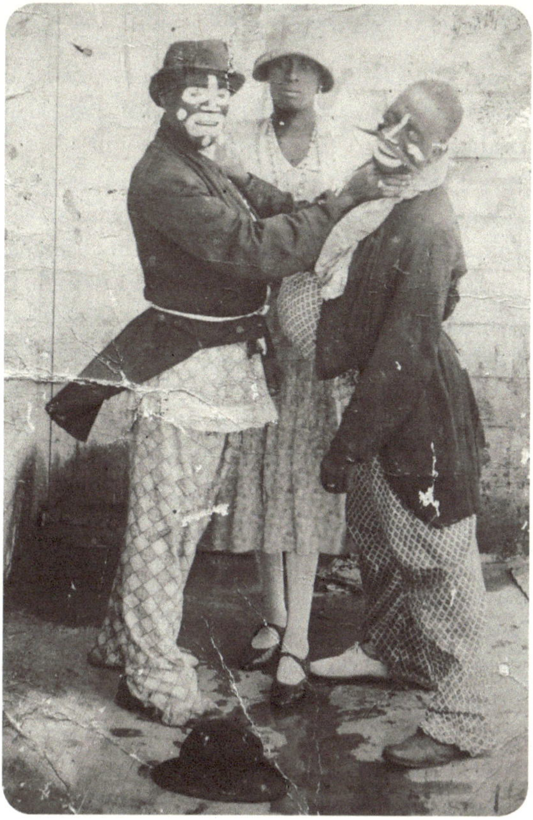

Figure 8.4. The Two Bobs and Their Carolina Girl, circa 1934 (from left to right): J. B. Ansah as the Gentleman, Charles B. Horton as the Lady, and Bob Johnson as the disruptive Houseboy "Bob," who in his behavior and large belly resembles the trickster Ananse. Courtesy of C. K. Stevens.

character, pictured on the far left, was supposed to be a well-to-do businessman who would speak only English. He was constantly taking on British affectations, and he wore a European suit, or at least a clown's version of a suit, rather than the traditional African cloth that Ghanaian men typically drape toga-style over their shoulders. Each of the concert party's stock characters was built on a core contradiction. For the Gentleman this was manifest in his speech and financial situation. Despite his Anglophilia, the Gentleman didn't actually speak English very well. So when he got flustered or angry—which happened often while he was dealing with the shenanigans of his houseboy—the Gentleman would explode with a torrent of Fante abuses, to the glee of the audience. And despite the fact that he pretended to be wealthy, the Gentleman didn't actually have much money. The humor of concert party skits often revolved around the elaborate ruses the Gentleman would deploy to disguise just how empty his pockets really were.

The second member of the trio, pictured in the middle of the photograph, was the Lady. Refined and restrained, the Lady in the concert party was typically beautifully clad in a British frock, hat, pearls, and gloves. Like the Gentleman, however, she too was created in such a way that there was a fundamental contradiction between her appearance and her underlying "true" nature. Though very convincingly feminine in her dress, voice, and comportment, the Lady was actually a man in drag. Unlike her husband, who would reveal in the course of concert sketches his poverty and limited English, the Lady never disclosed her true gender identity or, to be more accurate, the gender identity of the actor who played her. This was instead information spectators simply knew, or at least some of them knew, and their knowledge added further complexity to the love trysts that played out on concert party stages. A second contradictory feature of the Lady was that while she seemed to be prim and proper, a loyal "good wife" in a British-style nuclear family, she actually had a boyfriend (and sometimes several) on the side. A recurring concert party sketch from this era involves the Lady hiding her lover in a laundry basket when she hears her husband returning to the house. In the course of the sketch, her Houseboy ends up having to carry the laundry basket, with her lover in it, on his head. He would pitch and weave about the stage, cursing in pidgin English while struggling with the weight of his load. It's no accident that the concert party, a theatrical form very much about imitation of foreign ideas and customs, frequently told stories about infidelity, implicitly juxtaposing private notions of sexual fidelity with a larger question of African fidelity to custom and tradition.

The third member of the trio was the Houseboy who worked for the Gentleman and Lady. He was supposed to be a poor Kru laborer from Liberia, and he spoke comically mangled pidgin English. Selfish and mischievous, the Houseboy constantly irritated and outsmarted his masters. Like the other two characters, the Houseboy was constructed around a core contradiction: though supposedly uneducated, he was actually far more clever than his masters. Comic sketches often dramatized how this subordinate character would prevail in power struggles precisely because of his cleverness and verbal wit. The Houseboy was the first concert stock character to merge clearly with local lore, as he fused with the Akan folklore character Ananse, the trickster spider. Ananse is clever and mischievous, motivated as often as not by his appetite. A single-minded quest for food soon became a defining feature of the concert party Houseboy, and this aspect of his character was expressed in the performer's large stuffed belly, as we see in actor Bob Johnson's rendering of the Houseboy in Figure 8.4. Ananse's cleverness was exemplified in the Houseboy's ingenious manipulation of all situations to his own advantage.

One could say that all three of these characters were in some sense "foreign" to the Gold Coast: the Houseboy was from Liberia, and the Lady and Gentleman, though Fante, were obsessed with acting British. Over the course of the concert party's history, each of these stock characters in the trio became increasingly Africanized and localized, switching to local languages, dressing in ways identifiable as "African," or even more particularly "Fante" or "Akan," and portraying stories that had much deeper roots in Ghanaian culture, as the stories and their accompanying songs and proverbs dramatized conflicts over inheritance, the plight of orphans, and the strife typical in polygamous households with multiple wives. Interestingly it was the concert party character that was the *most* foreign, the Liberian Houseboy, who became the most quickly indigenized, if we consider how closely he fused with Ananse, the famous Akan trickster spider. The Houseboy also proved to be the most enduring character of the concert party trio. Even in contemporary plays, the Houseboy, often called Bob after the role's founding actor, Bob Johnson, continues to make cameo appearances.

What was it about these three stock characters that so appealed to colonial Ghanaian audiences? In a world of imitators, each member of the trio comically lampooned the gulf between aspiration and reality. The way these characters were drawn foregrounded imitation itself as a performative act. Since concert party shows were fictional as well as public, they provided a safe forum for public discussion about imitation as a fundamental feature of colonial culture. Spectators were able to rebuke and judge publicly, to editorialize about and laugh at the concert party's preposterously drawn characters, to discuss with fellow spectators how strangely or abominably these characters behaved, while at the same time studying the cut of a particular dress or the verbal mastery of English in order to imitate later these very attributes in daily life. According to Ghanaian values of indirection, spectators would typically have been far more cautious about publicly voicing critique of *real* civil servants, merchants, schoolmasters, and Christian ministers in everyday colonial life, no matter how preposterous the European affectations of these individuals appeared.[17]

Blackface as adopted in the Gold Coast quickly took on idiosyncratic, localized variations, especially when one compares the 1922 photo of Williams and Marbell (Figure 8.3) with the photograph of the Two Bobs and Their Carolina Girl from 1934 (Figure 8.4). The Houseboy and the Gentleman have faces blackened with a foundation not unlike what one sees in U.S. minstrelsy. But the white accents they use are quite distinctive. The Gentleman has white paint around his mouth, a white stripe down his nose, white rings around his eyes, and white dots on his cheeks and chin. Bob Johnson as the Houseboy has white lips below his most impressively distended moustache, and he also has white stripes on his nose and cheeks. This is a highly localized variation of blackface that draws from and incorporates Ghanaian customs of face painting that one might see during ritual occasions. By the time I did my research in Ghana in

1993–1995, all the actors pictured in this photo had passed away, so it is impossible to know for certain what led J. B. Ansah and Bob Johnson to modify the blackface they were copying from American movies in this particular way. But other veteran concert party performers I interviewed interpreted blackface painting in the concert party as being as much about local African body painting customs as about anything copied from abroad. At a gathering of concert party elders in 1995, Y. B. Bampoe, who was a leader of the Jaguar Jokers troupe, who studied and emulated the Two Bobs and Their Carolina Girl, offered this interpretation of blackface:

> [*In Fante*] I want to give some explanation. The fact is [with] some of our brothers elsewhere, we have been made to understand that if they see someone staging a show in Ghana or elsewhere with some paint applied to that actor's face, it means the actor is insulting them. I am referring to those who were sold into slavery. But that's not the idea. Here in Ghana are many occasions when people apply paint to their bodies. When the Krobos are undergoing Dipo rituals, the body is smeared with some paint. The Nzemas apply some colors to their bodies during the Kundum festival. The Akuapem have a ritual known as *bragor* for young girls who have had their first menstrual period. The young girl and her intimate friends have some colors applied to their bodies. The Abiriws, Guans, perform the same rituals for young girls. . . .
>
> When, therefore, we apply colors to our bodies, nobody should think that he or she is being made fun of. It's customary. We normally paint our faces. Some people apply paint to their faces before they attend some functions. We have the colors. We have all the colors: blue, green, red. . . . [*Switches to English*] Some people over the globe have different understandings or different interpretations that we are reminding them that they are slaves: is never true. It is completely out of gear. So nobody should think of that. We should all cooperate. When you see Africans painting their face, you should not be offended. It's for fun's sake. [*Switches back to Fante*] It is something we do, and people are happy about it.[18]

The speech in which he gave this explanation was delivered in the context of a conference I organized with veteran concert party performers about the history of their art form. What was especially striking about Bampoe's speech was that he actually left the conference proceedings momentarily as we were discussing the history and meaning of blackface, only to return a few moments later wearing a hastily improvised blackface costume. Bampoe had gone to the nearby market, where he purchased charcoal and chalk, and after blackening his face, whitening his lips, and tying a bandana around his neck, he gave the speech I have just quoted. Bampoe was speaking both to his peers at the conference and to the video camera we were using to document the event. As he spoke, Bampoe addressed the camera with full recognition that the video would be shown to people in America, including African Americans, who he had learned would likely be quite offended by Ghanaian performers' use of blackface.[19]

I have argued elsewhere that blackface in Ghana was not generally seen as racist. It was on some level *about* race, however, or at least about racial identification. Early colonial newspapers provide ample evidence that literate coastal Africans in the Gold Coast were very much aware of African American leaders and performers and about African American political mobilization against racial oppression. Some colonial Ghanaians tried to emulate their sisters and brothers overseas, seeing in African Americans a model for black identity operating within the constraints of vast, racialized power asymmetries. On some level, Africans in the Gold Coast did associate blackface with African Americans. Some of them even mistook Al Jolson as African American rather than a white Jew. In a world of imitators, signs such as blackface that travel transnationally can seem to divest themselves of previous meanings as rapidly as they assume new ones. Blackface must be read, therefore, as part of a general Gold Coast discourse among Africans about "Negroes" from America, but it is also deeply immersed in local discourses about a whole range of ethnic, gender, and class differences in which race was by no means the most salient marker of identity.

In the hall of mirrors produced by the minstrel masquerade enacted at nodal sites of imperial power, misapprehensions are typical. For instance, in 1993, when many African Americans were expected to come to Ghana as participants in the Pan-African Historical Theatre Festival, it occurred to the performers' guild known as the Ghana Concert Party Union that they could provide a fitting contribution to the Panafest ceremonies by reviving and featuring their practice of blackface. They knew in some vague way that the blackface makeup used in the concert party was associated with African Americans. So they offered to stage an old-time concert party with blackface in the Cape Coast Castle, where so many slaves had been held before the Middle Passage. Union members were completely unaware of the volatile and derogatory associations that blackface has in America and how offensive such a performance by Ghanaians in the Cape Coast Castle was likely to be.[20] Ghosted by the half-life of former meanings, the minstrel mask circulating globally is a highly unstable sign.

The story of blackface in West Africa, of how it arrived in colonial Ghana, was adopted there by schoolboys, blended with local folklore characters such as the spider trickster Ananse, combined with vaudeville sketches learned from foreign movies and visiting performers, and gradually indigenized through the use of African languages, proverbs, and songs, reveals much about the cultural and social transformation of this one particular colony within a vast empire. The story demonstrates the fluidity of the blackface sign as it moved from, say, New York vaudeville houses to Al Jolson's movies, which then played in cinema halls in places such as urban Accra in West Africa. The overdetermined meaning of blackface in segregated America became something quite different when re-performed by Africans and for exclusively black audiences in the colonial Gold Coast. There, ethnic, linguistic, and class differences resonated far more prominently than racial ones.

In thinking of the transnational circulation of blackface, the case of the concert party is instructive. The affinities, continuities, and profound differences between blackface in, say, the Optimism Club of Sekondi in 1934 and the Cape Town Coon Carnival in Cape Town, South Africa, in the nineteenth century demand far more comparative scholarly attention than they have yet received, as do the performances of *el negrito* in newly independent Cuba in 1902 and Ramón Rivero's character Alma Negra (Black Soul), who narrated in 1936 the various stages of Puerto Rico's political history through the medium of blackface.[21] The historiography of minstrelsy is so overwhelmingly dominated by American examples and interpretive frames that scholars who look at blackface elsewhere around the globe must actively resist a hegemonic interpretive imperialism that would see American referents as being the most important or salient. Often what is being played out through this complex masquerade is a theater of difference that is quite particular, idiosyncratic, and local. At the same time, there is a need for American studies scholars to consider how these global manifestations of blackface might transform and subvert the way they see minstrelsy practiced on North American soil. How must the historiography of minstrelsy change if we are truly to take account of the global and transnational reach of the form? Perhaps we will be forced to see America as both a colonized and a colonizing site, a quintessentially colonial place not just in 1820 but also in the present.

Compton Cookout Parties in San Diego

The peculiar work of this most mobile of signs—the blackened face and whitened lips—is distinctive not only for its affinity with border zones of contact but also for the ease with which blackface erases its path of travel as well as the consistency with which it becomes both a cynosure and a bellwether in the places where it takes root. I turn to a recent and, for me, comparatively local manifestation of blackface: a private party held in 2010 by individuals associated with a fraternity at the University of California, San Diego—or, to be precise, an event that was at least as "private" as any social event posted on Facebook generally can be said to be. This present-day manifestation of minstrelsy-derived stereotypes transpired in a very different border zone of contact compared to the coastal cities of colonial Ghana: on the tony shores of La Jolla, California, just fifteen miles north of the U.S.-Mexican border, the site of the extraordinary encounter between so-called first and third worlds. Home to U.S. Navy and Marine Corps bases, San Diego is also the base of one of the largest naval fleets in the world. In February 2010—during the seventh year of the occupation of Iraq (a.k.a. "Iraq war," "second Gulf War," "Operation Iraqi Freedom," "Operation New Dawn")—fraternity students at the University of California, San Diego, hosted an event called the "Compton Cookout," a costume party that they claimed was in honor of Black History Month. The name referred to Compton, a city to the north located in the center of Los Angeles County with a sizable African American population. Guests were invited to attend in costumes that evoked "ghetto" stereotypes. I have banished to an endnote the full invitation for this event, which took place on February 14–15, 2010.[22] Here is an excerpt: "For guys: I expect all males to be rockin Jersey's, stuntin' up in ya White T (XXXL smallest size acceptable), anything FUBU, Ecko, Rockawear, High/low top Jordans or Dunks, Chains, Jorts, stunner shades, 59 50 hats, Tats, etc. For girls: For those of you who are unfamiliar with ghetto chicks—Ghetto chicks usually have gold teeth, start fights and drama, and wear cheap clothes."[23]

Ghosts from nineteenth-century American minstrelsy haunt this text, such as Zip Coon, the urban dandy who was the antithesis of the southern bumpkin caricature, Jim Crow. The minstrelsy pedigree of the Compton Cookout stereotypes is evident to anyone who knows this history. Yet ignorance of minstrelsy's history is precisely what is so troubling not only about the Compton Cookout but also about the firestorm of controversy it provoked. Reader comments on news websites and blogs indicate that a large number of those posting saw the cookout as an innocent joke with no racist significance. "Innocence" is a notable condition for students in an elite institution of higher education, for it suggests these students have been taught very little about America's long history of theatricalized racial stereotyping and, more significantly, its pervasive and endemic racial violence. Exposing the underbelly of brutality and enslavement that was anything but innocent, Saidiya Hartman, in her analysis of the economy of enjoyment in nineteenth-century minstrelsy, writes: "Within this economy, the bound black body, permanently affixed in its place, engenders pleasure not only ensuant to the buffoonery and grotesqueries of Cuff, Sambo, and Zip Coon but above all deriving from the very mechanisms of this coercive placement; it is a pleasure obtained from the security of place and order and predicated on chattel slavery."[24] "Ghetto-fabulous" parties transpiring more than a century after the performances Hartman was writing about force us to consider the contrasting economic foundations of these performances. Those who live in America's contemporary ghettos must endure a structured nexus of poverty, exploitation, disenfranchisement, crime, and staggering rates of incarceration. This is different from chattel slavery, yes, but perhaps not so radically different when one considers the consistent bottom line: the pervasive and systemic dehumanization of black subjects.

When it comes to blackface in America, the forces of selective amnesia are as enduring as minstrelsy's stereotypes. Perhaps in its simultaneous erasure and rehearsal of history, the Compton Cookout *was* a quintessentially American performance. But was it also a quintessentially *colonial* one? In analyzing comparatively the concert parties of colonial Ghana and the Compton Cookout parties in San Diego, one finds it striking that the imperatives, styles, genealogies, and political potency of neo-minstrelsy performances—so often enacted within a border zone contact and in a milieu that has a "world of imitators"—can be as insidious and crude as they are many-layered and complex. It is with this capriciousness in mind that we consider the global reach of blackface as it has been adopted and revised in colonial outposts and present-day colonizing metropoles—whether Accra, West Africa, in 1923 or San Diego, California, in 2010. In the hall of mirrors where minstrel masquerades are staged at nodal sites of imperial power, misapprehensions proliferate.

The Compton Cookout invitation performs product placements in a distinctly contemporary, neoliberal fashion: "FUBU, Ecko, Rockawear, Jordans." The irony of naming "FUBU" in such a derogatory context is that this clothing line comes from an African American company that touts its apparel as being "For Us By Us."[25] The Compton Cookout was anything *but* for African Americans, by African Americans. Although there has been a long debate about who, exactly, threw the party at UCSD—where African American students constituted only 1.3 percent of the student population—party organizers would have had to work very hard for this to be a truly African American event.[26] In a context of gross radical underrepresentation of blacks at the school, such an event performs a particularly insidious dramatization either of the organizers' ignorance about or their willful disregard for the conditions under which African Americans attend their university.

The racism of the invitation is most potent in its address to women, which, as one blogger described it, "drip[s] with moralizing language sneeringly directed at an embodiment stereotyped as irrational ('cheap clothes' mistaken for 'high class couture,' 'cheap weaves' in 'bad colors'), uncivilized ('limited vocabulary,' 'cursing persistently'), and animalistic ('smacking their lips,' 'making other angry noises, grunts, and faces')—in other words, ugly."[27] The invitation performs intersectional oppression with breathtaking impunity. The dynamics at play in this text have a very long and ignoble genealogy in America, with minstrelsy its prime progenitor. UCSD's ethnic studies faculty pointed out this history in a statement they issued that illuminates the party's very predictable conflation of racism and sexism in its performance of power, as well as the way the invitation simultaneously dehumanizes African Americans while also denying the structural conditions that shape black life in America.[28]

The Compton Cookout was just the first in a whole series of polarizing events that transpired at UCSD in the early months of 2010. A few days after news of the party ignited protests and calls for the campus administration to censure the event's organizers, a group of students issued a second ghetto-themed party invitation: "Compton Cookout Part Deux."[29] Organizer Mike Randazzo stated, "We pretty much want people to just choose a culture and harmlessly poke fun at it," a position of innocence he further elaborated by saying, "If your intent is to make fun and not to harm anyone, and you really aren't trying to hurt anyone's feelings, then it's different from trying to cut someone down on purpose."[30] Randazzo wanted to claim that intentionality is critical in our reading of neo-minstrelsy performances and that there was no malicious intent with the Compton Cookout. Some UCSD students who broadcast on *The Koala,* a notoriously inflammatory satirical television show whose mission is "to crush all your hopes and dreams with comedy," left no doubt about their intentions.[31] Addressing African Americans who were up in arms about the Compton Cookout, they dismissed these members of the UCSD community as "you ungrateful niggers."[32]

As with the analysis of the concert party in colonial Ghana, interpretation of performance in San Diego depends on a careful consideration of context and local detail. We must consider, for instance, the location of the first Compton Cookout event, the Regents La Jolla, a luxury condominium complex sited in what its website describes as "an enviable enclave of world-class hotels, multi-million-dollar homes and private research facilities." The Regents has "gorgeous landscaping, open courtyards, impressive architectural design and much more, all within the coveted La Jolla zip code."[33] Although the name of the condo refers to the Regents of the University of California, the governing body of the ten-campus state university system, the complex is independent of both the campus and the UC Regents, and its location off campus severely restricted what the university could do in terms of a disciplinary response.

Context also leads us to consider the pervasive structural inequities that have led UCSD to have such an astonishingly low enrollment of African American students. In 2009–10, there were only 299 black students out of total student body of 22,500—1.3 percent. Blacks historically have never risen above 3 percent of UCSD's population. We must also consider the university's remarkably low yield rate, that is, the percentage of students offered admission who accept. Since 1997, UCSD's African American yield rate has hovered in the teens and low twenties.[34] According to a 2008 comprehensive study of African American students in the whole UC system, the reasons for UCSD's remarkably low yield rate have much to do with campus climate: "Anecdotal evidence suggests that many African American applicants perceive the racial climate at UCSD as a hostile one, opting not to attend the campus after being offered admission. Similarly, the low enrollment numbers for black admits reflect their fear of experiencing racial isolation at the university because of its exceedingly small African American population."[35]

If we expand the frame out from the Cookout parties (both "Un" and "Deux") and the inflammatory broadcast on the *Koala* program via the UCSD campus television station, we find numerous other incidents on the campus that indicate racial hatred: the discovery of a noose in the UCSD library not long after the parties, a KKK-like hood that was placed on a statue shortly thereafter, and a spate of coincident racist and hate incidents on other University of California campuses all within a matter of weeks, including the carving of swastikas and the vandalism of the Lesbian, Gay, Bisexual, Transgender Resource Center at UC Davis and an anti-gay physical assault at UC Riverside. This larger context in which neo-minstrelsy private revelries in San Diego were staged raises a host of questions about what peculiar work the twenty-first century's version of the minstrel mask is doing in the sunny state of California.[36] These events on California campuses arose during a year of great tumult in the whole UC system due to drastic budget cuts and a staggering 32 percent increase in student fees. These changes threatened to undermine the foundational principles of the fifty-year-old California Master Plan for Higher Education, Clark Kerr's vision that promised access to higher education for all, regardless of economic means.

We must ask: Was the Compton Cookout event, like the Ghanaian concert party, which arose in colonial schools, a performative expression of some deep underlying contradictions embedded in the local educational project? Schools in colonial Ghana promised to "civilize" black Africans, enlighten them with Western culture, and give them access to an advanced economy. And yet school graduates soon learned that their education prepared them, at best, to be underpaid clerks for the colonial administration. By way of contrast, California's system of higher education promises access across the socioeconomic spectrum; but the very exclusionary processes that are central to matriculation and graduation at this elite tier of higher education ensures social differentiation for a select few. The ghetto is the antithesis of the aspirations and dreams usually associated with a UC degree. And yet in a climate of escalating tuition hikes, students are assuming ever-increasing debt in order to obtain their undergraduate degrees. As a "hedge" meant to secure and/or elevate their class position—either attaining a place in the middle class or facilitating their upward mobility within and beyond it—a college degree is not the sure bet it once was.

Students who belong to what Anya Kamenetz has dubbed "Generation Debt" may find that their aspirations for upward mobility through higher education will instead ensnare them in an endless cycle of debt and even downward mobility.[37] In that regard, it may be that college students participating in "ghetto-fabulous" revelries imagine they have a new affinity with the ghetto, a sense that the game is stacked against them—as has long been the case for America's urban poor. "We have all become students of color now," says my UC Berkeley colleague and comrade in activism Ananya Roy about the massive divestment of the state in California's public universities.[38] As Chris Chen argues, "formerly insulated middle-class students and families" are now exposed to a "process of 'minoritization' in which older forms of cultural privilege" are stripped away.[39] Yet if privileged white students who attend the elite tier of California's public universities imagine they are now disenfranchised minorities—the "nouveaux poor"—what does this mean for the "old poor," people of color who have experienced disenfranchisement as a permanent and enduring condition of their lives in America? It hardly seems that racially themed ghetto parties are an act of solidarity.

An examination of neo-minstrelsy in semiprivate spaces of revelry attached to institutions of higher education in America reveals that this is by no means solely a California phenomenon. There have been dozens of racially themed parties like the Compton Cookout on campuses throughout the United States since at least the mid-1980s.[40] From schools such as Tarleton State in South Carolina and Auburn University in Alabama to liberal arts colleges like Macalester in Minnesota and law schools at the University of Texas and University of Connecticut, students are engaging in a kind of cross-racial transvestism at private parties often held in off-campus sites controlled by fraternities and sororities. These private parties have become exposed to the public eye because of social networking websites such as Facebook, where invitations and post-party pictures document a widespread practice that may well have been going on during prior decades but just flew under the public radar.

There is very little scholarship on these racially themed parties to date, though there is certainly a viable dissertation topic to be found here.[41] Tim Wise counted in 2007 over thirty such racially themed parties that had transpired during the previous decade, and his lists run the gamut from Ivy League to small-town colleges, from public to private, from small liberal arts colleges to sprawling research campuses.[42] The parties show variations on a theme. There was, for instance, the "Halloween in the Hood" party at the Sigma Chi fraternity at Johns Hopkins University in 2007, to which partygoers were invited to wear their best "bling, bling, ice, ice" in the "HIV pit."[43] Outside the fraternity house a plastic skeleton in a pirate costume hung from a noose, and inside the house, partygoers encountered a soundscape of gunshots.[44] Other parties include "Bullets and Bubbly" at the University of Connecticut School of Law in 2007, where white attendees flashed gang signs, gold teeth, and fake machine guns while slugging malt liquor.[45] "Gold chains, doo-rags, hats turned to the side" were also de rigueur at the "Straight Thuggin' Party" held at the University of Chicago in 2005.[46] "Ghetto Fabulous" appears to be a particularly popular theme, and one of the first of these seems to have been staged by the Zeta Beta Tau fraternity at Cornell University in 2004. Joseph J. Sabia, a sympathizer with the event and at the time a Ph.D. candidate in economics, explained the concept: partygoers were to impersonate "rappers who made the climb from rags (the ghetto) to riches (bling-bling)." Sabia elaborated, "A rapper's transformation from 'ghetto fabulous' is a lot like what happened in every Horatio Alger tale, except that it involves significantly more crack and murder."[47] In 2006, law students at the University of Texas, Austin, took up the "Ghetto Fabulous" theme to host a similar party, complete with photos posted online that depicted guests wearing Afro wigs and necklaces with large medallions.[48] The theme has become so popular that a website named "College Candy" offered a kind of prepackaged "Ghetto Fabulous" party kit which it touted along with kits for other theme parties such as "Little Kids' Birthday Party," "The Classy(ish) Holiday Party," and, perhaps with prescient insight in 2008, "The Tea Party." Of these, "Ghetto Fabulous" was the budget option: "All you need is $10 pack of Hanes men's white tank tops (affectionately referred to as beaters), a dark or colored bra, a baseball cap, cocked to one side. If you're feeling adventurous, invest in fake bling, and make your playlist all hard-core rap. Everyone starts the night with a 40 of their choice, and if you're feeling extra-classy, you can even go with malt liquor."[49] African Americans are not the only targets of derogatory impersonation. Similar parties have been held with "South of the Border" and "Tacos and Tequila" themes. There is even a Facebook page "Students for Racially Themed Parties," which has a counterpart site called "Students against Racially Themed Parties."[50] As of this writing, the former had eleven members and the latter 2,155.

The nature of impersonation at these parties varies: gold foil on teeth, padded derrieres, hip clothing labels overtly displayed along with flashy jewelry, and, yes, black painting on white skin, whether of the greasepaint, shoe polish, or burnt cork variety I don't know. Pictures I have found on the Internet show what appear to be white male students painting their faces and arms with black foundation while wielding forty-ounce malt liquor bottles, smoking cigars, and fondling their buxom girlfriends. This is in many ways the same old, same old: the libidinal economy that has long marked the white love and theft of blackness via minstrelsy. But one also sees new inflections in American college neo-minstrelsy that express how the prison-industrial complex has supplanted the former role of slavery: pants hanging down below the hips (or "sagging"), a reference to a black sartorial style some believe arises from the culture within prison, where belts are not allowed.[51] The violence of old is evoked by the white KKK hoods that some party attendees wear, but now they also bear props such as semiautomatic weapons. Whereas in former times the violence represented in minstrelsy was embedded in grotesque bodily acts, as Hartman says, such as "rolling eyes, lolling tongues, obscene gestures, [and] shuffling," in neo-minstrelsy the violence is far more overt. A photograph taken at a 2001 Alpha Tau Omega fraternity party at the University of Mississippi depicts "two students, both white men. One is in blackface, on his knees; he is picking cotton from a small bucket. The other, dressed as a policeman, is holding a gun to his head."[52]

According to Tim Wise, "whether racist parties like this are growing more common, or whether they're just gaining more attention thanks to websites like Facebook, MySpace, and others that allow the sharing of photo files is unclear. But in either case, the question remains: Why do so many whites engage in these kinds of activities, without giving their appropriateness a second thought?"[53] Wise posits two theories about this: one is that these students are ignorant about the history of blackface; the other is that participants in racially themed parties quite deliberately wish to insult and alienate students of color. Wise contends that both theories contain partial truths. When these events occur during Black History Month or the Dr. Martin Luther King Jr. holiday, which happened six times in 2007, it's hard to read these events as anything but deliberately racist. This is especially so when one considers that party hosts don't seem to seek co-sponsorship from entities such as the Black Student Union or La Raza. "After all, never did the sponsors of these parties make the mistake of inviting *real* black people to the ghetto celebration," says Wise.

Although lack of black participation may have been the case in 2007, this was not true with UCSD's Compton Cookout event in 2010, for which the Facebook invitation included an image of an iconic black figure, a "shock jock" comedian with the stage name of "Jiggaboo Jones," a.k.a. "the number one nigger in America," in "real" life a man known as Nipsey Washington from Las Vegas.[54] Jiggaboo Jones's website announces: "Man I'm Jiggaboo Jones! I eat fried chicken, I steal shit, I drink Olde English, I love Grape Soda, Watermelon and a good gang fight. All the things that people associate with a Nigger. That's what I do."[55] Jones issued a statement on his website about the whole Compton Cookout controversy, detailing his views on the strange twists and turns this story took. He claimed that the party was intended to mark the release of his new DVD, but when the video wasn't available in time, the Cookout went ahead anyway, with people "simply drinking a few beers and having a few laughs with a mixed crowd of people and laughing about the stupidity of racial tensions in 2010."[56] Jones makes clear that the genre of the event was very much in keeping with that of prior social events he had been associated with: "Nigga Nite 2009," which is not to be confused with "Nigga Nite 2008," which was held at the University of Southern California.[57] It appears that in the space between 2007, when Wise published his "Majoring in Minstrelsy" article, and 2010, when members of the Pi Kappa Alpha fraternity participated in the Compton Cookout at UCSD, the racially themed party had evolved to the point where organizers could strategically legitimate such revelries by hosting a colorful and outrageous token mascot from the minority group that is being travestied.

When historians look back on the neo-minstrelsy of our era, "Jigaboo Jones" may well appear as the Prince Bata Kindai Amgoza Ibn LoBagola (also known as Joseph Howard Lee from Baltimore) of his time. LoBagola is an extraordinary figure from early-twentieth-century minstrel history whose strange career Louis Chude-Sokei traces: "From America to Europe to Africa to vaudeville to the University of Pennsylvania; from the department of anthropology at Oxford to dressing in feathers, playing with fire, and landing in prison; from accusations of fraud to multiple charges of pedophilia and child molestation: this was the trajectory. And he never removed the mask."[58] Jiggaboo Jones likewise dons an endless profusion of masks that reflect and reverberate a depressingly tenacious racism while frustrating any attempt to find his "authentic" self behind the masks. Like LoBagola, Jiggaboo Jones traffics both in black American culture and in the sign of Africa: "Jones" is as generic a name as any given to an American slave, while "Jiggaboo" performs the sign of Africa through skin tone. Urbandictionary.com, which seems to have provided inspiration and actual copy for the Compton Cookout invitation, defines *jiggaboo* as "a term often used in the Southern regions of the United States in reference to African-American individuals that possess a darker than average skin pygment [*sic*] (Darkening skin color). These 'Jiggaboo's' often appear to be seen in the dark even in daylight hours, as the whitening of their eyes and teeth appear to glow through the darkness of their skin tone surrounding the eyes and mouth."[59]

Jones shares with LoBagola a prismatic refraction of Africa and black America as well as an oscillation between high and low, yet he seems adamantly and defiantly to relish the low. It is striking that Jones, as both a wild card and a race card in the whole Compton Cookout ordeal, did one thing that no one else within the orbit of this event seemed willing to do: he took responsibility for planning and participating in the Cookout, even if he did so without remorse or contrition. Other than Jones, the party's organizers remain underground and incognito. The *San Diego Union-Tribune* reported that it had obtained an e-mail from UCSD's assistant vice chancellor for student life, Gary Ratcliff, linking the Cookout to the Pi Kappa Alpha ("Pike") fraternity, writing, "It was not an official Pike event but the students who posted it on Facebook were members of Pike and other frats."[60] Nevertheless, Garron Engstrom, president of the UCSD chapter of the fraternity, denied any involvement by Pi Kappa Alpha in this event,[61] and in fact at this writing no UCSD fraternity has admitted any involvement with the party. In contrast with this endemic pattern of denial of responsibility for not just the UCSD Compton Cookout but also the dozens of racially themed parties all over America in recent years, Jiggaboo Jones's performance again stands out. He admits he was at the party and was one of its core planners. Addressing his audience as "Ladies, Gentlemen, people of the media & the element of sub human trash who started this crap," Jones laments on his website the way his unnamed party collaborators have been maligned:

> Some hate mongering black people . . . told a pack of lies about our event stating that a White Fraternity and several members of the KKK threw a Racist party that made fun of black people. This lie was quickly soaked up by people with some kind of political agenda to spread hate and discontent among people who attend UCSD. The divisive few told a "Woa [*sic*] is me" tale of how all blacks at UCSD are almost lynched in trees seemingly everyday. Members of the media ate this up because this type of story sells papers, gets people pissed off and keeps them tuning in. Blog sites went crazy and facebook fascists took their laptops and started the witch hunt that would ruin the reputations of several good hearted people and their families with their inaccurate statements.

Jones himself has proven an effective deflection for many in the blogosphere who see participation by this one black man in the Compton Cookout incident as evidence that the party could not possibly have been racist. Yet Jones provides a far from comfortable exoneration. Like the Yoruba trickster Eshu, Jiggaboo Jones unleashes forces that are both potent and of uncertain outcome: "I eat fried chicken, I steal shit, I drink Olde English, I love Grape Soda, Watermelon and a good gang fight. All the things that people associate with a Nigger. That's what I do."

The advent of neo-minstrelsy in contemporary American higher education may well be a continuation of long-standing American minstrel traditions. Although the historiography of minstrelsy has long focused on formal, professional theatrical stages, the reality is that much of the burnt cork in America was applied in private and semiprivate spaces such as charity balls, parties, and men's social clubs. Participants used widely published minstrelsy "how to" manuals (which are now preserved in many minstrelsy archives) to learn how to don burnt cork, procure a wig of nappy hair, and perform the antics of Tambo and Bones as well as the verbal witticisms of Mr. Interlocutor. Putting contemporary American neo-minstrelsy next to colonial Ghanaian concert parties, one notes how these geographically and historically distant manifestations of blackface have flourished in sites that are at once radically hierarchical, culturally heterogeneous, and economically destabilized.

Scholars C. Richard King and David J. Leonard see the rise of "ghetto-fabulous" parties on college campuses as being not only very much tied to a conservative backlash on college campuses in the wake of the civil rights movement, affirmative action, and multiculturalism but also symptomatic of a corporate takeover of America's colleges and universities. This corporatization manifests itself not just in the privatization of bookstores, food services, building names, and the endowed agendas of departments and research centers but in a utilitarian framing of knowledge production itself as being primarily about serving corporate interests and personal gain. According to King and Leonard, "that is why so many ethnic studies courses at universities are increasingly being displaced by diversity training programs, where rather than learning about persistent inequalities, students are taught about cultural competency and tolerance as skills that will serve them in the business world." As the economic and philosophical foundations of the academy are being undermined, dismantled, and reconstructed, students performing in racially themed parties might be said, in a very twisted sort of way, to be demonstrating "cultural competency." But the larger story is that, as King and Leonard argue, "White supremacy and its institutional supporters no longer enjoy secure futures; however the confluence of neoliberalism and neoconservatism allows White students one last chance to party like it's 1899."[62]

Colonial Ghanaian concert parties and contemporary American ghetto parties both transpire in a murky zone somewhere between public and private. Early colonial concert parties were performed in elite spaces such as the Optimism Club, an exclusive social sphere where access to membership was highly regulated and demanded conformity to certain norms of behavior, comportment, and values. This is also true of American college fraternities, which seem to have served as the fertile incubation sites for "ghetto-fabulous" festivities. For colonial Africans in the Gold Coast, participation in the concert party as a performer was a route to postsecondary employment that gave them far more economic autonomy than the colonial clerkships for which they had been trained. For audiences, which tended to be working class, the concert party provided public access to new cultures, manners, languages, and behaviors that were infiltrating the country and giving a tiny minority of elite

Africans heretofore unheard-of social and economic mobility and wealth. The concert party actually democratized knowledge about the performative aspects of the colonial project: how mobility within this new order seemed to require certain embodied behaviors and how it transformed social relationships, such as prioritizing the nuclear family over the extended matriclan. The masquerade of identity on concert party stages was performed by and for those who were relatively powerless in comparison to the larger business and government forces structuring Gold Coast society. What the concert impersonators and their buffoonery dramatized was the vast discrepancy between the rhetoric and reality of the colonial project itself: the pretentious, well-educated Gentleman stock character actually had no money and couldn't speak English very well; the immigrant Kru houseboy known as Bob was supposed to be stupid yet was far smarter than his masters, and with his conniving wit, he had an affinity with Ananse the spider that made him far more "indigenous" than his masters, despite his Liberian pedigree; and the Lady stock character wasn't actually a lady at all but a man in a woman's frock. Through impersonation and comic exposure of artifice, Africans in the Gold Coast interrogated social changes and selectively adopted and transformed ideas being imported into Ghana from the outside. Colonial concert parties, however, also portrayed a lifestyle and an upward mobility that many spectators *did* desire, even as they held it at arm's length and laughed at the performances that exposed this lifestyle's foundational contradictions.

In contemporary American ghetto parties, the masquerade is of a very different sort. The targets of mockery are people who live in blighted urban neighborhoods and public housing projects (for example, the "Party in the Projects" hosted by Pi Kappa Alpha at Texas Tech in 1992) or Mexicans living "South of the Border" and immigrants seeking a green card. At a party hosted by the Kappa Delta sorority at the University of Alabama at Tuscaloosa in 1991, the site of parody was simply "Who Rides the Bus?" to which two women in blackface came costumed as though they were pregnant.[63] For American student revelers, are these acts of impersonation a performance of disavowal—a disidentification with places, identities, and lived realities to which the upwardly mobile college student does *not* aspire? Or is this a performance of identification, a grasping for authenticity in a media-saturated world, and a sign that even the most elite college students see that a neoliberalized future has now put them in the "ghetto" too? Perhaps both are true.

Ghanaian concert parties and American ghetto parties, considered together, suggest that the masquerade of minstrelsy flourishes in worlds that are at once destabilized and highly stratified; worlds where aspirations for upward mobility are intense but their realization remains elusive; worlds in which the very act of impersonation seems to hold promise as a means of performative self-actualization, perhaps as important as the attainment of an actual degree or school certificate. The history of the concert party in Ghana was coincident with the rise and fall of the British Empire. The genre's rough boards, stock characters, improvised plays, mercurial plots, radically polyglot dialogue, and raucous comedy expressed something fundamental about the colonial occupation as it was experienced by Africans living in one West African British colony. Just as there was an enormous gulf between the colonial rhetoric of "civilization" and the reality of Africa's actual exploitation and underdevelopment by colonial forces, so too was there an enormous gulf between the aspirations and pretensions of each of the three stock characters of the concert party and the material and physical realities that lay underneath them.

Perhaps American ghetto parties, especially those staged in San Diego—a citadel of American military power, a place that hosts one of the largest navel fleets in the world and where the military infuses $26 billion into the local economy each year—should be read as expressions of an American colonization that is at once global (Iraq, Afghanistan) and local (Compton, Tijuana).[64] Of the actual city of Compton, scholar Josh Sides writes, "How Compton made this sweeping transition, from an exemplary African American suburb to an urban nightmare, is at once a story of social and economic historical transformation: de jure desegregation, shifting regional and global labor demand, declining retail sales, and changing municipal tax burdens."[65] That privileged students at UCSD—an elite and racially polarized university—chose to perform in their leisure hours stereotyped imagery of Compton in particular speaks to their insensitivity, surely. But it may also speak to an increasing economic stratification and volatility, the demise of the middle class, and an irrevocable epistemic change that the idyll of academe can no longer forestall or disguise for the members of Generation Debt. Like the concert parties among colonial Ghanaians, the "ghetto-fabulous" revelries are enacted in a world of mercurial shifts and a distinct sense of eroding promises. Rhetoric that affirms aspirations of upward mobility and ensures public access to a better future through education rings ever more hollow. As with the "Lady" in the concert party trio, things aren't what they seem.

Afterword: 3.49 Percent

Over 225 African American students at the University of California, Berkeley, gathered on March 1, 2010, on historic Sproul Plaza to stage a protest action called a "Blackout" in response to the spate of racist incidents in the UC system during the previous month, most notorious among these the UCSD Compton Cookout. Clad in black clothing, with black cloths over their mouths, hundreds of African American students sat and stood for two and a half hours in silence, arms linked, in the cold (Figure 8.5). Occasional drops of rain fell as they formed a human blockade across Berkeley's historic Sather Gate, an important conduit for foot traffic between north and south campus. During change of classes at noon and 1 PM, throngs of students were forced to queue up on either side of the gate, where they could pass through small portals of access the protesters had left open. A few protesters handed out flyers explaining, "We are brothers and sisters in a nonviolent, silent demonstration, standing in solidarity with the UCSD students who have been affected by blatant acts of ignorance and hatred."[66] The installation made full use of the space with two phalanxes of protesters facing in both directions. There was no front stage or backstage. If you wanted to cross campus on this day, the Blackout confronted you. Usually Sproul Plaza at noon is frenetic and cacophonous. On this day it was somber and silent. Some passersby stopped to watch in silence, read the flyers, or converse sotto voce with other bystanders trying to make sense of this visually stunning but initially enigmatic event. Others quickly scurried on to their destinations.

To assemble over two hundred African American students at Berkeley was no small feat. Black students represented only 3.49 percent of Berkeley's total population of 35,843 students, and the university did not have a Black Student Union. As I talked to faculty of color assembled at the edges of the protest, I learned that many of the participants had met one another only in the preceding forty-eight hours. Protesters were galvanized by their outrage over the racist events at UCSD, and they were guided by black alumni who had staged similar "Blackout" actions on the Berkeley campus in previous decades.

When the clock chimed two o'clock, the protesters processed in an orderly, dignified formation to California Hall, the chancellor's office. Moving in single file, a hand of one on the shoulder of another, the formation made me think of slaves in Africa processing to the coast. At one point the line of protesters extended all the way from Sather Gate to California Hall, about the length of two city blocks. The students then lined up in orderly rows, and here one could see another historical resonance: the Black Panthers.

By this point only a few onlookers remained. The action was transformed into a rather extraordinary and intimate formal meeting between this student

Figure 8.5. Silent protest at the University of California, Berkeley, in response to the "Compton Cookout." Photograph taken March 1, 2010, by Eddie Wright.

delegation and the campus administration. Executive Vice Chancellor and Provost George Breslauer was waiting outside to receive the students. Once the protesters assembled, a spokesperson read a letter that expressed the students' "disgust" with the Berkeley administration's response to the San Diego racist incidents. They found a campus-wide e-mail issued by Berkeley chancellor Robert Birgeneau to be woefully inadequate: it tepidly expressed "distress" when outrage was due. The student speaker then enumerated several racist incidents that had happened on the Berkeley campus, and identified the repeated failure of the administration to provide an adequate response. "Though these incidents seem isolated, they are in fact symptomatic of a deeper issue that plagues the University of California as a whole—a continued marginalization of the Black student body," the students declared.[67]

After the letter had been read, the students formed one large circle in front of California Hall, some standing on a rise of grass. At that moment, 225 African American students could see one another's faces and feel the energy their collective silent action had created among them during the previous two and a half hours. There was a brief reflection and exhortation, then a rallying chant led by two students. And everyone dispersed, with a few still lingering in small groups. Observers could also feel the energy and excitement of newly made friends who had shared a deeply transformative ritual.

NOTES

1. Ralph Ellison, *Shadow and Act* (New York: Random House, 1964), 48.

2. See ibid., 45–59; and Robert C. Toll, *Blacking Up: The Minstrel Show in Nineteenth-Century America* (New York: Oxford University Press, 1974). For more recent appraisals of blackface, see Eric Lott, *Love and Theft: Blackface Minstrelsy and the American Working Class* (New York: Oxford University Press, 1993); W. T. Lhamon Jr., *Raising Cain: Blackface Performance from Jim Crow to Hip Hop* (Cambridge: Harvard University Press, 1998); and Saidiya V. Hartman, "Innocent Amusements: The Stage of Sufferance," chap. 1 in *Scenes of Subjection: Terror, Slavery, and Self-Making in Nineteenth-Century America* (New York: Oxford University Press, 1997), 17–48.

3. On Australia, see Richard Waterhouse, *From Minstrel Show to Vaudeville: The Australian Popular Stage, 1788–1914* (Kensington: University of New South Wales Press, 1990). On Brazil, see Ron Conner, "Brazilian Blackface: *Maracatu Cearense* and the Politics of Participation," paper presented at the Fifty-fourth Annual Meeting of the Society for Ethnomusicology, UCLA, November 13, 2009. On Britain, see Michael Pickering, *Blackface Minstrelsy in Britain* (Burlington, Vt.: Ashgate, 2008). On Colombia, see Andrés Duque, "Blackface at Bogota Pride + Latin American Pride 2006," *Blabbeando,* July 3, 2006, http://blabbeando.blogspot.com/2006/07/blackface-at-bogota-pride-latin.html. On Cuba, see Jill Lane, *Blackface Cuba, 1840–1895* (Philadelphia: University of Pennsylvania Press, 2005). On Ghana, see Catherine M. Cole, *Ghana's Concert Party Theatre* (Bloomington: Indiana University Press, 2001). On Jamaica, see Errol Hill, *The Jamaican Stage, 1655–1900: Profile of a Colonial Theatre* (Amherst: University of Massachusetts Press, 1992). On Puerto Rico, see Yeidy M. Rivero, "Caribbean *Negritos:* Ramón Rivero, Blackface, and 'Black' Voice in Puerto Rico," *Television & New Media* 5, no. 4 (2003): 315–37; and *Tuning Out Blackness: Race and Nation in the History of Puerto Rican Television* (Durham: Duke University Press, 2005). On South Africa, see David Coplan, *In Township Tonight! South Africa's Black City Music and Theatre* (Johannesburg: Ravan Press, 1985), 37–42; Viet Erlmann, *African Stars: Studies in Black South African Performance* (Chicago: University of Chicago Press, 1991), 27–31; and Denis-Constant Martin, *Coon Carnival: New Year in Cape Town; Past to Present* (Cape Town: David Philip Publishers, 1999). On Trinidad, see Louis Chude-Sokei, *The Last "Darky": Bert Williams, Black-on-Black Minstrelsy, and the African Diaspora* (Durham: Duke University Press, 2006), 147–57. Chude-Sokei's book is one of the best sources in terms of beginning to think through the global economy of minstrelsy.

4. Veit Erlmann, "Spectatorial Lust: The African Choir in England, 1891–1893," in *Africans on Stage: Studies in Ethnological Show Business,* ed. Bernth Lindfors (Bloomington: Indiana University Press, 1999), 107–30. For a video clip of this South African form, see "Amazing Zulu ISICATHAMIYA Choirs," www.youtube.com/watch?v=hWkIsSKWhWc.

5. Rivero, "Caribbean *Negritos,*" 317. Within the Cuban teatro bufo, the negrito was a stock character based on stereotypes of Africans. The negrito embodied a Caribbean-mediated blackness.

6. Chude-Sokei, *The Last "Darky,"* 58.

7. Ibid., 160.

8. Lhamon, *Raising Cain,* 78.

9. This section of the chapter provides a distillation of key findings and arguments from my book *Ghana's Concert Party Theatre.* Readers familiar with that text may wish to move ahead to the next section, which focuses on racially themed parties in contemporary college settings in the United States.

10. Allister MacMillan, *The Red Book of West Africa* (1920; reprint, London: Frank Cass and Co., 1968), 176.

11. Lhamon, *Raising Cain,* 41.

12. Kobina Sekyi, *The Blinkards* (London: Heinemann, 1974), 21–22. "Brofusem" means matters relating to foreigners, or *oburonis.*

13. Rivero, "Caribbean *Negritos,*" 321–24.

14. Cole, *Ghana's Concert Party Theatre;* David Donkor, "Spiders in the City: Trickster and the Politics/Economics of Performance in Ghana's Popular Theatre Revival" (Ph.D. diss., Northwestern University, 2008).

15. Augustus Williams, interview with the author, filmed by Nathan Kwame Braun, Jamestown, Accra, Ghana, May 29, 1995. All quotations are from this interview.

16. Lawrence Cudjoe, interview with the author, filmed by Nathan Kwame Braun, Sekondi, Ghana, December 29, 1994.

17. On Akan indirection, see Kwesi Yankah, *The Proverb in the Context of Akan Rhetoric: A Theory of Proverb Praxis* (New York: Peter Lang, 1989); and *Speaking for the Chief: Okyeame and the Politics of Akan Royal Oratory* (Bloomington: Indiana University Press, 1995).

18. Y. B. Bampoe, speech given at the Concert Party Mpaninfo Reunion, organized by Catherine M. Cole and Nathan Kwame Braun, Sekondi, Ghana, January 21, 1995, trans. K. Keelson.

19. Bampoe's defense of blackface is a complicated speech act, as I have discussed elsewhere. See Catherine M. Cole, "Reading Blackface in West Africa: Wonders Taken for Signs," *Critical Inquiry* 23, no. 1 (1996): 183–215. See also Catherine M. Cole, "When Is African Theatre 'Black'?" in *Black Cultural Traffic,* ed. Harry Justin Elam Jr. and Kennell Jackson (Ann Arbor: University of Michigan Press, 2005), 43–58.

20. For a moving account of the conflicted processes of remembering and forgetting that characterize Ghanaian reflections on the country's slave trade history, read Saidiya Hartman, *Lose Your Mother: A Journey along the Atlantic Slave Route* (New York: Farrar, Straus and Giroux, 2007).

21. Rivero, "Caribbean *Negritos,*" 322.

22. The copy from the Facebook invitation is available online at "UCSD Frat Denies Involvement in 'Ghetto-Themed' Party," 10news.com, February 17, 2010, www.10news.com/news/22588063/detail.html#invitation. The full text of the invitation, as quoted in this link, reads:

> February marks a very important month in American society. No, i'm not referring to Valentines day or Presidents day. I'm talking about Black History month. As a time to celebrate and in hopes of showing respect, the Regents community cordially invites you to its very first Compton Cookout.
>
> For guys: I expect all males to be rockin Jersey's, stuntin' up in ya White T (XXXL smallest size acceptable), anything FUBU, Ecko, Rockawear, High/low top Jordans or Dunks, Chains, Jorts, stunner shades, 59 50 hats, Tats, etc.
>
> For girls: For those of you who are unfamiliar with ghetto chicks—Ghetto chicks usually have gold teeth, start fights and drama, and wear cheap clothes—they consider Baby Phat to be high class and expensive couture. They also have short, nappy hair, and usually wear cheap weave, usually in bad colors, such as purple or bright red. They look and act similar to Shenaynay, and speak very loudly, while rolling their neck, and waving their finger in your face. Ghetto chicks have a very limited vocabulary, and attempt to make up for it, by

forming new words, such as "constipulated", or simply cursing persistently, or using other types of vulgarities, and making noises, such as "hmmg!", or smacking their lips, and making other angry noises, grunts, and faces. The objective is for all you lovely ladies to look, act, and essentially take on these "respectable" qualities throughout the day.

Several of the regents condos will be teaming up to house this monstrosity, so travel house to house and experience the various elements of life in the ghetto.

We will be serving 40's, Kegs of Natty, dat Purple Drank— which consists of sugar, water, and the color purple, chicken, coolade, and of course Watermelon. So come one and come all, make ya self before we break ya self, keep strapped, get yo shine on, and join us for a day party to be remembered—or not.

23. See a screenshot of the Facebook invitation to this event at "RAGEnts Present: Compton Cook Out," http://cache.gawkerassets.com/assets/images/7/2010/03/comptoncookout.jpg.

24. Hartman, "Innocent Amusements," 31.

25. See "FUBU," http://en.wikipedia.org/wiki/FUBU.

26. Black Student Union of the University of California, San Diego, *Do UC Us? Campaign to Increase Numbers of African-American Students at the University of California, San Diego,* October 28, 2009, 4. This report was available at vceba.ucsd.edu/pdf/Do%20UC%20us%20Campaign%20Report.pdf but has since been removed.

27. Minh-Ha T. Pham and Mimi Thi Nguyen, "Campus Minstrelsy: On 'Compton Cookouts' and More," http://threadbared.blogspot.com/2010/02/campus-minstrelsy-on-compton-cookouts.html.

28. "Ethnic Studies Faculty and Student Response to UCSD Campus Crisis Precipitated by the Event Dubbed the 'Compton Cookout,'" February 19, 2010, www.ethnicstudies.ucsd.edu/currentissues.shtml, republished as "Statement by UCSD's Department of Ethnic Studies," in *Another University Is Possible,* ed. Another University Is Possible Editorial Collective (San Diego: University Readers, 2010), 120–26.

29. Michelle Wayland, "'Compton Party Part Deux' Organizer Defends His Actions: Racial Tensions Boil in San Diego," NBC San Diego online, February 21, 2010, www.nbcsandiego.com/news/local-beat/UCSD-Fallout-Invite-Mocking-Other-Cultural-Stereotypes-Surfaces-84851882.html.

30. Quoted ibid.

31. *The Koala,* Center for Student Involvement, UCSD, http://wailua.ucsd.edu/studentorg/StudentOrgDetail.aspx?frmID=2290.

32. See Wayland, "Compton Party Part Deux." See also "UCSD Black Student Union Address! State of Emergency!" February 2010, http://complex-systems.ucsd.edu/antiracism/node/1, reprinted in *Another University Is Possible,* 1–8.

33. See the website for Regents La Jolla Condominiums, http://regentslajolla.net/.

34. Robin Nicole Johnson, Cynthia Mosqueda, Ana-Christina Ramón, and Darnell M. Hunt, "Gaming the System: Inflation, Privilege, and the Under-representation of African American Students at the University of California," research report (Ralph J. Bunche Center for African American Studies at UCLA) 4, no. 1 (January 2008): 21–22.

35. Ibid., 21.

36. Nanette Asimov, "UC Regents Sorry for Acts of Hate on Campuses," *San Francisco Chronicle,* March 25, 2010. On UC Riverside, see the report "Anti-Gay Hate Crime Committed at UC Riverside," dated March 3, 2010, posted on the UC Regent Live blog, http://ucregentlive.wordpress.com/2010/03/03/anti-gay-hate-crime-committed-at-uc-riverside/.

37. Anya Kamenetz, *Generation Debt: Why Now Is a Terrible Time to Be Young* (New York: Riverhead Books/Penguin, 2006).

38. Ananya Roy quoted in Tad Friend, "Protest Studies," *New Yorker*, January 4, 2010, 26.

39. Chris Chen, "'We Have All Become Students of Color Now': The California Student Movement and the Rhetoric of Privilege," *South Atlantic Quarterly* 110, no. 2 (Spring 2011): 559.

40. For an article that offers a table of twenty-seven such events from 1986 to 2010, see Gina A. Garcia, Marc P. Johnston, Juan C. Garibay, Felisha A. Herrera, and Luis G. Giraldo, "When Parties Become Racialized: Deconstructing Racially Themed Parties," *Journal of Student Affairs Research and Practice* 48, no. 1 (2011): 5–21.

41. See C. Richard King and David J. Leonard, "The Rise of the Ghetto-Fabulous Party," *Colorlines Magazine*, October 5, 2007, http://colorlines.com/archives/2007/10/the_rise_of_the_ghettofabulous_party.html; see also Brendesha M. Tynes and Suzanne L. Markoe, "The Role of Color-Blind Attitudes in Reactions to Racial Discrimination on Social Network Sites," *Journal of Diversity in Higher Education* 3, no. 1 (2010): 1–13.

42. Tim Wise, "Majoring in Minstrelsy: White Students, Blackface, and the Failure of Mainstream Multiculturalism," *Lip Magazine*, June 22, 2007, reproduced at www.racismreview.com/blog/2010/02/26/majoring-in-minstrelsy-white-students-blackface-and-the-failure-of-mainstream-multiculturalism/.

43. "Racist Parties on the Rise," *The Hilltop Online: The Daily Student Voice of Howard University*, November 15, 2006, www.thehilltoponline.com/2.4799/racist-parties-on-the-rise-1.463332.

44. Ron Cassie, "Johns Hopkins Fraternity Suspended after Racially Themed Halloween Party," *The Examiner* (Washington, D.C.), October 31, 2006.

45. For photographs of this event, see "Another Celebration of Black Culture," www.thesmokinggun.com/archive/years/2007/0125072uconn1.html.

46. David Pilgrim, curator, Jim Crow Museum of Racist Memorabilia, Ferris State University, "Question of the Month: Ghetto Parties," March 2007, www.ferris.edu/jimcrow/question/mar07/.

47. Joseph J. Sabia, "Cornell Thought Police Haze a 'Racist' Frat," *FrontPageMag.com*, March 18, 2004, http://archive.frontpagemag.com/readArticle.aspx?ARTID=13763.

48. Associated Press, "'Ghetto Fabulous' Costume Party Latest Racial Incident at University of Texas," *Diverse Issues in Higher Education*, November 2, 2006, http://diverseeducation.com/article/6595/.

49. K-NYU, "Pre-Partying Just Got Better," CollegeCandy.com, July 27, 2008, http://collegecandy.com/2008/07/27/lhpre-partying-just-got-better/.

50. For the Facebook group that supports these racially themed parties, see www.facebook.com/group.php?gid=2219731845&v=wall. The Facebook group in opposition can be found at www.facebook.com/group.php?gid=2215137633.

51. Michael Eric Dyson and Meta DuEwa Jones, "An Interview with Michael Eric Dyson," *Callaloo* 29, no. 3 (Summer 2006): 786–802; see also Paul Butler, "Much Respect: Toward a Hip-Hop Theory of Punishment," *Stanford Law Review* 56, no. 983 (April 2004): 983–1016.

52. Hartman, *Scenes of Subjection*, 30; Thomas Bartlett, "An Ugly Tradition Persists at Southern Fraternity Parties," *Chronicle of Higher Education*, November 30, 2001, A33.

53. Wise, "Majoring in Minstrelsy."

54. Steve Schmidt, "Performer: Off-Campus Party Not Offensive," *San Diego Union Tribune*, February 26, 2010.

55. For all quotations, see Jiggaboo Jones, "The Number One Nigger in America," www.jiggaboojones.com/.

56. For Jones's "official statement," see www.jiggaboojones.com/Compton_cookout_Final_Official_Statement_jiggaboo_jones.htm.

57. See a video of the USC event at www.youtube.com/watch?v=tA3E5JcH624. As of April 2011 this footage included a note at the beginning that read, "Due to negative Political actions from UCSD Jiggaboo Jones declined to show the faces of any Compton Cookout participants."

58. Chude-Sokei, *The Last "Darky,"* 128–40.

59. See www.urbandictionary.com/define.php?term=jiggaboo. On the influence of the Urbandictionary website on racially themed parties, see Earl Ofari Hutchinson, "Lots of Cooks Prepared the Compton Cookout Racial Insult Stew," *American Chronicle,* April 24, 2010, www.americanchronicle.com/articles/view/143032.

60. Eleanor Yang Su, "UCSD Party Mocks Black History Month," *San Diego Union-Tribune,* February 16, 2010.

61. Copy of letter published online in "UCSD Frat Denies Involvement in 'Ghetto-Themed' Party."

62. King and Leonard, "The Rise of the Ghetto-Fabulous Party."

63. Bartlett, "An Ugly Tradition Persists," A33.

64. Jeanette Steel, "Top Admiral: San Diego Has Military Muscle," *San Diego Tribune,* August 26, 2010.

65. Josh Sides, "Straight into Compton: American Dreams, Urban Nightmares, and the Metamorphosis of a Black Suburb," *American Quarterly* 56, no. 3 (September 2004): 584.

66. For a further write-up of the event, see Riya Bhattacharjee, "UC Berkeley Students Protest UCSD Racist Acts," *Berkeley Daily Planet,* March 1, 2010.

67. Ibid.

Notes on Contributors

Louis Chude-Sokei is a writer and scholar at the University of Washington, Seattle. His writing has been widely anthologized and ranges from the scholarly/academic to public venues like the *Los Angeles Times* and the *San Francisco Chronicle*. His work includes the monograph *Dr. Satan's Echo Chamber: Reggae, Technology and the Diaspora Process* (1997) and the book *The Last "Darky": Bert Williams, Black-on-Black Minstrelsy, and the African Diaspora* (2006) which was selected as a John Hope Franklin Center book and was a finalist for both the 2007 Hurston/Wright Legacy Award and the Theater Library Association's George Freedley Award. Forthcoming books are *The Sound of Culture: Diaspora and Black Techno-Poetics* and a work of creative nonfiction.

Dale Cockrell is director of the Center for Popular Music at Middle Tennessee State University and professor of musicology emeritus at Vanderbilt University. He is the author of *Demons of Disorder: Early Blackface Minstrels and Their World, Excelsior: Journals of the Hutchinson Family Singers, 1842–1846, The Ingalls Wilder Family Songbook* (a critical edition of the music referred to in the *Little House* books), and more than one hundred other books, articles, papers, and monographs. A former president of the Society for American Music, he is at work on *Blood on Fire: Music, Dance, and Sex in Victorian America.* Cockrell is also founder and president of The Pa's Fiddle Project, an educational, scholarly, and musical program dedicated to recording the music of the *Little House* books and to reconnecting children with the rich musical legacies embedded in them.

Catherine M. Cole is a professor of theater, dance, and performance studies at the University of California, Berkeley, where she runs the Graduate Program in Performance Studies. She is the author of *Performing South Africa's Truth Commission: Stages of Transition* (2010) and *Ghana's Concert Party Theatre* (2001), which received a 2002 Honorable Mention for the Barnard Hewitt Award for outstanding research in theater history from the American Society for Theatre Research and was a finalist for the Herskovits Prize in African Studies. She co-edited the book *Africa after Gender?* (2007) as well as a special issue of *Theatre Survey* on African and Afro-Caribbean performance, and she recently served as editor for *Theatre Survey.* Her dance theater piece *Five Foot Feat,* created in collaboration with Christopher Pilafian, toured North America in 2002–2005. Cole has published articles in *Africa, Critical Inquiry,*

Disability Studies Quarterly, Research in African Literatures, Theatre, Theatre Journal, and *TDR,* as well as numerous chapters in edited volumes.

Stephen Johnson is director of the Centre for Drama, Theatre and Performance Studies at the University of Toronto. His publications include *The Roof Gardens of Broadway Theatres, 1883–1942,* and an edited volume of forty essays for Performing Arts Resources, *A Tyranny of Documents: The Performing Arts Historian as Film Noir Detective,* as well as numerous book chapters and essays. He was co-editor of *Theatre Research in Canada* for ten years. His research into blackface minstrelsy, including a database and website, is available at link.library.utoronto.ca/minstrels. He has been developing a Web-based project focusing on performance in southern Ontario during the nineteenth and early twentieth centuries, link.library.utoronto .ca/ontheroad/canadawest.

W. T. Lhamon Jr. has written a cultural history of the 1950s in the United States, *Deliberate Speed: The Origins of a Cultural Style in the American 1950s,* and he has published three books on blackface performance: *Raising Cain: Blackface Performance from Jim Crow to Hip Hop; Jump Jim Crow: Lost Plays, Lyrics, and Street Prose of the First Atlantic Popular Culture;* and *Jim Crow, American: Selected Songs and Plays.* He is working on a book titled *Secret Histories,* on cultural transmission, popular performance, and the slow delivery of democracy. Lhamon lives in Vermont and north Florida.

Alice Maurice is an associate professor of English at the University of Toronto. She is the author of the forthcoming book *The Cinema and Its Shadow: Race, Apparatus, Meaning* (2013). She has also been associate producer of two documentary films, *A Healthy Baby Girl* (1997) and the Academy Award–winning short *Defending Our Lives* (1994).

Nicholas Sammond is an associate professor of cinema studies and English at the University of Toronto. He is the author of *Babes in Tomorrowland: Walt Disney and the Making of the American Child, 1930–1960* (2005), as well as articles on media and culture, early animation, and media and childhood. He is currently working on *Biting the Invisible Hand: Blackface Minstrelsy and the Industrialization of American Animation.*

Linda Williams's first book, *Figures of Desire* (1981), was a study of the cinematic surrealist avant-garde. Much of her research has since centered on popular American genres and modes of moving pictures, particularly those that make a strong appeal to the bodies of viewers. In 1989 she published *Hard Core: Power, Pleasure, and the "Frenzy of the Visible,"* a feminist study of hard-core pornography that has been widely translated and issued in a new edition (1999). In 2001 Williams published *Playing the Race Card: Melodramas of Black and White from Uncle Tom to O. J. Simpson.* More recently, she has published *Screening Sex* (2008). She is currently writing a book about *The Wire.*

Index